PRAYER
IN THE
NEW
TESTAMENT

OVERTURES TO BIBLICAL THEOLOGY

Editors

WALTER BRUEGGEMANN, McPheeder Professor of Old Testament, Columbia Theological Seminary, Decatur, Georgia

JOHN R. DONAHUE, S.J., Professor of New Testament, Jesuit School of Theology at Berkeley, California

SHARYN DOWD, Professor of New Testament, Lexington Theological Seminary, Lexington, Kentucky

CHRISTOPHER R. SEITZ, Associate Professor of Old Testament, Yale Divinity School, New Haven, Connecticut

PRAYER IN THE NEW TESTAMENT

Oscar Cullmann

 FORTRESS PRESS   Minneapolis

PRAYER IN THE NEW TESTAMENT

First North American edition published 1995 by Fortress Press.

Translated by John Bowden from the German *Das Gebet im Neuen Testament*, published 1994 by J. C. B. Mohr (Paul Siebeck), Tübingen. Copyright © 1994 J. C. B. Mohr (Paul Siebeck), Tübingen.

English translation copyright © 1994 John Bowden.

Library of Congress Cataloging-in-Publication Data available

Manufactured in Great Britain   AF 1-2944

99 98 97 96 95   1 2 3 4 5 6 7 8 9 10

To the memory of my dear sister

Louise Cullmann,

without whose loyal companionship and radiant spirit
and without whose sacrifice to relieve me of all cares
I could not have pursued the theological work
which she followed with such interest.

Contents

Preface

I planned and began this book a long time ago, but its completion has been delayed, despite my desire to achieve my aim of writing on this important topic. For after all, prayer is a quite central theme in the interpretation of the New Testament, which has been the focus of my theological work in teaching and research. The main reason for the delay has been the considerable demands made on me by my ecumenical work, in particular the composition and discussion of a proposal which is equally close to my heart. I am concerned that now further progress should be made beyond the necessary and very welcome, yet still not decisive, steps that have been taken towards unity by the formation of an incomplete yet concrete association of all Christian confessions which recognizes the variety of their charisms and tolerates those divergences which have not yet been reconciled.

However, even during these efforts I have never stopped reflecting on the prayers and the instructions for prayer in the New Testament, all the more so since shared prayer is indispensable to the cause of unity and in fact for a long time has been a bond which has held Christians together.

The fact that this book has been in preparation for so many years has meant that on the one hand I have constantly had to take into account new monographs which have kept appearing; on the other hand it has been easy for repetitions to arise. In my last reading of the manuscript I tried to eliminate these and tighten up the extensive material – a process which I have found increasingly important.

In most of my works on the theology of the New Testament I have come near to dogmatics without crossing the frontier. That is also the case here. However, this time I am going further in this direction, since I am deliberately trying to find the answer to dogmatic problems of prayer in the New Testament. But I believe that in so doing I have not left the sphere of New Testament research, since I have tried always to keep to answers which arise from exegesis rather than from other scholarly discussions, whether dogmatic or philosophical, justified though such discussions are.

Apart from my gratitude at having been able to bring my plan to a conclusion, I have many people to thank on a human level. It will emerge from this book where I have learned from the publications of others which I have cited, even where disagreement has clarified my own position. In addition, I have been stimulated by both conversations with and communications from colleagues. I hope that they will excuse me for not mentioning them all by name, for fear of forgetting one or other of them; I shall limit myself to mentioning the help that I have been given by some specialists on the Semitic environment of the New Testament: Professor Dr Ernst Jenni, Professor Dr Max Philonenko, and Dr Max Wagner.

I need especially to express my thanks to two doctoral students, Matthieu Arnold of Strasbourg and Christoph Schrodt of Basel and Erlangen, not only for sparing no pains over bibliographical details, but also for taking on the time-consuming technical work of putting my manuscript text on computer, checking my biblical and bibliographical references, providing the index, and so on.

Nor can I forget my publisher Herr Georg Siebeck here. By accepting my works for his old and distinguished house he has ensured their wide dissemination, and in showing his interest in their content he has always been a stimulus for me.

Basel, New Year 1994
Oscar Cullmann

Foreword

To write a book on prayer is a questionable enterprise, for believers or for unbelievers. Believers who are convinced that they are speaking with God in prayer will be somewhat reluctant to talk about their prayer, even if they feel compelled to bear witness to it. They must even ask themselves whether they will trivialize what they experience in the course of their prayer as a positive expression of their faith if they subsequently make it the object of analysis and theoretical discussion. Isn't it presumptuous, shamelessly to show off what should take place in their room and not at street corners (Matt.6.5f.)? So does that mean that believers should be silent about prayer?

The so-called non-believing scholar of religion is not faced with such questions. For in fact there are aspects of prayer which may be subjected to psychological analysis or studied in terms of modern depth pyschology by those who have not prayed or longer pray. Nor do such constraints exist for theologians who in talking about prayer deliberately confine themselves to these aspects, as they do not for those who think that they can explain totally in terms of depth psychology an encounter with a transcendent Other which believers are convinced that they experience. However, such people should ask themselves whether they have the right simply to ignore or to deny experiences going beyond what can be explained by depth psychology which they themselves have never had but others claim to have had. For those who pray and who believe with Max Scheler that the reality of this experience is 'removed from all psychology', the experience of prayer is what seems to forbid them to do any theorizing.

However, on the other hand the need to defend the authenticity of their experience not only gives those who pray the right to treat prayer, which Origen called the 'heart of all piety' and Luther 'the real calling of the Christian', as a topic to be dealt with by theology, but indeed imposes such a treatment of it on them as a duty. And indeed all Christian doctrine is indissolubly bound up with this topic.[1]

This theological reflection not only serves as a defence but should also be a help to all those who honestly try to pray, but find the 'hiddenness' which is a characteristic of God's properties a tribulation preventing them from having the encounter with God which they seek. Few of those who pray will have been totally spared such a tribulation, especially in connection with prayers which have not been heard.

Not always, but often, this is the consequence of the wrong kind of prayer, which must be recognized as such. Praying is at the same time both the greatest gift of grace vouchsafed to us and a difficult task which has to be learned. 'Lord, teach us to pray', the disciples say to Jesus (Luke 11.1). This, too, is a reason for reflecting on prayer. Jesus himself, who would not profane the holiness of his conversation with God and therefore carried it on in solitude,[2] not only taught his followers to pray the Our Father but constantly incited them to pray, in order to preserve them from wrong behaviour, to admonish them to persist and to promise them that their faith would be heard. Paul, too, knows the difficulty of praying: 'We do not know how to pray as we should' (Rom.8.46), but he refers to the support of the Holy Spirit and in all his letters shows by his own example and by teaching how we should pray with its help. The whole of the Pauline and Johannine writings, and most others in the New Testament, present prayer in connection with their theology, but on the other hand their theology is rooted in prayer.

So we are justified in discussing the question of the nature of all prayer by means of an objective account of what is in the New Testament. Here we should not fail to notice that New Testament prayer is rooted in the Old Testament. Although in this book we shall be concentrating completely on Christian prayer, from this centre we may speak of 'biblical prayer'. In a wider context we should not forget that prayer has a firm place in Islam and in different manifestations in other religions.[3]

Thus the main part of this book will be devoted to the New Testament. But so that at the same time it can serve as an answer to all the problems of prayer, this main part will be framed with a short introduction and conclusion, without these influencing the exegetical account. The introduction is meant to offer a survey of the objections to prayer, the problems it raises and what nowadays tend to be called the crises of prayer. In the conclusion I shall attempt to sum up the various New Testament statements in a synthesis which at the same time should contain implicitly the answer that is being sought.

Without striving to be as complete as a concordance, in three long chapters on the Synoptic Gospels, Paul and John and a shorter chapter on the other writings, I shall attempt not to ignore any p:ssage which is important for our topic, but to emphasize those statements from which a perhaps rash attempt at a coherent New Testament doctrine of prayer can be ventured.

I have not provided a bibliography proper. In connection with my remarks I shall simply cite a number of often valuable investigations with which I have been able to compare and contrast critically the view which is presented in this book and which I have arrived at in my many years of working on the New Testament. This applies particularly to New Testament commentaries.

However, here I must mention at any rate the detailed monographs of which special account should be taken. I shall confine myself to the more recent ones, though I owe important insights to the fathers of the early church,[4] above all Origen,[5] the Scholastics, the Reformers and authors of the seventeenth and eighteenth centuries.[6]

Among the monographs on prayer in the New Testament there are very few which have investigated the whole of the New Testament, like the exhaustive and well-documented work by the French Franciscan A.Hamman,[7] which sometimes goes beyond the narrow framework of prayer. The much shorter book by the late Lausanne New Testament scholar C.Senft,[8] which puts forward personal views, is much shorter. The other New Testament monographs are on individual writings, and particularly on the Our Father. An older work by Ernst Lohmeyer should be mentioned as still worth consulting.[9] More recently the French Catholic theologian J.Carmignac has applied his deep philological knowledge to the exegesis of the Our Father, and in a major work has put forward sometimes original and interesting explanations, though these have not been generally accepted.[10] Most recently the Basel Reformed theologian J.M.Lochman has devoted a deep theological study to the

Lord's Prayer.[11] On prayer in Paul we have above all the older and
very thorough work by G.Harder[12] and now the dissertation by
R.Gebauer[13]. The latter contains a complete and excellent history of
the exegesis of Pauline prayer which also covers all the non-German
literature. In the chapter on the Pauline corpus I will engage in a
critical discussion of the explanations which he offers.

Of course all the dogmatically orientated monographs on prayer
in general also discuss New Testament texts, especially the now older
work by the former Strasbourg Lutheran dogmatic theologian
F.Ménégoz, whose book, which is not taken sufficiently seriously in
the German-speaking world, demonstrates the relevance of prayer
for Christian doctrine.[14] Whereas later the well-known Basel
theologian and pastor E.Thurneysen still complained that [Protest-
ant] dogmatic theologians were neglecting the doctrine of prayer and
leaving pastors and preachers on their own here, not only does
prayer finds its due place in the great *Dogmatics*, like those of
Barth,[15] Brunner, Tillich, Ebeling, Pannenberg and so on, but since
his time several separate studies have appeared in connection with
the deepening crisis over prayer. Authors include the Swiss Reformed theologian A.de Quervain, of whom insufficient note is
taken,[16] the Geneva professor Henry Mottu,[17] the Norwegian
professor O.Hallesby,[18] very much orientated on the New Testament, G.Ebeling, whose work has already been mentioned,[19] and
most recently the Reformed emeritus professor R.Leuenberger,[20]
who surveys the New Testament texts and goes into the problems of
prayer, but also brings in psychological explanations and from this
perspective draws the concept of prayer very wide. The an-
throposophist H.W.Schröder[21] expounds biblical texts, above all
the Lord's Prayer, in a book on prayer which is well worth noting.
The dogmatic part of the article 'Prayer' by Gotthold Müller in the
Theologische Realenzyklopaedie, 84ff., is also very valuable.

From the Catholic side, special mention should be made of the
concentrated but profound book by the well-known theologian
R.Guardini,[22] and also of the work on intercessory prayer in which
the Catholic Swiss student chaplain H.Schaller[23] not only makes a
critique of Kant and Bernet[24] but also clearly expounds Thomas
Aquinas' view of prayer and takes it over. He has clearly recognized
that it gives an answer to these central questions which is inspired by
the New Testament. The 1990/3 issue of the international theolog-

ical journal *Concilium* entitled *Asking and Thanking* contains important contributions. The *Catechism of the Catholic Church*, which appeared after my manuscript was completed, has a chapter on prayer which is particularly worth reading – perhpas the best in the book. The references to the church fathers and the quotations from them are very valuable. But due attention is also paid to the New Testament.

The Zurich emeritus professor W.Bernet[25] discusses the question of prayer not from the perspective of the New Testament but particularly from that of depth psychology. Of course the radical criticism which he makes here also applies to New Testament prayer: prayer, he argues, is not dialogue, not an I-Thou relationship, but only reflection on oneself. The position of D.Sölle, who has written about prayer in several books, is less consistent.[26] She begins only partially from the New Testament, and more particularly from the modern experience of reality, and the view of the world and God which derives from that. But she retains prayer and creates for it the model of 'expressing oneself before God', orientated on this world, for which she appeals to the New Testament.[27]

Part One

Introduction: Difficulties in Praying and Objections to Prayer

The 'crisis over prayer' which is so often spoken of today is nothing new.[1] There has been a crisis at all times, even already in non-Christian antiquity, i.e. independently of present-day scientific progress, new insights and their effects, including depth psychology, which is usually seen as the sole and decisive ground of all the problems of prayer. In reality any reflection on prayer as such raises questions. As I have already said, just as prayer itself not only brings joy but is also difficult, so talk about prayer produces objections which can lead to categorical rejection.

The fact that in the present work we are looking for the answer to the questions in the New Testament certainly does not mean that New Testament prayer, considered theoretically, contains only answers and not also questions. On the contrary, the difficulties and objections (including distortions introduced by human beings) which I shall be enumerating in the introductory part of this book also affect Christian prayer as we recognize it in the New Testament, although on the other hand it is precisely in the New Testament that we find the answer to the problems of prayer which are posed in all religions.

So the difficulties that I shall be going on to describe are the kind that we experience as members of our Christian churches. The objections certainly arise in part from those who do not regard themselves as Christians, but the prayer that they contest is usually the Christian prayer that they encounter in the environment in which they live.

I. The Difficulties

I shall distinguish between on the one hand the difficulties which make the practice of prayer difficult, in other words which are an obstacle for believers who have prayed, still pray or attempt to pray – difficulties which often lead to giving it up – and on the other the repudiation of prayer in principle, objections which in theory are made to all prayer or particular forms of prayer.

The difficulties are primarily legitimate questions which are raised by prayer and then those which are caused by human weaknesses.

1. Questions raised by praying itself

First and foremost comes the painful experience of prayers which are not heard, an experience which is often expressed in the more or less resigned complaint, 'I prayed, but it wasn't any use'. Emphatic statements in the New Testament, words of Jesus himself which promise that all the prayers of believers will be heard, make the problem much worse. When a war threatens there are prayers for peace in all the churches, but more often than not war then breaks out.

The Bible itself, and particularly the New Testament, reports prayers which are not heard. The experience that God remains silent and is hidden often leads many people who have prayed honestly to the despairing conclusion that prayer is useless. Only rarely does a 'nevertheless' about prayer remain, an attitude which I noted in a remark by a good woman, a simple soul whose honesty and sound common-sense I valued. Troubled about what was going to happen to a mutual friend, she said to me: 'Do you believe that prayer is any use? I don't. Nevertheless, I shall pray for him.' Certainly this was no thoughtless prayer. The occurrence of unheard prayers in the New Testament will allow us in such cases to seek the answer from the New Testament.

I have spoken of prayers for peace. But apart from the fact that such prayers go unanswered, the fact of war itself, like that of natural catastrophes, is a tribulation for those who pray. We know from the history of the eighteenth century how the Lisbon earthquake which took many human lives generally shook people's faith. We ourselves can think of events in the wars of our time which deepen the crisis over prayer. From the last months of the First World War I have a personal memory of the effect of the news that one of the shots from the remote-controlled German bombardment hit a Paris church and the congregation gathered in it for prayer. I was sixteen years old at the time, and can still remember how much this news shook me. For me (and not just me) the burning question was, 'What conclusion are we to draw for prayer from something like this?' Similar questions arose after the fearful events of the Second World War, like the often-heard 'How can one still pray after Auschwitz?'[2] The reason given is the impossibility of believing in the goodness of God in the face of such an event: in fact without this faith, it is impossible for those who pray to be ready to bow to the will of God, which as we shall see is what the New Testament calls for.

Here in part we are already anticipating the objections associated with a particular view of God, which will be discussed in the next section. But mention can already be made of this tribulation here, in the context of the difficulties which emerge without being particularly the fault of human beings. We shall be returning to it in the last chapter.[3] For the problem posed to faith by evil, the problem of theodicy, is also a problem of prayer.

A further question which those who pray are constantly tempted to ask is also connected with the view of God which we shall be going on to discuss: how can God, who rules the universe, be bothered about my petty concerns? Why pray at all if God knows everything in advance? How can God attend to the demands of so many fellow human beings who pray, all at the same time? How in a war can God attend at one and the same time to the prayers of one people for their victory and the prayers of the enemy for theirs?

An answer to that may also be attempted in connection with the New Testament.[4]

2. Difficulties arising from human inadequacy

Prayers tied to appointed times and customs should and could be a help in praying.[5] They become dangerous only when human weakness turns them into thoughtless habit, precisely because they are so regular. We succumb to this danger when we do not see it and do not react against it. Here I am thinking of the evening and morning prayers and grace before meals to which children are brought up in Christian families and which even adults often continue throughout their lives. Monastic rules prescribed the 'hours of prayer', and they are certainly a helpful incentive to prayer. Like the customs mentioned earlier they make it easier to stand aside from all busy-ness. They are an encouragement to take 'time' to recollect.[6]

But at the same time they can all too often become mere ritual practices engaged in as a matter of habit. Thus Franz Overbeck, Nietzsche's friend who taught the beginnings of Christianity in the theological faculty of Basel University without actually professing Christianity himself, wrote in his 'Notes on My Life, Especially Concerning my Public Office as a Theologian' that he had already lost his childhood faith as a nineteen-year-old in the course of his first year of theological study at Leipzig. He continues: 'At the beginning of 1857 I finally gave up the habit of daily evening prayer before going to sleep. Hitherto I had prayed kneeling by my bed. I stopped out of disgust at an action from which I increasingly felt myself absent and in which I could not take part with any enthusiasm.' In a note at this point he adds that no one led him to make this decision 'except myself, in a silent conversation with myself'. He could date it almost to the day.[7]

Many people reject grace at meals, which is attested in the Bible, for the same reason, and in fact it often becomes a thoughtless habit. Adults then think that all prayers have the same character. It has to be conceded that it is not always easy to collect one's thoughts before a table laid for a meal. Is talk with God, which is what prayer is meant to be, possible there? The difficulty cannot be denied. But we must ask whether it is not the result of our own inadequacy that we allow what should be carried on with inner involvement to become a mere habit.

The custom of offering silent private prayer in church before taking one's place for a service is another of those intrinsically meaningful practices which all too easily degenerate into a merely external gesture that is devoid of content.[8] Generally speaking, in any prayer distraction leads to a devaluation.

Not only thoughtlessness but also erroneous, and especially simplistic, thinking are to blame for doubts which encourage people to turn away from prayer.

Today prayer is made more difficult by the rush of modern life which leaves no time for it; and if the question of prayer is put at all, it is made to seem a waste of time. Clearly a general laziness about concentrating is to be attributed to human weakness, as is forgetting to pray, which finally leads to its abandonment: a disinclination to prayer in periods of 'spiritual drought', of the *taedium spirituale* which the mystics strove to combat. Luther dealt at length with precisely such difficulties in a work from the year 1535 which is full of good advice: *A Simple Way to Pray. To A Good Friend, Barber Master Peter*.[9]

Above all it takes courage to pray,[10] and we often lack this courage. Talk of the necessity 'which teaches us to pray' certainly fits the facts.[11] But we should not forget that the opposite also often happens: an emergency may paralyse prayer.[12] A dreadful event may cause despair and a lack of courage which then has to be fought against. Prayer in emergencies should not just be described with cheap slogans as cowardly 'substitute action' addressed to a 'God of the gaps'.[13] It can also be a very bold practice to which one has to stir oneself.

In an emergency, courage to act is certainly necessary, but so too is courage to pray. This is the other side of the scene cited from Brecht's *Mother Courage* which plays off action against prayer.[14] Here farmers pray helplessly to God in the face of preparations for a surprise attack on the neighbouring town, whereas the dumb girl Kattrin gets up in the middle of the prayer and beats her drum to warn the people in the city; she sacrifices her life, but saves the inhabitants.[15]

II. Fundamental Objections to Prayer

Here we shall first discuss the relationship between the objections and belief in God, and then survey specific objections, first to all prayer, and then to particular forms of prayer. Finally we shall attempt to see whether several objections do not really apply to the wrong kind of prayer.

1. Objections and belief in God

Attitudes to prayer, to talking *with* God, are closely connected with views about God, with talking *about* God. Where the possibility of talking about God and the reality of talking with God are affirmed, each nourishes the other. So there is a reciprocal effect: prayer presupposes a particular view of God, and at the same time this arises from prayer. Luther sees prayer in particular as a means of knowledge: 'That through our prayer we teach more ourselves than him.'[16] We shall see that prayer in the New Testament, which is the subject of this book, presupposes a particular view of God, just as everything that is said there about God and Christ is rooted in the prayer attested in the New Testament.

Conversely, repudiation of belief in God results in the repudiation of all prayer. So we shall see that the sharpest opponents of belief in God, like Nietzsche, are particularly fond of citing the prayer of believers to illustrate the absurdity of belief in the existence of God, thus confirming in a negative way the indissoluble link between prayer and belief in God.

It can be disputed that all prayer is meaningless for atheists only if the words 'atheists' or 'prayer' are not understood in the usual sense: atheists not as those who deny the existence of God, and prayer not as speaking with a transcendent Other. We find the former in the title of Dorothee Sölle's much-read book *Believing Atheistically in God*. Here she understands 'atheistic' as non-theistic or 'post-theistic',[17] and also brings into this view of atheism a polemic against 'religion' which goes back to Karl Barth and was taken over by Dietrich Bonhoeffer, and which was also engaged in by John A.T.Robinson in *Honest to God*.[18] But she is hardly correct in appealing to the pagan designation of Christians in antiquity as 'atheists',[19] for Christians were not accused of rejecting 'theism', but of rejecting the state gods.

Prayer is compatible with atheism (in the authentic or in the derived sense described above) if the character of prayer as dialogue is replaced with 'reflecting on oneself' (thus W.Bernet) or 'talking to oneself' (D.Sölle).[20] Here Bernet does not specially discuss the relationship to belief in God, whereas Sölle associates her remarks about prayer with the view of God which she puts forward.[21] The main criticism of prayer as a conversation with a transcendent Other is fuelled by opposition to belief in a God whom in accordance with customary theological terminology we call the personal God; as we shall see, that means the faith of the New Testament and of the Bible generally. Since, as I have indicated,[22] the objections which we usually encounter in Western culture relate to biblical prayer, they are primarily directed against prayer to a God who is at the same time omnipotent, remote and near, to whom we may bring our intimate concerns,[23] a God who watches both over creation, cosmos and nature and over the history of the peoples, a 'good Father who dwells above the firmament', a God who 'gives way and course to clouds, air and winds'[24] and who according to the well-known hymn at the same time cares for us; who according to the Psalmist 'knows when we sit down and when we rise up' (Ps.139.2), and who also, according to Jesus, 'numbers the hairs of our head' (Matt.10.30). This God, as the conversation-partner in our prayers, is the object of many often sarcastic objections, both from those for whom there is no God and those who replace this 'theistic' picture with another one: that of a God who is denied these properties, which are thought unworthy of him, as they cannot be accepted by modern men and women. Talk of the 'death of God', which is already old, but some years ago became a modern slogan, and which Eberhard Jüngel calls the 'dark word',[25] often occurs here.

   This notion of God is meant to retain its value through reduction, i.e. through the elimination of other properties and functions attributed to God by Bible and 'tradition'. As we shall see in considering the objections to particular forms of prayer,[26] such a reduction is based on a particular mode of thinking which puts forward a view with a consistency which is pressed to the point of simplification, so that no juxtaposition of opposed statements is allowed to stand. Thus properties of God which cannot be separated by biblical faith are maintained, but only these, with the exclusion of the paradoxical presence of others which apparently contradict them. This applies, for example, to the assumption of a God who is either only near or only remote. The same applies to the immutability of God. This is indisputably presupposed in the Bible, but in the objections made to it, it is taken on its own with no reference to the way in which it is combined with another biblical presupposition which equally cannot be disputed, that of the divine freedom.[27] Many objections to intercessory prayer, which as such seeks to have an effect on God, to make God 'change his mind', are based on this reduction. Among many others,[28] Kant and Rousseau fought sharply against such a view. So too to a certain degree did Friedrich Schleiermacher, but his polemic was indirect; he used other arguments and only opposed certain petitions. According to

Kant, God has bound himself to the moral law; according to
Schleiermacher, to the law of nature.

Here mention should also be made of all the efforts which rest on a
particular view of God, which allow prayer only as meditation[29]
after the manner of Eastern religions.[30] They, too, do away with an
aspect that is indispensable for biblical prayer, which rests on
childlike trust in God.

2. Objections to all prayer

Here I shall choose by way of example just two great names from
among all those who down to the present day have repudiated
prayer;[31] they attacked prayer particularly sharply and passionately
and with powerful remarks which are often quoted. The first is the
great Immanuel Kant, whom the Protestant theology which was
dominant in the nineteenth century chose as its philosophical
sponsor.[32] What he said in his book on *Religion within the Limits of
Reason Alone*[33] and in his articles on prayer,[34] in the interest of
preserving the purity of the moral law which he put at the forefront,
are among the sharpest attacks on that practice without which there
is no religion, without which, as Guardini says, in the long run one
cannot be a Christian any more than one can live without
breathing,[35] and which according to Luther is the very calling of the
Christian, just as making shoes is that of the cobbler.

In Kant's works mentioned above we find quite an accumulation
of taunts to denote prayer: 'A fit of madness', a 'kind of madness in
which there can be method', superstitious illusion, idolatry, fetish-
faith, religious enthusiasm, hypocrisy. Kant regards seeking privacy
for prayer, not as an expression of religious purity but as something
of which one should be ashamed: 'Everyone will . . . expect a man
thus surprised [praying] to fall into confusion or embarrassment, as
though in a situation of which he should be ashamed; for he is
suspected of having had a slight attack of madness.'[36] 'Those who
pray talk with an imaginary being as though this being were present.'
All prayer is simply a matter of talking to oneself, and those who
engage in it imagine that they are dealing with a God imagined by the
senses, in order to be able to secure his 'favour', out of a concern to
influence him which is incompatible with his immutability.

Those who pray use their prayer as it were as an excuse for not fulfilling their duty to act morally. According to Kant, rather than praying, it is important to lead a moral life.[37] Thus he plays action off against prayer, as we find Dorothee Sölle doing today with different arguments.[38] Instead of acting morally themselves, people want help from God. Now there are passages in Kant[39] in which he at any rate allows the validity of prayer for those who are not capable of developing the moral disposition without imaging God in a sensual way, who thus need prayer to strengthen their moral self-awareness. However, his repudiation of prayer is hardly weakened by these concessions made in connection with his doctrine of the moral law.[40]

Friedrich Nietzsche had no occasion to make any concessions, given his radicallly negative verdict on Christianity and religion. His mockery of prayer in *Thus Spoke Zarathustra*[41] far surpassed anything said by Kant. The following quotations show how the prayer of believers can provoke not only incomprehending rejection but real tirades of hatred.

'What is happening? What are they doing?' he asked himself . . . 'They have all become pious again, they are praying, they are mad', he said . . . It was a strange, pious litany in praise of the worshipped and praised ass. The litany went thus: 'Amen! And praise and honour and wisdom and thanks and glory and strength be to our God for ever and ever.' The ass, however, brayed, 'Ye-a.'[42]

'We have grown pious again' – thus these apostates confess; and many of them are still too cowardly to confess it. I look into their eyes, then I tell them to their face and to the blushes of their cheeks: You are those who again pray! But it is a disgrace to pray! Not for everyone, but for you and me . . . You know it well: the cowardly devil in you who would like to clasp his hands and to fold his arms and to take it easier: – it is this cowardy devil who persuaded you: 'There is a God!'[43]

At another point we hear that those who pray choose the night to do so: 'And truly, you have chosen well the hour: for even now the night-birds have again flown out.' And again, 'Wherever there are closets, there are new devotees in them and the atmosphere of devotees.'[44]

Apart from such a total challenge related to prayer itself, of course mention should be made of all the repudiations which refer to the difficulties of prayer mentioned above, in particular the charge that prayer goes unheard ('How can one still pray after Auschwitz?').[45]

3. Objections to particular forms of prayer

Among the various forms of prayer, we distinguish between petitionary prayer or intercession, thanksgiving and praise. As thanksgiving and praise come very close to each other, in what follows we can reduce the three forms to two. For petitionary prayer differs from praise and thanksgiving, and we have already seen that it poses the greater problems and provokes the most objections. On the other hand, however, petitionary prayer and prayers of thanksgiving are connected.[46] Intercession fundamentally presupposes thanksgiving and praise.

If, as we shall see, one of the main characteristics of New Testament prayer is union with God's will, this aim will be striven for not only in intercession but particularly clearly in thanksgiving and praise, which provides the background to most Old Testament psalms, in which creation, too, joins in the hymn of praise (Ps.148.3ff.).

Prayers of intercession and praise are offered both by individuals and in worship. Thanksgiving is a fixed part of the church's liturgy.

Praise is usually attacked less than petitionary prayer because to those who attack the latter, it alone seems appropriate to the divine dignity and majesty, and exalted above all petty and even selfish earthly wishes.

As representatives of this trend I shall cite here simply three famous thinkers who play off thanksgiving and praise against intercession in a particularly consistent and emphatic way. First, there is Jean-Jacques Rousseau, though he is concerned more with contemplation than with real praise. In his great work *Émile* he writes:[47]

> I consider the ordering of the universe, not to explain it by any futile system, but to revere it without ceasing, to adore the the wise Author who reveals himself in it . . . I bless him for his gifts but I do

not pray to him. What should I ask of him – to change the order of nature, to work miracles on my behalf? Shall I desire the disturbance of that order on my account? No, that rash prayer would deserve to be punished rather than granted. Thou source of justice and truth, merciful and gracious God, in thee do I trust, and the desire of my heart is – Thy will be done.

The great Protestant theologian Friedrich Schleiermacher is much less radical. In his *The Christian Faith*[48] he does not contest intercessory prayer as such, but prayer the subject of which is earthly, material wishes, though this, as we shall see, is a constituent of New Testament prayer.

Within the framework of his view of religion as the feeling of absolute dependence he attacks any expectation on the part of the individual of having an effect on God's will and the immutable natural law that is willed by God. There is no reciprocal action between creature and creator.[49] Only one intercession is justified: that of the church. It is meaningful only as an expression of the members of the church, and then only as a petition for the coming of the kingdom of God.

I do not seek anything earthly either for myself or for my brothers; my sole concern is that the work of the Lord should ever more be fulfilled, and that alone is the object of my prayer, that his kingdom may be built up more and more.[50]

Although Protestant theology is indebted to Schleiermacher for important insights, nevertheless he must be reckoned among those who, as we shall see, have manifestly robbed New Testament prayer of essential ingredients by reducing it in a one-sided way.[51]

Albrecht Ritschl, who decisively shaped the Protestant theology of his time at the end of the nineteenth and beginning of the twentieth century, goes yet further in this direction. He accuses Schleiermacher, whom in general he follows, of still having regarded petitionary prayer as admissible, albeit within limits. For Ritschl any petitionary prayer is contrary to God. Only thanksgiving and praise are worthy of God. Thus he writes:

In the concept of prayer as a whole, petition and thanksgiving are not equal parts. For otherwise the error would be encouraged that self-seeking petition may serve as justifiable worship of God, and that one has to return thanks to God only when one's petitions are heard. Instead, prayer is represented as a whole and under all circumstances as thanksgiving, praise and recognition and worship of God.[52]

In combatting petitionary prayer Ritschl even goes so far as to interpret the Lord's Prayer, which of course he retains, as a prayer of thanksgiving and praise. But little proof is needed to show that in reducing prayer to thanksgiving and praise he is not in line with the New Testament. Martin Kähler, the cautious Protestant critic of the theology of his time, writes:

> On those Christians who merely want to voice thanksgiving rather than intercession, we simply pass the verdict of the one who knows men's hearts: the Pharisee gives thanks, the publican prays.[53]

However, it would be a mistake to believe that in the New Testament only the Pharisee gives thanks. The opposite reduction of prayer in the direction of a repudiation of thanksgiving and praise would deviate as far from the New Testament as the contesting of petitionary prayer. Although the latter is more strongly attested in the case of Jesus than the prayer of thanskgiving and praise, it is not absent from his words, as we shall see,[54] and in Paul it even predominates. Moreover there are hardly any examples of an exclusive, direct polemic against the prayer of thanksgiving and praise, of the kind that we have noted against petitionary prayer.[55]

More general objections to certain forms of prayer which are firmly associated with the New Testament, objections which go beyond the repudiation of one of the two genres (praise and intercession), also belong in the context of objections to particular forms of prayer. These exaggerate and isolate a genuinely New Testament view of prayer and the view of God which underlies it in such a way as to exclude and contest, contrary to the New Testament,[56] another view which is also represented in the New Testament, as being incompatible with it.[57] Or they adopt the New Testament condemnation of false prayer, but exaggerate this, too, in such a way that they extend it to prayers which are an ingredient of New Testament prayer.

In both cases the repudiation of the form of prayer in question rests on the application of a logic on the basis of which, on the one hand the juxtaposition of different views is regarded as contradictory, and on the other, it is not asked whether contradictions which arise in the human sphere can be transferred to God.

So in the first instance the focus is so exclusively on the nearness of God brought about by the incarnation of Christ and its effect on prayer that the transcendent God who has communicated and still communicates his transcendent being in Jesus Christ fades into the background.[58] In the second instance the New Testament opposition to anthropomorphic notions of God who is compelled to listen by 'many words' (Matt.6.7f.) turns into polemic against prayer to the 'theistic' God who is attested throughout the Bible.[59] The attack on prayer which does not lead to absolutely necessary action or on 'only praying in an emergency' suggests a certain devaluation of all prayer in favour of action. In other words it suggests a dissolution of the Benedictine rule *ora et labora*, work and pray,[60] inspired by the Bible, which joins the two together.

Part Two

What the New Testament says
about Prayer

Introduction

I have gathered together the difficulties about praying and the
objections to prayer without attempting to give an answer.
Independently of the problems raised, in accordance with the main
topic of this book we shall now investigate the relevant passages in
the various writings of the New Testament which speak of prayer.
Already at this point the New Testament answers to the questions
will already emerge; we shall then make a synthesis of them in the
third and final part.

Granted, in the New Testament there is opposition only to the
wrong kind of prayer. We shall not find any mention of objections
to prayer in principle, of the type that I have cited above.[1]
Nevertheless, the New Testament itself allows us to adopt a
standpoint towards them. For the New Testament opposition to
the wrong kind of prayer, the positive statements that it makes
about prayer, and the examples that it offers, show the manifold
deep roots of all prayer and with them indicate a solution to
modern problems.

We shall be concentrating on the New Testament and attempting to see where it is a new development from other religions in
whose prayers we find common elements. At the same time,
however, we must not forget that New Testament prayer presupposes prayer in the Old Testament,[2] some of which it indeed takes
over.

Here the special trends of marginal Judaism represented by the
so-called 'inter-testamental literature' and the newly discovered

texts in Qumran should be noted, because Christianity has close connections with this Judaism.[3]

I. Prayer in the Synoptic Gospels

We begin with the prayers that we can infer from Jesus' preaching as contained in the three Synoptic Gospels. Where it seems necessary, at this point I shall already introduce the Gospel of John to elucidate them, especially since in my view some parts of this Gospel go back to old testimony.[4] However, since the words of Jesus contained in it are rooted in the whole of Johannine theology and coloured by it, we shall be devoting a separate chapter to the prayer of the Johannine Jesus.

I shall not discuss the Synoptic sayings in each of the three Gospels separately, but in general combine them as far as content is concerned. The question of what is 'authentic' and what is not is of less importance here, as most of the sayings about prayer are among those the 'authenticity' of which is least challenged. Of course we need to take account of the deviations between the Gospel. If they cannot be explained on the basis of form criticism in terms of different traditions, then on the basis of redaction criticism we must attribute them to the different kinds of explanations offered by the evangelists, and come as close as possible to Jesus' view by comparing them. It will emerge that the author of the Gospel of Luke in particular is the evangelist of prayer.

In addition to Jesus' instructions about prayer, the reports in the Synoptic Gospels about his behaviour when praying and especially the prayers which he uttered will help us to grasp the depth of his belief in prayer. As prayers of Jesus, we have not only the Our Father, which is contained in the Gospels of Matthew and Luke, but also prayers which Jesus himself addressed to God. We shall already use petitions of the Our Father to help in understanding these prayers, but we shall also be discussing the whole of the Our Father in a separate section at the end of this chapter.

On semantics in the Synoptic Gospels: contrary to our modern languages, in Greek we find a large number of words for prayer. For a list of them and their different nuances see A.Hamman, *La*

Priére I, *Nouveau Testament*, Tournai 1959, 135f. The difference
in meaning is not fundamental.

1. Prayer as a conversation with God.
The experience of God's presence

The essence of all prayer is that it is a conversation with God as the
partner. As soon as purposes creep in which distract from this goal,
prayer is profaned, and if it is then supposed to be talk with God, it
becomes blasphemous hypocrisy. None of the opponents of prayer
who want to dismiss true prayer by referring to this wrong kind of
prayer has characterized this distortion and censured it as sharply as
Jesus did.

The parable of the Pharisee and the publican (Luke 18.10ff.) is an
example of this criticism. The Pharisee is pretending to himself and
others that he is thanking God. In reality, in his prayer he only has
himself and other human beings in view. Feuerbach's verdict on
prayer, that it is worship of one's own heart, applies to this form of
prayer which is censured by Jesus. The Pharisee is not talking with
God, whereas the publican with his petition for pardon, in awareness
of his sin, is seeking to make contact with God.

In the Sermon on the Mount (Matt.6.5), Jesus paints the
unforgettable picture of those who pray hypocritically, wanting their
prayers to be seen by others in the synagogue and on the street
corners. They are play-acting (indeed the Greek word of which
'hypocrite' is a precise rendering means 'actor'). They want to be
seen by their fellow men, and indeed they are. They get what they
want: 'their account is settled', as the Greek word has it.[5] They have
nothing to expect from God.

Then there is the positive instruction: 'When you pray, go into
your room and shut the door.' The Greek word for 'room'[6] used here
denotes a remote room in the house (treasury or store chamber), safe
from thieves, which no one enters. There the person who prays is
alone with God. It is said here, as with almsgiving, not only that God
sees in secret (Matt.6.4), but according to a very good, though not
unanimously attested, reading[7] that God *is* in secret. There God is
present for us in a special way. Indeed God is everywhere,[8] but there

are places where it is easier to find God, away from all distractions, in such a way that he is ready to carry on a conversation with any individual. That is the important thing. Even in the temple, which is defined as a house of God, a 'house or prayer', as Jesus says following Isa.56.7 (Mark 11.17), concentration is to be invited. Even there people are to pray in such a way that it is possible to be alone with God, who, even in the temple, wants to be present to each individual, as he is for the publican in the parable (Luke 18.10). For the one who is outside us at the same time takes up his abode in us, in secret.

God reveals himself where we do not expect it, in secret. We might think of the appearance of God to Elijah in I Kings 19.11f.: '. . . and a great and strong wind . . . but the Lord was not in the wind; and after the wind an earthquake, but the Lord was not in the earthquake; and after the earthquake a fire, but the Lord was not in the fire; and after the fire a still small voice.' That was when Elijah heard the divine voice. Here is the great biblical paradox. God's hiddenness, which is so often a stumbling-block for faith, but is part of God's holiness,[9] goes with God's communication of himself in love: the Holy and Hidden One condescends to his creature as the loving Father. Underlying this paradox is Jesus' admonition to seek a conversation with God, in secret, in *prayer*.

In the Gospels, Jesus himself sets an example in the choice of a place for his own prayer. The fact that the evangelists refer to this specially each time indicates that they recognized Jesus' special intention to seek solitude, to be alone. Mark 1.35, 'In the morning, a great while before day, he rose and went out to a lonely place, and there he prayed' (cf. Luke 4.42); Matt.14.13, 'he withdrew to a lonely place'; Luke 5.16, 'he withdrew to the wilderness and prayed'; Luke 9.18, 'When he was praying alone'; Luke 9.28, 'he went up the mountain to pray' (Mark 9.2 and Matt.17.1, 'a high mountain apart'). Jesus also seeks the solitude of the hills (Mark 3.13; Luke 6.12; Mark 6.46; Matt.14.23) on the Mount of Olives. Luke 22.39 observes that he went there 'as was his custom'. The disciples follow him into Gethsemane, but then he himself goes 'a little farther', Mark 14.35; Matt.26.39; according to Luke 22.41 'he withdrew from them about a stone's throw' to pray.

The conversation not only presupposes that God sees in secret but also that he hears in secret, whether the prayers are spoken loudly or softly,[10] just as those who pray want to hear God there, and God's hearing is intrinsically listening to. Therefore in Mark 11.24 Jesus can invite the disciples to believe while they are praying that they 'have already received' what they are praying for. This faith is part of the conversation. The experience of the presence of God who sees and hears is already fulfilment.

> The copyists already failed to understand the aorist *elaben*. By replacing it with the present or the future they robbed this saying of Jesus of its depth. We shall see[11] that Paul develops this view in Rom.8.15; Gal.4.6f. theologically in connection with the picture of us as children with the argument that in our prayer God speaks to us as children if his Spirit impels us to call on him as Father.

In mentioning the need to concentrate in the temple we have already seen that Jesus' own preference for solitude and his admonition to the disciples to pray to God in secret does not exclude the view, held throughout the Old Testament, that God can also be encountered in the temple, the 'house of prayer' (Isa. 56.7), where several are gathered together. In Matt.18.20 Jesus promises his own presence where two or three are gathered in his name, and if two bring their petition to God in accord, it will be granted to them by the Father (Matt.18.19). But here, too, it is presupposed that they exclude all that could keep them from their effort to hear God in their prayer.

2. God has no needs, but God wants human prayer

In Matt.6.7 Jesus censures 'babbling', as Luther translated the rare Greek word,[12] the use of 'many words' and the expectation of getting a hearing with them. The reason he gives (v.8) is particularly important for his understanding of prayer. 'For your Father knows what you need before you ask him.' This saying describes one of the main characteristics of all prayer – one of the main theses of the present book. We have seen that the objection that prayer is useless relates specifically to this saying of Jesus. 'Why pray when God knows everything in advance and – many people go on to conclude – carries out his plan independently of this prayer, so that any attempt to want to influence him is absurd?' In reality Jesus' saying only presupposes the certainty that God does not in fact need our prayers, since God knows the needs which we ask to be fulfilled, but from that it follows only that according to his will the wrong kind of prayer is to be rejected, not prayer generally (v.7: 'When you pray . . .'[13]).

Similarly, in Isa.65.24 we read about God's foreknowledge: 'Before they call I will answer, while they are yet speaking I will hear.' But these prophecies apply only to the end time: to the new heaven and new earth. By contrast, what Jesus says applies in principle to all prayer. For quite apart from the consequence envisaged, that God does not need our prayers, he implies that God nevertheless wants his creatures to pray to him.

This development of the significance of the saying is not only permissible but necessary. The presupposition of the independence of God from human behaviour which it contains holds for Jesus quite apart from its use in Matt.6.7.[14] But in the context of his instructions to pray it is to be connected with the emphatic imperatives which call for persistence in prayer: 'Ask, and it will be given you: seek, and you will find; knock, and it will be opened to you' (Matt.7.7). This demand, combined with the promise of being heard, clearly shows that Matt.6.8 must not be misused as a proof of the uselessness of prayer. Along with the statement that being heard does not depend on the use of many words, the saying spoken against the background of the invitation to pray at the same time presupposes that a hearing is gained by prayers as such. That is the paradox of petitionary prayer: God knows what we need, yet nevertheless he wants us to pray to him for it.

Here is a paradox, but not a contradiction, in God. I mentioned above (5f.) that the objections to prayer are connected with attitudes to views about God. So the apparent contradiction that on the one hand God does not depend on our prayer but on the other that it is God's will that we should nevertheless pray to him, which is also fundamental to Jesus' preaching about prayer, is rooted in the biblical view of God the Father and the Creator, who is at the same time the holy and infinitely loving one. By freely communicating himself, God has created free human beings out of love, for them to become united with his loving will. God wants a bond to be maintained with them through their thanksgiving and praise, and especially through their intercession.[15] This biblical image of God is the basis of the consciousness of the distance between creator and creature[16] which is so important for all prayer, and at the same time of the childlike trust of the creature in its creator. The awareness in prayer of being a creature and the trust which is expressed in prayer are not opposites; the one flows from the other.

Jesus grasped just how radical is the unconditional will of God that we should pray to him. Hence the repeated invitation to persist in prayer, issued so urgently. The need for this persistence corresponds to the divine will. The parables of the friend in need (Luke 11.5ff.), the importunate widow and the unjust judge (Luke 18.1ff.) make this clear. God wants those who pray to be persistent. Because of this (the Greek word used in Luke 11.8[17] means something like 'shameless'), we are told that 'the friend will rise and give him whatever he needs' (Luke 11.8).[18]

In connection with prayers being heard we shall return to the basic notion, of which insufficient notice is taken, that while God does not need prayer, he does want it. Paul Gerhard clearly expressed the thought that God want us to pray to him in his hymn 'Put thou thy trust in God' (Psalm 37.5):

> With crying and with grief,
> and pain so hard to bear,
> the gracious God will not be moved,
> he must be asked in prayer.

3. The subject of prayer: petitionary prayer

As I remarked above,[19] praise and thanksgiving are often played off against intercession. Only they, and not it, are said to be compatible with reverence for God's majesty. How can God be concerned for human petitions in his immutable counsel? Petitionary prayer is rejected particularly if it is for material things.

First of all let us investigate the variety of things which are asked for. It might seem natural here to limit ourselves to the Our Father, which in fact contains the different kinds of petitionary prayer.[20] But in pursuit of the plan which underlies this whole chapter, we shall begin from the witness of the Synoptic Gospels generally. Then in the light of the results of this investigation, in the course of which I shall already be referring briefly to the petitions of the Our Father, we shall treat this prayer separately and thoroughly.

(a) Requests for material things

The rejection of requests for material things cannot be justified in terms of the New Testament. Biblical faith in God the Creator (in both the Old Testament and the New) requires respect for the material world, and this is also the faith of Jesus, who in contrast to John the Baptist was called a 'glutton and a winebibber' (Matt.11.19).[21] So he would not have agreed with exegetes who from antiquity to the present day have spiritualized the petition for bread in the Our Father (see below, 51f.).[22]

Matt.7.9f. is certainly a parable, and from what the son asks of his human father, namely bread and fish, we may not immediately conclude that the 'good' gifts that God gives to those who pray, mentioned later in the same verse, are also material nourishment. However, the comparison can suggest this.[23]

The assumption that Jesus also regarded material things as a subject for prayer does not mean that these have priority. But in view of the objections already mentioned, it must be emphasized quite specifically that their inclusion in prayer is justified. Absolutely nothing is excluded from Jesus' prayer. Philippians 4.6, which will be quoted in another context (see below, 54), really corresponds to Jesus' invitation: God is to be prayed to in *all* things.[24]

We can add here:

(b) Prayer for help in material need

Bert Brecht's play, already mentioned above, with peasants praying in the face of an attack on the town of Halle, while Mother Courage's dumb daughter Kattrin loses her life by drumming out a warning, is often quoted.[25] If this illustration is really meant to censure doing no more than praying in an emergency in which action is called for, then it is quite correct. But tacitly it also criticizes with gentle or open irony recourse to prayer in *any* emergency. There are cases in which in fact human action is no longer possible – who is not aware of them? – where no Kattrin can beat her drum and where really our power can do nothing. I shall also return to another example mentioned in a note (151 n.60), in which the captain says at the height of the storm, 'Now we can only pray', and the pastor replies 'Is it that bad?'[26] We may rightly mock the attitude of the pastor and the assumption that prayer is resorted to only in distress and without any sense of responsibility. But does that mean that the captain, who really sees no human possibility of help, must be censured for the words that he speaks and must be chastized for his illusion? One may do this with a sense of having got beyond a naive and infantile stage of believing in God's omnipotence. But if so, it would be wrong to suppose that one was in line with Jesus.

I want to counter this error here. But in so doing I must also counter the arbitrariness with which a verdict on the 'authenticity' or 'inauthenticity' of the words of Jesus is made on the basis of a view of God derived from elsewhere, which is not the issue here, instead of with arguments which have a merely exegetical foundation.

Playing off action against prayer cannot be justified with an appeal to the Jesus who is accessible to us in the Gospels. Jesus himself prayed in distress. In Gethsemane, in his conversation with God, in a quite human way he expressed the wish that the cup (the hour) might pass, 'if it is possible' (Mark 14.35f.), and did so in childlike trust: 'all things are possible for you' (ibid.).

We shall be returning to this narrative several times in the present chapter. It clarifies many questions about how to understand Jesus' view of prayer, particularly the one which is pressing here: what sense can a prayer for the fulfilment of a purely human wish have for Jesus if God is carrying out his will according to his eternal plan?

Jesus sees the danger of his arrest approaching. He knows that by human calculation it can hardly be averted. He takes into account that whether or not it happens lies in God's will: 'not what I will, but what you will', in other words that his wish will not be fulfilled – and it is not fulfilled. The evangelists have given us a unfulfilled desire expressed in prayer. And yet Jesus expresses it in readiness to remain committed to the will of the Father: 'if it is possible'; 'all things are possible for you'. That means that even a human wish could be inserted into God's unchangeable plan. The prayer spoken in distress, in which the human wish not to suffer clashes with the readiness to be at one with God's will, represents a *struggle in prayer*, and as such remains a model for us.

There can hardly be any doubt about the 'authenticity' of this struggle in prayer. Granted, time and again it has been objected that no one could have heard the prayer, since the disciples were asleep. Even Eduard Schweizer mentions it, though only in passing.[27] In refuting this we might content ourselves by pointing out that their sleep cannot have been very deep, since they were repeatedly aroused and addressed by Jesus, especially if Hebrews 5.7 has preserved a good tradition in saying that Jesus prayed 'with loud cries and tears'. It is decisive that the evangelists would neither have invented nor handed down a prayer which shows Jesus in such a human state had it not existed. Eduard Schweizer writes that we should not doubt that Jesus did struggle in prayer.[28]

The information in Hebrews about 'loud crying and tears' which has already been mentioned, and which goes beyond the Synoptic narrative emphasizes the distress even more strongly. In it Jesus expresses his wish in prayer, and does so without any illusions, since he takes into account the possibility that it will not be fulfilled. But he prays. He admonishes the disciples to watch: to pray, and not to arm themselves to fight against the Roman cohort[29] and those with it: 'Put your sword in its sheath' (Matt.26.52).

On the cross Jesus prays the beginning of Psalm 22 in his desperate need: 'My God, my God, why have you forsaken me?'

I mentioned above that distress not only teaches prayer but can also paralyse the strength to pray. In the passion narrative of the Synoptic Gospels Jesus gives an example of how we should, indeed may, pray even in extreme need, where there seems to be no human way out and where we are not even certain that our prayer will be heard.

(c) Requests for spiritual gifts

Prayer for spiritual gifts has a special, if not exclusive, place in the Gospels.[30] Here mention should be made above all of prayer for the forgiveness of sins. In the parable of the Pharisee and the Publican (Luke 18.10ff.) it even seems to be the embodiment of all true prayer, and in the Our Father we read it in both Matthew and Luke.

The petitions for spiritual gifts are summed up in the prayer for the coming of the kingdom of God. We have seen that the great nineteenth-century Protestant theologian, Schleiermacher, allowed only this as a petition (see above, 11). The repudiation of this one-sidedness which the New Testament necessitates should not lead us to forget that in the Our Father this petition is one of the first three in which this prayer is rooted. All saving events are kingdom of God events. The kingdom of God for which Jesus teaches the disciples to pray and for whose coming he himself prayed is eschatological, future, and at the same time has already been on the way since his earthly ministry.[31] Of the kingdom of God which is already being realized on earth, Jesus says to his disciples: 'Pray to the Lord of the harvest that he may send labourers into the harvest' (Matt.9.38). Although it is God who performs his saving work with a view to his kingdom, we should pray for it, and this is confirmed by the fact that according to Jesus' preaching God not only needs, but wants, our prayer.

Thus in Luke 6.12 Jesus himself spends a whole night in prayer on a mountain before selecting, the next day, the twelve apostles from the host of disciples. For the decision about their calling which is important for the progress of the saving event he seeks God's will.

(d) Intercession. Healing miracles

We shall be discussing the long intercession in the Gospel of John which since the seventeenth century has been called the 'high-priestly prayer' (John 17) in the chapter on prayer in the Johannine writings. It has no real parallel in the Synoptic Gospels. But in the latter the disciples are urged to make requests, and this is rooted in Jesus' own intercession for the disciples whom he has chosen in prayer and for all human beings, just as indeed his whole work prompts intercessions.[32]

In the Sermon on the Mount Jesus calls on the disciples to pray for their persecutors: 'Pray for those who persecute you' (Matt.5.44). The reason he gives for this admonition is that they are to show themselves to be sons of the Father who is the Father of all human beings, even of our enemies. 'He makes his sun rise on the evil and on the good, and sends rain on the just and the unjust.' God has created them, too, and has included them in his loving will. According to many textual witnesses Jesus himself prayed before his death for those who put him on the cross, not knowing what they were doing (Luke 23.34). Our prayer for our fellow human beings establishes an invisible bond with them which binds us to them by binding us and them to our mutual Father.

Jesus' admonition to the disciples also to pray for their enemies is based on his certainty that they may count on the boundless loving will of the Father for *all* human beings, which is infinitely greater than theirs. The power of any intercession is that those who pray unite themselves with God's will and thus contribute towards building a bulwark of love for those for whom they pray. Here, too, it is true that God loves all human beings, but he wants us as his creatures to pray for one another. We are to be perfect, as our Father in heaven, who has made us in his own image, is perfect (Matt.5.48).

This power of intercession is behind the miracle of Jesus' healing of the sick. It is capable of repelling death. For any illness is an invasion of life by death, and therefore any healing is an anticipation of victory over death: an anticipation (but only an anticipation) of the future resurrection of the body. This is the meaning of the healings, and also of the raisings of the dead in the Synoptic Gospels (for those who are raised will die again). This anticipation of the conquest of death is brought about by Jesus' own prayer. His 'looking up to heaven' mentioned in the narrative about the deaf mute (Mark 7.34) is part of the attitude of prayer (see Mark 6.41; see also John 11.41; 17.1). The commands *ephphatha* (Mark 7.35) and *talitha kum* (Mark 5.41), preserved in Aramaic, are probably to be understood as invocations in prayer.

In the narrative about the epileptic boy in Mark 9.17ff., Jesus commands the spirit to come out of him (v.25) after the disciples, who had been asked by the boy's father, had failed to achieve this. Again we are reminded that Jesus shows his disciples what they themselves are to achieve through their intercession. After Jesus has complained about their unbelief (v.19) and they have asked why they were incapable of healing the child, Jesus answers: this kind can only be driven out through prayer (textual variants add 'and fasting'). All sickness is connected with the sphere of the demons.

But in the Synoptic Gospels Satan also attacks people in a different way, by tempting them.

(e) Requests for preservation in and from temptation

Since we shall be returning to temptation in very much greater detail in connection with the sixth petition of the Our Father (58ff.), I can be briefer here. So I shall speak of temptation only in so far as it is the subject of prayer in the Synoptic accounts apart from the Our Father. To understand fully what the object of this prayer is, a preliminary comment is necessary.

We must distinguish between preservation *in* temptation and preservation *from* temptation. Moreover, we should distinguish between divine temptation, the aim of which is the healthy testing, proving and strengthening of those tempted, and diabolical temptation, the aim of which, on the contrary, is to subject them to evil. In discussing the petition in the Our Father we shall see that in both instances (in other words in the second, too) God retains his omnipotence over the devil, who is conquered but not yet destroyed, and how although the aims are opposite, the two are fused together in the biblical stories about testing. God makes use of the evil which still exists[33] to put people to the test: in the Old Testament, for example, in the framework narrative of the book of Job (1–2.13; 42.7ff.); more rarely in the New Testament.

Prayers in the Synoptic Gospels which are about temptation are the prayer for Peter in Luke 22.32 and the prayer to which Jesus admonishes the disciples in Gethsemane according to Mark 14.38: 'Watch and pray, that you do not enter into temptation.'

According to Luke 22.31, Satan has 'demanded' the disciples: 'Simon, Simon, behold Satan demanded to have you, that he might sift you like wheat.' The word 'demand'[34] shows that here, as in the Old Testament, God has some involvement in the temptation, though this in the background; in other words, a divine testing is presupposed, though this is not mentioned specially. By contrast, the object of Jesus' prayer here is clear. This is a petition for Peter to be preserved *in* temptation (not *from* temptation): 'I have prayed for you that your faith may not fail.'

The object of the prayer to which Jesus summons the disciples in Gethsemane is less clear. Are they to pray that the temptation should not come upon them at all, or that they should remain strong in a temptation which is unavoidable?

Here we might consider whether the sixth petition of the Our

Father should not already be used to answer this question, if, as several commentators assume, Jesus' admonition to the disciples refers to this petition. This is all the more possible (but not absolutely certain), since in Matthew (26.42) the third petition of the Our Father, 'Your will be done', also appears in Jesus' own prayer in Gethsemane (see below, 48). Nevertheless, we shall discuss the question here only in the framework of the Gethsemane narrative, and save a comparison of Mark 14.38 with Matt.16.13 for the chapter on the Our Father. For the point of reference of the prayers is not the same in the two texts: in Gethsemane it is to a quite special concrete situation, whereas in the Our Father it is to the everyday need to make temptation the subject of prayer. Above all the difference in wording requires a special investigation.

If we consider the continuation of the passion narratives in the Synoptic Gospels, the flight of all the disciples and Peter's denial, it seems most obvious to assume that the prayer here is about preservation in the temptation that is to be feared. Certainly Jesus himself, as I shall emphasize later, prays for the event to be averted, but after he has spoken the words 'not my will, but yours be done' he accepts the inevitability of his arrest, by admonishing the disciples to watch.

Nevertheless, I do not exclude the possibility that the prayer which Jesus demands of the disciples also contains the petition that they may not find themselves in the situation of temptation (to flee and to deny). The prayer spoken by Jesus himself, which I have just mentioned, backs this up. Granted, the petition for the cup to pass him by does not relate to the temptation but to the suffering, but it does relate to the event that leads the disciples into temptation. If Jesus himself prayed for this event not to happen, in the prayer to which he admonishes the disciples there may be at least the hint of a wish that they shall not be put into the position of having to flee or to deny him.

Jesus knows the weakness of the disciples. In the light of this knowledge the invitation to pray that the temptation shall not come upon them also makes sense. How justified the note about their weakness is becomes evident from their conduct after the arrest: 'then they all forsook him and fled' (Mark 14.50; see also John 16.32).

That leads us to the conclusion that on the surface the prayer required of the disciples in Gethsemane is about preservation in unavoidable temptation, but in the light of the whole narrative and especially Jesus' own prayer we cannot exclude preservation from temptation.

4. The subject of prayer: thanksgiving and praise

So far we have only discussed intercessory prayers. As has rightly been remarked, these stand in the foreground in the Synoptic Gospels, whereas thanksgiving and praise occur rarely. By contrast, in the letters of Paul (and also in the Gospel of John), praise and thanksgiving predominate. But we have already seen that it cannot be inferred from this (see above 12f.) that thanksgiving and praise were unimportant for Jesus. If these are mentioned less frequently, it is because Jesus probably followed the common Jewish practice of prayer. Prayers of praise often, though not exclusively, have stereotyped wording and thus a liturgical character. They include Jesus' thanksgivings before meals (the Last Supper, Mark 14.22; Emmaus, Luke 24.30; the Feeding, Mark 6.41; 8.7f.). Although the doxology of the Our Father is missing from the early manuscripts, it was always added, as it was to all Jewish prayers (see 67f. below). So prayers of praise in particular are spoken together. We hear in Mark 14.26; Matt.26.30 that on Jesus' last journey to the Mount of Olives he sang psalms with the disciples. The Psalms are largely prayers of praise. One prayer of praise and thanksgiving uttered by Jesus has been preserved in Matt.1.25 and Luke 10.21: 'I thank you, Father, Lord of heaven and earth, that you have hidden these things from the wise and understanding and revealed them to babes; yes, Father, for such was your gracious will.' Exegetically we can hardly declare this logion inauthentic because of its closeness to the statements of the Johannine Jesus. Luke has connected it with the mention of the return of the seventy disciples and their report on the subjection of the demons (Luke 10.17ff.), and with Jesus' saying about 'Satan falling like lightning from heaven' (v.18). We shall see that in Paul the prayers of thanksgiving and praise similarly relate to the saving event.

That Jesus does not rate thanksgiving any lower is also shown by

the narrative about the ten lepers, of whom only one praises and
thanks God for his healing – and he was a Samaritan (Luke
17.12ff.).

5. The hearing of prayer according to the Synoptic Gospels

Here we come to the most difficult problem of prayer. I shall
discuss it under its different aspects: Jesus' promise that prayer will
be heard; the need for faith; the need to submit to God's will (the
prayer in Gethsemane, 'if it be possible', which is not heard); God's
immutability and freedom; the need for belief in God's goodness.

(a) Jesus' promise that prayer will be heard

In many of his sayings in the first three Gospels Jesus promises that
prayers will be heard with an unlimited certainty which is almost
bold in its absoluteness: 'Ask, and it will be given you; seek, and
you will find; knock and it will be opened to you' (Matt.7.7; Luke
11.9), and the next verse adds even more unconditionally: 'For
everyone who asks, receives' (Matt.7.8; Luke 11.10). The promise
is reinforced by the examples which follow, of a son asking for
bread or a fish and his father not giving him a stone or a serpent
instead (Matt.7.9ff.; Luke 11.11ff.); and then the parable which
comes before this in Luke (v.5) of the friend making a request, who
receives his wish because of his 'importunity', and that of the
importunate widow to whom the 'unjust' judge gives her due rights
so that he will no longer be burdened with her (Luke 18.11f.): 'And
will not God vindicate his elect, who cry to him day and night?'
(v.7).

The last-mentioned parables are not meant to demonstrate that
God is influenced by the 'importunity', since this would contradict
Jesus' remark about divine foreknowledge, but they are meant to
impress vividly on those who pray the certainty that they will be
heard and to encourage them to persist: 'And he told them a
parable to the effect that they ought always to pray and not lose
heart' (Luke 18.1). But that means that if prayers are to be heard, a
certain attitude is required of those who pray.

(b) The need for faith

Jesus knows that some prayers of the disciples will not be heard. This knowledge leads him not to leave his promises in an unconditional form but to combine them with the need for faith. We shall be talking about another need later. In the instructions to the disciples he envisages only this one demand for an unshakable faith, and we shall see later that this raises a question for us.

Time and again Jesus emphasizes this need for faith. In Mark 11.22 (Matt.21.21), after cursing the fig tree, he says: 'Have faith in God. Truly, I say to you, whoever says to this mountain, "Be taken up and cast into the sea," and does not doubt in his heart, but believes that what he says will come to pass, it will be done for him. Therefore I tell you, whatever you ask in prayer, believe that you have received it, and you will.' We have already seen (above, 19) that the past form 'that you have received' implies that hearing takes place in the praying itself, in so far as it is a matter of being united with God.

In the narrative about the epileptic boy in Mark 9.14ff. the father asks, 'If you can, help us.' ' "If you can?"' retorts Jesus, 'everything is possible to the one who believes' (v.23). As Jesus had heard (v.18) that the disciples had not succeeded in healing the boy by driving out the dumb spirit, which according to v.29 is possible only through prayer, he complains about the 'unbelieving generation' that he has had to 'bear' for so long. So prayer is effective only if it is offered in unshakable faith. Thus at the parallel passage in Matt.17.20 Jesus gives as an answer to the disciples' question why they could not drive out the demon, 'because of your lack of faith'. Evidently he sees almost no faith at all in their 'lack of faith'. For he continues: 'If you had even as much faith as a grain of mustard seed you would say to this mountain, "Remove yourself . . ." And nothing would be impossible for you.' Luke also produces the image of the grain of mustard seed, which is evidently rooted firmly in the tradition (like the saying about moving mountains), but in a variant (Luke 17.6), as an answer to the petition of the disciples, 'Increase our faith.' (Here the moving of the mountain becomes the planting of the sycamine tree in the sea.)

(c) The need for submission to God's will (Jesus' prayer in Gethsemane)

The sayings of Jesus which I have quoted mention only faith as a fundamental condition of being heard. There the petitions refer to the performance of an action. But if we connect them with the whole testimony of the Synoptic Gospels on prayer, while faith always remains a requirement in the attitude of those who pray, it is not an all-sufficient one.

For even prayers addressed to God in full faith are not heard: Jesus' prayer in Gethsemane (Mark 14.35 par.) for the cup (Mark 14.35 'this hour') to pass him by was not heard. The words of prayer spoken by Jesus there, 'not what I will, but what you will', show what else is necessary: unconditional readiness to submit to the will of God. This must be added to faith. Certainly the wish expressed in the prayer is not fulfilled. But because it is combined with submission to God's will, the edge is taken off this fact by its being illuminated by the light of the divine will which seeks our salvation. At this new level the prayer is heard.

The scandalous contradiction between on the one hand Jesus' categorical promise that those who pray in faith will be heard and on the other the fact that petitions addressed to God in faith are not heard can be removed only if we take into account the teaching that is contained in the Gethsemane prayer. We may and must take account of this prayer,[35] since it is part of the testimony of the Synoptic Gospels about praying.

However, a difficulty arises from the fact that not only does Jesus not mention submission to the divine will in his words about the need for faith mentioned above, but he almost seems to rule out the fact that the believer must reckon with the possibility that God's will could be opposed to the wish of believers: the disciples are not to 'doubt' (Mark 11.23). However, this is connected with the fact that the absolute demands made on the disciples to believe by Jesus relate, as I have already said, to the performance of an action, whereas in Gethsemane (and consequently in all prayers which involve the will of God) the issue is more one of deliverance from a situation which is regarded as misfortune. But the boundaries are blurred, and in noting the teaching of the Synoptic Gospels about prayer we must combine Jesus' admonitions to the disciples to pray with his own readiness to submit to the will of God.

We could find one explanation of the fact that we hear of submission to God's will in prayer only in connection with suffering and death in Hebrews 5.8, where the author writes that Jesus learned obedience from his suffering. But the union of Jesus with the will of God may have shaped all his prayers. The saying 'no one knows the Son but the Father, and no one knows the Father but the Son' (Matt.11.27f.; Luke 10.22) points to the oneness of Jesus with the will of the Father.

Jesus' union with the will of the Father in prayer is a model for all prayer because it is rooted in the character of prayer as dialogue, which we have recognized as its essential feature. In any prayer the encounter of the creature with the Creator, quite apart from the fulfilment of any wishes, is already an attainment of the basic goal, and all prayers must find a place in the framework of this encounter. Where this is encounter is absent and is not sought, prayer becomes suspect of being a magic formula.

Even in the deepest forsakenness on the cross the bond between Jesus and the Father remains, as he cries out with the opening words of Psalm 22 (v.2), 'My God, my God, why have you forsaken me?' (Mark 15.34 par.). For he addresses the question to God, like the Psalmist, who seeks to answer it in the continuation of the psalm (see below, 126):

Certainly human sin is not an obstacle to union with God's will. However, Jesus combines forgiveness of sin with prayer in Mark 11.25: 'And whenever you stand praying, forgive, if you have anything against anyone; so that your Father also who is in heaven may forgive you your trespasses.' Those who pray must put themselves within the sphere of forgiveness, which is the deepest expression of God's will. Hence the basic prayer of the publican, 'God be gracious to me a sinner' (Luke 18.13), and the place of the prayer for forgiveness in the Our Father, which strives for the utmost brevity.[36]

Submission to the divine will is expressed in the Gethsamene prayer in the two additions to the petition: 'if it is possible' (Mark 14.35; Luke 22.42: 'if it is your will') and 'not what[37] I will but what you will' (Mark 14.36, introduced with 'but'[38]; in Matt.26.69 and

Luke 22.42 with the contrast between wish and submission made even more emphatic by 'however'[39]). The addition of these words presupposes that a deep inward unity of will between Jesus and God already exists.[40]

We must take note of the uniqueness of this in our attempt to derive a requirement for all those who pray from the conduct of Jesus. The strength needed to be ready to accept the rejection of any petition and even to pray that 'God's will be done'[41] is as great and as difficult to attain as the faith that Jesus requires of the disciples (even if it is only like a mustard seed). It is infinitely difficult to add to an ardent prayer for deliverance from terrible distress the words 'But not what I will.' This strength can be striven for only by seeking and finding a conversation, an encounter, with God in prayer. Those who pray must themselves have this encounter in prayer. Then the fact that a request is not fulfilled no longer means that prayer is not heard. The power to unite oneself with God's will is itself the hearing of a prayer.

But in that case, isn't it enough simply to ask for this power of union with God, without presenting the specific wish to him? Indeed many prayers have only this main intent. But does that mean that prayer for the fulfilment of particular wishes is ruled out? We have seen (see above, 11f.) that Schleiermacher in part and Ritschl radically denied that it was legitimate to engage in petitionary prayer. The Gethsemane prayer gives a positive answer here, since Jesus includes the readiness to bow to God's will whether or not it corresponds to his wish, in the petition 'let this cup pass from me'. We have indeed noted (see above, 19ff.) that the starting point for his instruction on prayer is that while God does not need prayer, he wants it. That also applies particularly to petitionary prayer. It is part of God's loving will that his creatures should also present their wishes to him, whether he can grant them or not, just as parents want their children to ask them trustingly for a gift, even if they are not certain of getting it.[42]

The words 'if it is possible' in fact presuppose that God can not only reject but also fulfil a request: 'all things are possible for you' (Mark 14.36). In particular, in this case of fulfilment God does not need the human request, but wants those whom he has created out of love to unite with his loving will if he grants their wish. Only in this sense can we say that a request of ours has an effect on its being heard. But here a question arises about the view of God that is held.

(d) The hearing of prayer in the light of God's unchangeable plan and God's freedom

Like the prayer of Jesus generally, so too the addition 'if it is possible' to his prayer in Gethsemane is connected with his view of God. How is it compatible with God's unalterable plan that God can accede to human wishes? The words 'if it is possible' relate to God's freedom to grant or not to grant the petition, but they also relate to the freedom of the children of God to bring their requests to him. In God's communication of himself, which proceeds from his loving will, he has created free men and women, and he wants them to accede to his loving will in freedom.

But doesn't that put in question the 'immutability' of God (to use a philosophical term[43]) which is presupposed by the foreknowledge that is important to Jesus (see above, 19). In the Old Testament there is emphatic mention of God's 'repentance'.[44]

That 'everything is possible for God' (Mark 14.36) means that God can combine the plan for his kingdom with his freedom to grant the petitions of his creatures.

The problem we encounter here is one which I have discussed in *Salvation in History*,[45] continuity and contingency. The contingency is taken up in the continuity. Human conduct, human resistance to God's plan, does not change this, but God does take it further by including this conduct. However, there it is a matter of human rebellion through sin. The positive attitude of those who pray is a factor in the inclusion of their petitions in the divine plan.

God has foreseen that his hearing of prayers granted in freedom will find a place in his plan of salvation by not abandoning his plan because of them but incorporating them into its development.[46] The answer to the question raised here certainly belongs more on the periphery of our New Testament investigation, but it does affect the doctrine which follows from the Gethsemane prayer and which ultimately raises this prayer that was not heard to the level where it is brought into the light of the divine plan of salvation and thus reaches a higher order in the sphere of being heard.

But the presupposition is that the will of God which is expressed in this plan, to which those who pray submit, is for the good, for salvation. We must look at this presupposition even more closely in the last section of this chapter, which follows.

(e) Belief in God's goodness

The strength which Jesus had in his conversation with God in Gethsemane to add to his wish for the cup to pass from him the words 'not what I will, but what you will' is rooted not only in his oneness with God's will (see above, 33 and below 42), but also in his certainty that God wills the good. His emphatic promises that prayer will be heard, 'Ask and it will be given you . . .', are based on faith in God's goodness. He wants to impress this on the disciples with the example of the son who asks his father for bread or a fish (Matt.7.9ff.; Luke 11.11ff. has 'a fish or an egg') and is not given a serpent. If human beings ('who are evil', Matt.7.11 par.) give good things, 'how much more will your heavenly Father give good things to those who ask him'. Granted, it is not specifically said at this point that those who pray participate in the good even if they wish some other good than what is resolved in God's plan, but it is presupposed, and in the Gethsemane prayer it is clearly expressed in the added phrase.

Although we shall not be attempting to give the answer of the New Testament to the objections raised at the beginning of this book until its final part, here already in connection with the need presented by the Gospels to believe in God's goodness when praying, a question arises which is often asked: 'How can one still pray after Auschwitz?' How can one incorporate the non-fulfilment of our wishes in prayer in submission to God's will even there?

In the light of the Synoptic Gospels we can find an answer in another question: how can we still believe that God wants the good in the face of the crucifixion of Jesus? Here we might think not only of the particularly painful death by crucifixion but also of all the torture that went with it, including the mocking and scourging (Mark 15.19ff.; Matt.27.26ff.). We can infer from the Synoptic Gospels, as from the New Testament as a whole,[47] the indirect answer that redemption comes about through suffering, that God brings good out of the evil which causes the suffering. This applies not only to suffering but also to temptation by evil as the way in which God tests the good (see above 27f. and below 137). God uses the evil which exists to produce good.

However, the New Testament does not put a question which arises here and which cannot be avoided, namely whether it is also compatible with God's omnipotence for evil to exist in all its terror, since divine omnipotence is everywhere presupposed as a property which is inseparably bound up with belief in God. Nevertheless, in the last part of this book (137ff.) I shall attempt also to find in the New Testament an indirect answer to this question which it does not raise, in the temporal tension between 'already' and 'not yet', between the evil which has already been conquered and the evil which has not been destroyed. This indication is unavoidable in this context.[48] In fact the tension runs right through the New Testament, but I am mentioning it briefly at this point in the chapter on the Synoptic Gospels, since we shall see that it is also present in the sayings of Jesus (*already*: Matt.11.2ff.; Luke 7.18ff.; Luke 10.18; Matt.12.28; Luke 11.20; *not yet*: Mark 13 par.; Mark 14.62, and passim).

6. The Our Father

(a) Introduction

We have already taken note of the Our Father throughout this chapter on prayer in the Synoptic Gospels in connection with Jesus' many sayings about prayer. But it is important to treat it as a whole.

(i) Its special position within the Synoptic Gospels

The Our Father has a unique significance within the tradition of the first three Gospels, for since Jesus sought solitude for prayer, it is understandable that apart from the prayer in Gethsemane; the prayer of thanksgiving (Matt.11.25ff.; Luke 10.21ff.); and the cry on the cross which consists only in a quotation of the beginning of Psalm 22 (Mark 15.34; Matt.27.46), together with three disputed prayers on the cross present only in Luke[49] (in contrast to the Gospel of John), no other texts of prayers of Jesus have come down to us.[50] The Our Father gives an application of his instructions on prayer, and we shall investigate it particularly from this perspective. Moreover Matthew has put it in this context (6.9, following his systematic ordering of the traditional material), whereas Luke (11.1) gives as the occasion on which it was spoken the request of one of the disciples that Jesus should teach them to pray, as John the Baptist taught his disciples.[51] However, in the same chapter, other parables and sayings about prayer (vv.5ff.,9f.,11ff.) are then combined with the Our Father.

In this prayer we can hear Jesus himself. Its 'authenticity' has never seriously been doubted. If 'hearing' is important for all prayer,[52] this is particularly true of the Our Father. We shall attempt at this point as it were to hear Jesus' voice quite concretely. On the other hand, for the same reason, despite the confidence needed in all prayer, this prayer should be spoken with a pious reverence, a feeling which has been retained in the later church liturgies by the use of the term 'be bold' in the introduction, which particularly envisages the Lord's Prayer.[53]

It may have been prayed by individual disciples, not as though it were meant to exclude or replace all independent individual prayers, but as a model and stimulus for these, and, where it was impossible to formulate a personal prayer, also as a means of self-expression. However, Jesus gave it to the disciples especially so that they could pray it in their community – perhaps also *with* him[54] – not as a liturgy, but together.[55] If for him the goal of prayer is union with God, and it is God's will that people should pray to him, then striving for this goal will be as it were reinforced and simplified 'where two or three are gathered together'. The Lord's Prayer became a congregational prayer at a very early stage in the earliest community, as is indicated both by the old collection of prayers in the Didache[56] and also by echoes in the letters of Paul and in the Gospel of John,[57] and to the present day it has rightly remained *the* prayer in all the Christian confessions.[58]

(ii) Bibliography

From antiquity to the present day the Our Father has been the subject of many theological investigations, and it has often been regarded as a compendium of Christian prayer.[59] Of course it does not have this character, since it was Jesus' intention to teach the disciples a prayer. I shall not offer a survey of the extraordinarily extensive literature here.[60] I mention only some important more recent works to which I shall be referring frequently and which have already been mentioned on p. xv above: the now quite old work by E.Lohmeyer, *The Lord's Prayer* (1952), London 1965; J.Jeremias, 'The Lord's Prayer in the Light of Recent Research', in *The Prayers of Jesus*, London 1967; id., *New Testament Theology*, I, *The Proclamation of Jesus*, London 1971, 193ff.; J.Carmignac, *Recherches sur le 'Notre Père'*, Paris 1969; J.M.Lochman, *Unser Vater*, 1988. For the Matthaean version see the commentary on Matthew by U.Luz, Evangelisch-katholischer Kommentar zum Neuen Testament, I, ²1988.

(iii) The relationship between the two versions (Matthew and Luke)

The Our Father has come down to us in the New Testament in two different variants, in Matt.6.9ff. and Luke 11.2ff. Moreover it is contained in the old collection of liturgies to be found in the Didache (8.2ff.), mentioned above, though apart from unimportant details and the addition of a doxology, this reproduces the Matthaean text, so that we need not take special account of it. No global decision can be made between the two texts in the Gospels, the longer one of Matthew used in our liturgies (six, or seven, petitions) and Luke's shorter one (five petitions).[61] Rather, with each petition we have to ask which form is the earlier and has most faithfully preserved the prayer spoken by Jesus.[62] Since we shall have occasion at some points to prefer Matthew and at others Luke, both texts as a whole must be regarded as old. Origen's explanation (*On Prayer*, XVIII.3) that Jesus spoke the Our Father twice, on different occasions, saying it once in a complete version and at another time in an abbreviated form, is not impossible, but all too simple. Nor is it likely that the two evangelists are responsible for the difference; the explanation may be that we have two old traditions, or community usages, one adopted by one evangelist and one by another.[63] We should also note that in contemporary Judaism prayers – certainly unofficial ones – were not firmly fixed, but spoken freely, with additions and omissions.

(iv) The original language

It is almost universally assumed that the original language of the Our Father was Aramaic.[64] However, recently Carmignac (30ff.) has taken special pains, with reference to numerous Hebrew Qumran texts, to demonstrate that the original text was composed in

Hebrew.[65] He bases his view on the fact that Hebrew had to be used for official Jewish prayers. However, Grelot,[66] one of the main opponents of Carmignac's theory, emphasizes that the Our Father must be classified among the private prayers to which this obligation did not apply.[67] He himself attempts a back translation from Greek into Aramaic, but makes the important point that all back-translations are hypothetical.[68] This should also be noted in connection with the numerous other back-translations, since these are often regarded without further ado as the original version as spoken by Jesus. That is the case if they are not attested in the Gospels, even more so since there are several Aramaic dialects. This brings us to the last preliminary remark:

(v) *The relationship between the Lord's Prayer and Jewish prayers*

In the exposition we shall see that in Matthew the first three, in Luke the first two petitions – those in the second person singular, which form the first part[69] – resemble the so-called Kaddish in Aramaic; indeed they reproduce this, albeit in a rather different form. What was later called the 'Eighteen Benedictions' is equally relevant. Parallels to the individual petitions can also be adduced.[70] Jesus took over the precious prayer material of Judaism, just as he sang the psalms, which are also prayers, with the disciples (Mark 14.26; Matt.26.30) and prayed the beginning of Psalm 22 on the cross (Mark 15.34; Matt.27.46). But apart from individual peculiarities for which Jewish examples are hard to find (for 'Abba' as a designation for God see below), the new feature is that what can also be found in Judaism, without being typical there, takes on a special depth in the Our Father, by being rooted not only in Jesus' instructions about prayer but in the whole of his preaching. This is also true of the brevity of the Lord's Prayer (Matt.6.7) which is also emphasized, though short prayers can also be found in Judaism. Generally speaking, we should note not only what is present in the Our Father and in Judaism, but also what belongs among the main elements in Judaism and is absent from the Our Father.[71]

(b) The form of address

Instead of the form of address 'Our Father in heaven', which is familiar to us from the text of Matthew (6.9), the Gospel of Luke has only the word 'Father' (*pater*). A great many exegetes, probably rightly, regard the Lukan text as original. In support of this is the fact that in his own prayers, in the Greek text Jesus says only 'Father', or 'my Father' (Mark 14.36 par.;[72] also Matt.11.25; Luke 10.21[73]), and also in particular the underlying Aramaic word 'Abba', which in this form stands in the prayer in Gethsemane alongside the Greek translation *ho patēr*, and was evidently Jesus' special way of addressing God.

As Joachim Jeremias has shown,[74] specifically as a form of address in prayer this word gives us the key to Jesus' special understanding of the word 'Father'.[75] Even without taking note of the Aramaic 'Abba', we can see from the Synoptic tradition, for example in the parable of the prodigal son (Luke 15.11ff., especially v.20), what a deep significance Jesus attaches to the word 'Father'. In Judaism, too, God is called 'Father' outside prayer. But he is rarely addressed as 'Father', and according to Jeremias the Aramaic word 'Abba' is not used like this, so that it is unique to Jesus.[76] However, more recent studies have applied further texts from the intertestamental liter- ature and especially also from the Qumran discoveries to 'Abba' and the address 'Father'.[77] Although it seems to emerge from these that not only the Aramaic 'Abba' but also other Semitic substrata could underlie the address 'Father' in the New Testament, we should accept Jeremias' main thesis to the degree that the word 'Abba' is particularly typical of Jesus, if not unique to him, as a form of address to God. Jeremias has demonstrated[78] that adult sons and daughters said 'Abba' to their fathers,[79] and that the word was also used as a form of respectful address to older persons.[80] The fact that Jesus used this familiar form of address to God in his prayers must have resulted from his own personal experience of prayer, and his disciples must have sensed this. That explains how later the term was still used in its Aramaic form even in the Hellenistic world as a form of address in worship, as Paul presupposes in Rom.8.15 and Gal.4.6, whether he is referring to the beginning of the Our Father or to prayer in general. The term was used with special reverence because the recollection remained alive that Jesus had addressed God in this way and taught his disciples to pray similarly.

This intimate form of address confirms that in his conversation with God, Jesus found himself in a quite specially close and unusual union. It gave him the power to submit to God's will in prayer (see above, 32ff.). Given this understanding of sonship, we can understand how the prayer that Jesus teaches his disciples begins with 'Abba'.

The fact that in Matthew this is translated *our* Father (*patēr hēmōn*)[81] and that, following Jewish prayers, this is given the addition 'in heaven' (as also similarly in Matt.11.25; Luke 10.21[82]), does not go against Jesus' attitude in prayer, even if probably he only said 'Abba'. For Jesus, the familiarity expressed in the use of this word goes with his adoration of the holiness of God, with the 'hallowing of his name', which is the subject of the first petition that follows immediately. One can even said that the addition of the words 'in heaven' followed as a necessary expansion of Jesus' meaning precisely because of the form of address 'Abba'. In that case the reference to 'heaven' does not so much emphasize the difference from a physical father, far less liberation from the tie to Zion or Gerizim,[83] as the transcendence of God.[84]

The fact that Jesus also teaches the disciples to pray 'Abba' means that despite his extraordinarily intensive awareness of sonship, he also wants to lead them to an intimate conversation, into union with God.

So like Luz (*Matthäusevangelium* [p.39], 340), I do not share the view put forward by Jeremias ('Abba' [p.39], 44ff.) that Jesus expressly distinguished his own uniquely close bond with God from that of the disciples. It is certainly the case that in the Gospels he says 'my God' and 'your God', but we can hardly conclude from this that he could not also say 'our God'. Nor can we follow Jeremias (ibid.) in regarding the words which follow the 'cry of jubilation' on the return of the disciples, 'No one knows the Father but the Son' (Matt.11.27; cf. Luke 10.23), as an indication that Jesus could not have included himself with the disciples in union with God as 'our Father'. Like Jeremias (and also Albert Schweitzer[85]), I regard these sayings as authentic, as their 'Johannine' stamp does not allow us to deny them to Jesus. But they only confirm his unique oneness with God, especially in prayer;[86] they do not attest his intention to distance himself from the disciples in this respect.

(c) The first three (or two) petitions

The Our Father is rightly divided into two parts: the first part is marked by the second person singular, 'you', 'your', the second by the first person plural, 'we', 'our'. The first part relates to a divine event, though it is also for our benefit and, as we shall see, we take part in it, but it does not lie directly in the human sphere. The second part relates to a divine event which is directly concerned with human beings. But the link between the two parts is that on both occasions these are saving acts to be requested from God.

The petitions in the first part are very close to the Jewish, Aramaic Kaddish prayer. The wording of this prayer, which is spoken at the end of the synagogue service, has gone through different stages, but a constant feature is that the prayer for the hallowing of God's name and that for the coming of God's kingdom are closely connected: 'Magnified and sanctified be his great name in the world which he has created according to his will . . . may he establish his kingdom . . . speedily and soon',[87] a link which also occurs in other Jewish prayers.[88] As in Luke, here only these two petitions stand side by side, whereas in Matthew a third follows, for the divine will to be done.[89]

Jesus took over an abbreviated form of the prayer familiar to him from synagogue worship, and it has been said, probably rightly,[90] that the really new element in the Our Father is the group of 'we' petitions. This does not mean that by adding this second part Jesus wanted to criticize the Kaddish prayer; nor, however, does it mean that the second-person petitions used by him have precisely the same sense as in the Kaddish. Rather, what was said above on p.40 applies here: the same petitions, spoken by Jesus, must be understood in connection with his whole preaching, and here in particular we should also note the abbreviation: what Jesus does not say (see Matt.6.7 on 'using many words'). We shall note in detail the way in which the Our Father is rooted both in Jewish prayer and in the preaching of Jesus.

(i) The first petition: Hallowed by your name

In the New Testament, as in Judaism, in contrast to our present-day usage, the 'name' has a deep, full meaning. Origen already wrote in his treatise *On Prayer* (24.2) that the name denotes the essential property of the one who bears it. There is no need here to cite all the countless biblical texts from the Old and New Testaments. When, for example, we read in Isa.43.1 'I call you by your name', the reference is to the deep significance of the one who is called on: 'You are mine' (ibid.). In Luke 10.20 Jesus calls on the disciples to 'rejoice that your names are written in heaven' (cf. Rev.3.5). In the Gospel of John (10.3), the Good Shepherd calls the sheep by name.

So the name of God denotes his innermost being: Exod.3.13f. 'What is his name?' . . . God said to Moses, 'I am who I am.' If this name is to be 'hallowed', it means that God is to be recognized as the Holy One, for holiness is God's being. But the paradox of the divine holiness consists in the fact that the holy God who is the hidden and unfathomable one reveals himself precisely in his holiness.

It goes with this that 'hallow' and 'glorify'[91] are quite kindred concepts.[92] So in John 12.28 we read 'Glorify your name.' We hear very often in the Old Testament and also in extra-biblical Jewish texts of God hallowing his name. In a number of passages the hallowing of God's name is mentioned in connection with its profanation, with blasphemy. According to Ezek.36.20ff., the house of Israel has profaned God's name among the nations, so 'I will hallow my great name again' (v.22); in Lev.22.32, 'You shall not profane my holy name, but I will be hallowed among the people of Israel.'

There is much discussion of the question whether the hallowing of the name of God according to first petition is to be done by God himself or by human beings. The evidence of the Old Testament and extra-biblical Jewish texts is that the two belong together, and that hallowing by God himself stands in the foreground: God makes use of human beings. The petition is both eschatological and ethical at the same time.

In his posthumous work *The Christian Life* (p. 157, n. 75), Karl Barth emphatically and impressively stresses that the first petition derives its significance from the fact that human beings constantly desecrate the name of God (212f.). He puts the petition for the divine name to be hallowed in the framework of the unholy egoism which is deeply rooted in human nature, seeing it already at work in the indifference to fellow men and women which is ultimately always present, and which is masked by talk of 'neighbour' and 'friend'. Against this background, the need to take seriously the petition 'Hallowed be our name', which is often spoken so thoughtlessly, becomes clear.[93]

The link between the hallowing by God and the hallowing by human beings is emphasized in the Old Testament by a statement which is repeated in Lev.11.44; 19.2; 20.6: 'You shall be holy, for I am holy.' Changing these Old Testament passages, but probably taking them up, in the Sermon on the Mount Jesus says, 'You shall be perfect as your heavenly Father is perfect' (Matt.5.48).

In connection with ethical hallowing, the possibility has also been considered of regarding the petition at the beginning of the prayer as an imperative which we address to ourselves: 'let us hallow God's name'.[94] However, I would prefer also to include the uttering of the petition in this imperative. Hallowing takes place in the utterance. Here reference should be made to the 'Holy, holy, holy is the Lord of Hosts' (the *trishagion*) which Isaiah in the temple hears the seraphim round the throne of God calling out (6.3). This is probably what Jewish prayers for the hallowing of the name have in mind.[95] Sanctification takes place in prayer: not in empty speaking, but when we really take seriously our longing for the realization of the immeasurable holiness of God. This is to be prayed for everywhere, so that the name of God is hallowed in the offering of prayer. We are to contribute to this event each time we utter the first petition.[96] As we have seen, that something happens in prayer itself is part of the essence of all prayer, if it really becomes conversation.

I shall discuss later the possibility that in the text of Matthew the words 'on earth as it is in heaven' relate not only to the third but to all three petitions of the first part. In that case the hallowing which we must still ask for the earth has already been realized in heaven.

(ii) The second petition: Your kingdom come

The Greek word *basileia*, kingdom, can be understood statically as a place or dynamically as kingly rule. Both meanings are attested in Judaism, but the second occurs far more often. In the words of Jesus the one occurs approximately as often as the other. When, for example, Matt.7.21 speaks of 'entering the kingdom of heaven' or Matt.8.11 of 'eating in the kingdom of God', we have the spatial view. By contrast, the preaching that the kingdom of God is at hand

(Mark 1.14; Matt.4.17) and that it has already come (Matt.12.28) refers more to the kingly rule of God. When the Our Father prays for the coming of the kingdom, we are probably to think primarily of the latter sense. The rule which God exercises in heaven, in his kingdom, is to become reality everywhere, on earth as well.[97]

Here, however, we need to take another tension into account, namely the chronological tension, fundamental to the whole of the New Testament and especially also to the preaching of Jesus, between 'already fulfilled' and 'not yet fulfilled'. It is particularly relevant to our understanding of the second petition. The disciples are to pray for the future coming of the kingdom of God which has already dawned. I must emphasize this view once again here. For Albert Schweitzer's view, which only takes into account Jesus' expectation of a future kingdom of God, is one-sided, as is that of C.H.Dodd, who by contrast sees the hope for the kingdom of God as already having been realized.[98] With W.G.Kümmel I would emphasize that for Jesus the kingdom of God is at the same time both already there and has not yet arrived. It has already dawned, is already growing,[99] but has not yet been accomplished. This applies not only to Luke, as scholars are now fond of claiming, but also to Jesus himself.

This can be backed up by sayings of Jesus which can hardly be disputed.

That it has already dawned is evident from Jesus' answer to the John the Baptist's question whether he is the one who is to come or whether another should be expected (Matt.11.2ff.; Luke 17.18ff.). Referring to Isa.35.5ff. and 51.1 it is: 'The blind see, the lame walk, the lepers are cleansed, the deaf hear, the dead are raised up, the poor have the good news preached to them.'[100] In Luke 11.20 (Matt.12.28) Jesus says explicitly: 'If I by the finger of God (this is probably secondary; Matthew has 'spirit') cast out demons, then the kingdom of God has already come upon you', and as a sign has the experience 'I saw Satan fall like lightning from heaven' (Luke 10.18). That the kingdom of God in its fullness is nevertheless also expected by Jesus is indicated by many purely eschatological sayings which he shares with the Jewish expectation and which need not be listed specially here.[101]

I hope that it will not be seen as a burdensome and inappropriate repetition of a hobby-horse which is dear to me if to clarify matters here I recall an image which I used in my *Christ and Time* (1944), and which was very topical at the time: the decisive battle has been fought, victory has been secured, but the cease-fire – Victory Day, as we said at the time – has not yet come.

An eschatological waiting for the future is common to both Judaism and the New Testament – and this advent expectation also links present-day Judaism with Christianity. For Judaism, too, the future hope is grounded in the past, in the mighty acts of God for the people of Israel, which in the New Testament similarly form part of salvation history.[102] However, for Christians the decisive moment of time has been reached in Christ, whereas for Jews it is still to come. In the New Testament the future is no longer decisive, but can only bring the completion.[103] The meaning of the span of time which remains is to be defined in this light.

So when Christians pray 'Your kingdom come', they are uttering this prayer with Judaism, but following Jesus they are praying for the completion of a kingdom which has already come with him. Precisely because it has already come, they must suffer all the more from the fact that – because of their human guilt – it is so remote, when it ought to be near. So as disciples of Jesus we should pray 'Your kingdom come' much less thoughtlessly and far more ardently, and as we do so also think of our ethical tasks.[104] But on the other hand, precisely because it has already come, we can ask all the more confidently for its coming. When Jesus taught the disciples to include this petition in their prayer, he could not have forgotten what he preached to them about the kingdom which had already dawned.

(iii) The third petition: Your will be done, on earth as it is in heaven

This third petition appears only in Matthew, and not in the Lukan version. The question which of the two texts is the earlier in *this* case, and probably the question which is the original text, would be resolved from the start if we followed some scholars, today above all Joachim Jeremias,[105] in seeing the short Lukan version as the earlier and the longer, Matthaean version as a liturgical extension; or if, conversely, with others, now especially J. Carmignac,[106] we regarded the Lukan Our Father as an abbreviation of the Matthaean version (following the tendency of this evangelist). Although in general there is much to be said for preferring the thesis advanced by Jeremias, in the case of this petition (is it an addition or an omission?) as generally (see p.39 above), the question does not seem so simple to resolve. Here, too, we shall investigate the relationship between this petition and the Synoptic testimony generally about Jesus' attitude to prayer, and see what the Our Father adds to this.

Here the Synoptic narrative about Gethsemane, which has already been discussed above in the chapter on whether prayer is heard, offers itself as a parallel, and indeed it is cited in most explanations of the Our Father. In all three Synoptic Gospels, in fact the prayer of Jesus culminates in the subordination of human wishes to God's will: 'not what I will, but what you will.' Only in Matthew (26.42) does the second prayer spoken there by Jesus contain the precise wording of the petition of the Our Father, 'Your will be done'. So according to Matthew, Jesus himself addressed to the Father in Gethsemane the prayer which he had taught the disciples.[107] This also fits, even if in the framework of the Our Father, where the petition belongs with those for hallowing the divine name and the coming of God's kingdom, at any rate primarily we define God's will without contrasting it with the human will. Indeed the Gethsemane prayer, 'Your will, not mine', specifically involves this contrast.

As we shall see, we must not overlook the difference, which need not necessarily be a contradiction. So first of all we shall ask: when in the Our Father we pray that God's will shall be done (on earth as it is in heaven), what is this will? A discussion of the thesis developed in a very clear article written by G.Lohfink for the *Festschrift* for Rudolf Schnackenburg[108] seems to me to be particulary helpful in answering this question, especially as it has a particularly thorough discussion of the third petition of the Our Father. Taking up Schnackenburg's own view of the petition in terms of carrying out the divine plan of salvation,[109] Lohfink investigates it exegetically with reference to Acts 22.14 and Eph.1.3, and historically by citing Jewish views about this plan of salvation,[110] especially those in the Apocalypse of Abraham, which probably comes from the second half of the second century and has been preserved only in Slavonic.[111] In this work Abraham is shown God's plan in advance, as it exists in heaven and is developing in history on earth.

This notion also casts light on the words 'on earth as it is in heaven', which are not immediately clear. They can be understood to mean 'both in heaven and on earth'. There is evidence for the view that the divine will must also establish itself in heaven. But philologically and in terms of content the words are probably to be understood more in terms of a parallel: what already exists in heaven is to be realized and prayed for on earth.[112]

Lohfink is concerned to show that in the Our Father the will of God does not relate to the ethical fulfilment of God's commandments or to the fate of the individual either, but to the realization of God's plan of salvation, just as Paul in Acts 22.13 is an instrument of that divine will which underlies his saving way towards the Gentiles.

I largely agree with Lohfink. But I cannot see such an abrupt opposition between the individual human fate and the earthly realization of the heavenly plan of salvation. Certainly in the light of the petition in the Our Father, everything that happens to and is endured by the individual is clearly subordinate to the plan as a whole. This applies to Paul's task, and in Gethsemane the will which Jesus accepts despite his wish for the cup to pass from him is the redemptive work which he is to fulfil in accordance with the divine plan. The words 'if it is possible' refer to a possibility that this saving plan does or does not allow. But in the Gethsemane prayer the doing of the divine will which Jesus accepts in humility is the last answer to a human wish to be preserved from suffering, which he expresses as a human being. The fate of the individual cannot be bracketted off from the saving will of God, but has to be integrated into it.

At the end of his article (p.139), Lohfink defines the ethical task which follows from the limitation of the petition to the pre-existent plan of God which he defends so consistently as a 'life that leaves room for God's plan'. This corresponds to the formula 'fitting into salvation history at the point where we are', which I proposed in my *Salvation in History*.[113] According to this remark of Lohfink's, the divine plan of salvation with its development in wider earthly history does seem to me also to include the life of the individual who prays.

So it is certainly a development beyond the third petition, in the perspective of which the whole plan of God stands, but not an illegitimate one, to connect this with a prayer expressing a human wish, as in the Matthaean narrative in 26.42.

This development is justified by the Synoptic preaching of Jesus. For on the one hand the 'cry of jubilation' in Matt.11.25f.; Luke

10.21f. which Lohfink also cites, is for Jesus attached to the 'will' of God[114] in a plan of salvation the revelation of which is entrusted to him as a task along with 'all that is given him'. To this degree the petition in the Our Father is very much in the style of Jesus, even if, as in the Lukan version, it was not spoken by Jesus. But in particular according to the passage cited above, God's will for salvation relates not only to salvation history generally, but in and with it to what happens to individuals: the 'wise and understanding', from whom God has hidden it, and the 'innocent', to whom he has disclosed it. The integration of the individual into the divine plan of salvation is presupposed in particular in Jesus' belief in providence, which is vividly expressed in the saying Matt.10.30; Luke 12.7: 'even the hairs of your head are numbered.' If the disciples are to pray that the plan of salvation which has been completed in heaven shall be developed on earth, all that happens is to be brought into this light.

In that case, in the application of the petition of the Lord's Prayer, we may and should take into account what was said above (p. 34) in connection with the prayer in Gethsemane, despite its different orientation. We have seen that submission to God's will in prayer does not exclude the freedom of the one who prays to express a human wish to God, even if it may be uncertain to that person whether or not the wish accords with the divine will; on the other hand, this presupposes the freedom of God to incorporate this wish into his eternal counsel without changing it. The combination of the immutability of the divine will, the expression of which is God's plan of salvation, with God's freedom to hear or not to hear human wishes, emerges from the will of God as Creator, who in his communication of himself which is rooted in love wants the human beings created by him to accord with his will in freedom.[115]

Lohfink rightly shows that with reference to the divine plan of salvation, in terms of content the third petition of the text of Matthew fits into the framework of the whole of the first part of the Our Father, as the subject of the first and second petitions is the same: what is taking place in heaven (hallowing, kingly rule) is to be realized on earth. In that case we should not a priori rule out a suggestion made by Origen (*On Prayer* 26.2) that the addition 'on earth as it is in heaven' should be applied to all three petitions.[116] In other words, we should put a point or a dash after 'Thy will be done' and then regard the addition, which is to be applied to the whole of the first part, as its conclusion. It is difficult to make a final decision here. If Origen's thesis is right, then the three petitions would correspond not only in content but also in their summary structure: 'May the hallowing of your name, the coming of your kingdom, the doing of your will take place', the emphasis in all three instances echoing the second-person 'your'.[117]

(d) The fourth petition: Give us today bread for tomorrow

Although to the innocent ear this fourth petition would not seem to present any problems, since antiquity it has prompted very different explanations. This is connected with the understanding of the word 'bread', and that in turn is closely connected with the problem of the meaning of the preceding adjective,[118] which in the wording familiar to us and according to ancient tradition[119] has been translated 'daily'.

Quite apart from the difficulty of translating this Greek word, which will be discussed later, the divergence in interpretations derives from the fact that since the first century the application to material bread, which is the first thing that immediately springs to mind, has been thought to be incompatible with the deep spirituality of the other petitions in the Our Father, especially those of the first part. Evidently, taking up what was said on p. 22 above, people had difficulty in belieivng that in giving this prayer Jesus included needs like eating, which were thought to be base: here was a tendency towards of docetism.

Given the spiritualizing which can be seen particularly in antiquity and the Middle Ages, but also even today, we must put this petition, too, in the framework of the overall witness of the Synoptic Gospels, and thus return to the question of Jesus' attitude towards material food.

Jesus is far from despising food in any way. The quotation of Deut.8.3 in the temptation story (Matt.4.4; Luke 4.4), 'Man does not live by bread alone', to which reference is often made, really belongs there only in connection with the suggestion made to Jesus by the devil that he should turn stones into bread. In a comparison of his conduct with that of John the Baptist,[120] who fasted ascetically and was therefore regarded as being 'possessed by a demon', Jesus was called 'a glutton and winebibber' by the people (Matt.11.19).

Precisely on this point of fasting he deliberately differed from John the Baptist, whom he had first followed, and the Baptist's disciples (Mark 2.18 par.), though he did not exclude fasting in special circumstances (the temptation story, Matt.4.2; Luke 4.2; also Mark 9,29, but only according to some witnesses).[121]

Nowdays we note a reluctance to attribute a prayer for material bread to Jesus, especially within the Our Father, which otherwise focusses on the supreme aims of faith, in particular among those who believe that the whole prayer is directed only towards the future.[122] Such interpreters think of the future bread in the kingdom of God, and, as we shall see, refer the all-important defining adjective to the future. But the spiritual interpretation is often combined with the material interpretation, so that this latter is given a higher dignity.[123]

On the other hand, at any rate a considerable number of scholars take only material food into account, as I would propose here.[124] Between 1519 and 1528, after a good deal of hesitation, Luther changed from the spiritual to the material explanation.[125] Without concessions, in the *Institutes* Calvin accepts only material bread; so does Bucer in the *Enarrationes perpetuae* (1536). However, Bucer adds to his own view, and to his comments on other views, that he will not oppose those who defend a spiritual interpretation, provided that they do not think it unworthy that Jesus should have prayed for material bread.

So given the testimony of the Synoptists generally, an unprejudiced hearer of the fourth petition cannot contest the understanding of the word bread which immediately springs to mind. However, this must be confirmed by an investigation of the interpretation of the Greek adjective *epiousios*, which has been discussed so often.

The difficulty arises from the fact that this word does not occur anywhere else, so its meaning cannot be derived from another usage. Origen already writes that no Greek scholar used the word, and that it is not used even in the vernacular (*On Prayer*, 27.7ff.). Granted, an Egyptian papyrus containing the word was found in 1889.[126] However, it was already mutilated, and it has now been lost. For want of an explanatory context the meaning is uncertain, but as the papyrus seems to be a list of tasks, one can understand it as meaning 'what is necessary for the (day's) ration'.[127]

Quite apart from this papyrus find, *epiousios* has often been connected with the Greek word *ousia*, 'subsistence'. But leaving aside the philological difficulty,[128] it has rightly been said that more common words for this would have been available to the Our Father.[129]

The earliest of the countless explanations of the problematical adjective is the one preferred by Origen (see above) and then developed further by the church fathers, especially Jerome (*Commentary on Matthew*, on Matt.6.11). It, too, begins from the substantive *ousia*, but understands this as 'substance'; taking up the preposition *epi* = 'in addition', attached to it, Jerome translates the word *epiousios* as *supersubstantialis*, i.e. 'supernatural', bread.

This explanation, which was popular in the subsequent period and in particular was related to the eucharist,[130] is made philologically more difficult by the fact that the *i* of *epi* should have been elided before *ousia*, resulting not in *epiousios* but in *epousios*. The same difficulty arises in the derivation of the word from *ousa hēmera* = today.

The difficulty just mentioned does not arise if *epiousios* is derived from the verb *epienai* = follow. For here the *i* belongs to the root of the verb and cannot be elided. That produces the meaning 'for the following day, the morrow'. This derivation is reinforced by the report of the church father Jerome that in the Gospel which he calls the Gospel of the Hebrews[131] he read the Hebrew word *mahar* = 'tomorrow' for *epiousios*. A large number of exegetes have followed this explanation.[132] However, many of them, in accordance with their eschatological interpretation of the whole of the Our Father, understand 'tomorrow' in the sense of 'future', an interpretation which can be attested philologically. But in the last resort this is also a form of spiritualization of the fourth petition and is subject to a criticism which is hard to suppress; it does not allow the understanding which springs to mind and which also retains its validity within the framework of the New Testament expectation of the future. Moreover the pronoun 'our' (our bread) tells more against the spiritualization of this petition, which, precisely because it is so concrete and deals with everyday necessities, is characteristic of Jesus. Food for the next day is an obvious necessity to ask for.

The word 'today' is quite appropriate here. It is to be preferred to 'for every day', which we read instead in Luke (11.3). The Lukan version is more abstract, and envisages the bread that we always need.[133] So the Vulgate translates *epiousios* as 'daily' (*quotidianus*).[134]

An objection has been made to the translation 'for tomorrow' on the basis of Matt.6.34, 'Take no thought for the morrow ... Let the morrow look after itself.'[135] I think that this objection is unjustified, since 'taking thought for the morrow' is not the same thing as 'praying for the morrow'.[136] One could even say that because we must not and should not be anxious about the morrow, we should pray; or, to put it another way, because we pray, we need not and should not be anxious. The reason given, that the Father knows our needs, is the same in both cases: for not being anxious about food for the next day (Matt.6.31f.) and not using many words in praying (Matt.6.7). But that the reasons are identical does not mean, as I have said, that praying for the next day is ruled out here. The reference to the 'knowledge' of the Father is made only to warn against 'using many words' in prayer, and not directed against prayer in itself.

So the translation of the adjective *epiousios* as 'for tomorrow' seems to me to be justified by the connection between praying and not being anxious which is rooted in the preaching of Jesus.[137] Paul clearly saw the distinction between not being anxious and praying when he wrote in Phil.4.6, 'Have no anxiety[138] about anything, but in everything by prayer and supplication with thanksgiving let your requests be made known to God.' The verse from the hymn by Paul Gerhardt which I quoted above (p. 21) rightly contrasts 'anxiety' with prayer.

Carmignac adduces arguments which are often worth considering in favour of connecting the 'bread' for which we pray with the manna. Here he refers to Exod.16.4ff. ('until tomorrow'). Although we also find this explanation among some other notable interpreters of the Our Father,[139] it does not seem to me to commend itself because of the reasons I have given. The simple request for food for the next day corresponds far more to the nature of Jesus' instructions in the Synoptic Gospels.

(e) The fifth petition: Forgive us our debts, as we forgive our debtors

Matthew has 'debt' and 'debtors', Luke 'sins' (and then also debtors). There is no difference in meaning here, and the two Greek terms go back to the same Aramaic word.[140] Matthew's more concrete translation here is probably to be seen as the more original, especially as Jesus was fond of using the situation of financial indebtedness as an illustration.[141]

Much more important is the relationship of the subordinate clause ('as . . .') to the main clause. This is the real problem raised by this petition. Does the statement in the subordinate clause form the basis of a human claim to the divine forgiveness for which we ask? First of all a difference between Matthew and Luke needs to be mentioned. Whereas in Matthew the subordinate clause is introduced by 'as',[142] Luke writes 'for',[143] which further accentuates the problem to be dealt with. It is possible that here, too, we simply have variant translations.[144] But the problem remains.

In particular the tense of the verb in the subordinate clause is an important factor in a solution. Usually insufficient attention is paid to the fact that the Greek text of Matthew on which our modern translations are based has 'as we have forgiven', whereas Luke has 'as we forgive'. We usually forget that in translating 'as we forgive' we lapse into the Lukan version (see also Didache 8.2), whereas otherwise we follow the text of Matthew. The question of the original Aramaic or Semitic form which we have to assume for Jesus is of fundamental significance in this case, as it points a way towards answering the problem of this petition. The fact that Matthew has the past and Luke the present tense can be explained from a grammatical peculiarity of Semitic languages.

Specialists in Aramaic and Hebrew have pointed out the peculiar character of the Semitic perfect, which, as P.Joüon shows,[145] underlies Matt.6.12. The Aramaic perfect denotes an action which is complete at the moment of speaking or writing, which is actually having an effect during the statement. This coincidence, i.e. the present use of the perfect, is regular not only in Aramaic but also in Hebrew.[146] Thus Joüon translates the Aramaic *sebuqnem* which is here taken to be the underlying verb in the fifth petition of the Our Father 'as we now forgive'.[147] With reference to Joüon, Jeremias suggests as a translation 'as we hereby forgive'.[148] Moreover the same Aramaic verb form (present perfect) is translated in Matthew literally with the Greek past (aorist), whereas Luke's present more correctly reproduces the Aramaic sense.

I have dwelt on this philological discussion because it leads to a solution of the theological problem mentioned above. On the basis of the Semitic temporal 'coincidence', the subordinate clause 'as we forgive . . .' relates to the past and present and even to the future.[149] In that case it need not be emphasized that we must forgive *before* God forgives us by hearing our prayers, so that our forgiveness would be a condition making a claim on which God's forgiveness depended, in other words that we would be defining God's forgiveness by our behaviour. Regardless of whether our forgiveness takes place before the divine forgiveness, at the same time, or afterwards,[150] the only thing that matters is that with our petition for forgiveness, we always stand in the sphere of, or, as Lochman well puts it following Jeremias,[151] in the field of force of, the forgiving God.

Here it is of fundamental importance for the theological problem – and this is the main thing – that the subordinate clause 'as we forgive . . .' does not relate to the divine fulfilment of our petition but to our human petition itself, i.e. to our inner attitude when uttering the prayer. We can ask for God's forgiveness only if while we pray we are ourselves in the realm of the forgiveness that he wills.[152] We must know that God's forgiveness is not some property, but belongs to his innermost being, his infinite love. Faith in God is faith in the forgiving God. So we must know that when we ask for forgiveness, in the light of this forgiveness we must forgive those who do harm to us, just as in general, in the light of God's love we must practise love. Otherwise we do not know what we are doing when we utter the fifth petition of the Our Father.[153]

Moreover, with this understanding we can derive from Matthew's past form (the Greek aorist, 'as we have forgiven') a meaning which is compatible with what has been said, although Luke's present is more correct. We must also know from our past experience how difficult it is to forgive if someone has done us a very great injustice. We must know what we are doing when we ask God honestly for forgiveness for our much greater sin.

The honesty of our prayer requires that we ourselves should stand in the sphere, in the 'field of force', of forgiveness. In that case, any human claim to God's free forgiveness is excluded. However, we ourselves stand outside this divine field of force unless we are also ready on our part always to forgive; for unless we are, it is meaningless to utter this petition.

The understanding of the subordinate clause which is given philological support here is confirmed by the whole Synoptic preaching. First of all by Mark 11.25: 'And whenever you stand praying, forgive, if you have anything against any one; so that your Father also who is in heaven may forgive you your trespasses.' Here too the forgiveness of God rests on human prayer, which must take place while standing in the field of force of divine forgiveness. According to this saying, not only the petition for forgiveness but any prayer requires that we should stand in the sphere of divine forgiveness. For God's forgiveness is not only one expression of his loving will alongside others but is fundamental to his relationship to his creatures. That is also confirmed by Jesus' saying about the offering which is to be brought to the altar only if reconciliation with one's brother has taken place (Matt.5.23ff.).

Since all prayer, as we have seen, is to be encounter with God, union with his will, it is indispensable that forgiveness should bind us to God. Where this bond is destroyed through our refusal to forgive our fellow human beings, as in the parable of the unmerciful servant (Matt.19.23ff.), our encounter with God is destroyed, and all prayer and petitions for the forgiveness of our sins are meaningless.

The words in Matt.6.14f. which immediately follow the Our Father, 'For if you forgive men their trespasses, your heavenly Father also will forgive you; but if you do not forgive men their trespasses, neither will your Father forgive your trespasses', could only suggest, read independently of the context of the prayer, that God's forgiveness depends on our forgiveness. But Matthew has put these words in the context of the Our Father so to speak as a 'postscript', because he was aware that for Jesus forgiving and praying belong together.[154] The view that God depends on our conduct would contradict the whole proclamation of Jesus, for example the parable in Matt.20.1ff. about the labourers at the eleventh hour who receive the same reward as the first. Verse 15 emphasizes the freedom of the lord of the vineyard: 'Can I not do what I want with my own?' This also applies to forgiveness: God is not dependent on us, but he wants us to be united with him in prayer for forgiveness in the power to forgive our fellow human beings.

We can conclude that saying the fifth petition presupposes that each time we pray, from God's perspective we put ourselves once again in the realm of forgiveness and are ready to remain in this sphere in our relations with our fellow human beings.

(f) The sixth petition: Lead us not into temptation

This petition has always provoked the most discussion, so I shall spend rather more time on it, particularly as the interpretation which I shall propose differs from the usual ones and will meet with criticism. So contrary to my concern for brevity, this section will be relatively long, especially as I cannot avoid going into the different and extraordinarily numerous explanations.

The petition should not be connected over-hastily with James 1.13: 'God does not tempt anyone.'[155] In this book I shall explain the sixth petition in the framework of the Synoptic Gospels, where it belongs. But here, too, we have to ask the question: what does it mean for us to pray to God not to lead us into temptation? Can God, who alone is good (Mark 10.17), associate human beings with what is radically evil? As the Greek words stand,[156] they not only suggest, scandalously, that we should answer this question in the affirmative; they hardly allow any other interpretation.

Time and again since antiquity theologians have tried explanations which cannot be justified by the Greek text in order to remove this offence. Thus for example Marcion, Tertullian and also Augustine bent the sense of the petition, as though it read 'do not allow us to succumb to temptation'. Lochman rightly speaks of 'manipulation' and 'evasion'. If initially we keep to the Greek wording – afterwards we shall look at a grammatical peculiarity of the Aramaic of the fifth petition – in both Matthew and in Luke it clearly says 'Do not lead us'.

Now there is an explanation which leaves the verb 'lead' but gives it a philological significance which comes close to 'allow to succumb'. Distinguished exegetes emphasize the first syllable of the verb, 'into' (Greek *eis*), in such a way that the whole weight of the verb rests on it:

so we ask that we shall not totally fall victim to temptation, i.e. succumb to it.[157]

Those who advance this interpretation refer to the Gethsemane narrative. As we already saw on pp. 28ff., and as I shall argue later to justify my own explanation, despite the difference in situation this is certainly to be related to the petition in the Our Father. These exegetes emphasize that in the Gethsemane narrative, in both Matthew (26.41) and Luke (22.46) there is a composite verb with *eis*: Jesus admonishes the disciples to watch and pray that they do not 'enter into temptation'.[158] Later (pp. 60, 63) we shall have to ask whether the identification of 'lead into' with 'succumb' which these exegetes propose with reference to Semitic texts is really certain.

Furthermore, Carmignac refers to another Semitic peculiarity: what is usually called the causative use of verbs, 'make to do' something. In this case this produces 'cause us not enter into temptation'.[159] The recent work by Ernst Jenni[160] offers basic philological support for this causative character:

> He begins from the justified question why the prayer does not simply say 'do not tempt us', but expands this into 'lead us not into temptation'. Using the philological works of Germanists,[161] he designates the expanded form of expression, with a somewhat clumsy term, a 'functional verb structure'. It is important that this gives the simple verb a causative meaning (applied to this petition of the Our Father again, 'do not cause us to enter' into temptation). Jenni finds many examples of a parallel to this philological phenomenon, which appears in Indo-Germanic terminology, in the possibility or necessity in Aramaic in some cases to understand the verb as a causative.

This demonstration is important for the solution which I shall go on to propose. It differs from the usual explanation, but is not considered by Jenni, either, as a consequence of his argument. He believes that his investigation only supports the interpretation put forward by the scholars mentioned above (58f.), but I cannot agree with their presupposition that 'enter' = 'succumb'.

Certainly it has to be recognized that the explanation given by Carmignac and Heller (also followed by Lochman) removes the problem mentioned above which makes God the author of the temptation to evil, so that the 'entering = succumbing' could not be

God's work. But although it also has the advantage (in contrast to the earlier 'manipulations' of the text, which do not have a philological basis) of leaving the Greek verb as it is, it suffers from requiring presuppositions which in my view are not sufficiently established, that 'enter into temptation' must mean something like 'succumb to temptation'.[162] Even if we recognized the justification of the emphasis on the syllable 'into', the need to identify the expression 'enter the sphere of the devil' with 'succumb' does not follow.

The scholars mentioned above a priori exclude the possibility that in the petition of the Our Father 'be led into' can refer to temptation as a trial, to which we may succumb but which we may also withstand. Certainly they emphasize the presence and the importance of the meaning 'tempt = try', but for a reason which needs to be discussed later and at first is illuminating (see below, 63f.), they do not apply it to the petition not to be led into temptation (or, as Heller and Carmignac understand it, 'not to be caused to enter into').

To understand better what follows we must look at the double or even multiple meaning of the Greek word *peirazein* (tempt).[163]

First of all the eschatological meaning. The advocates of an eschatological interpretation of the whole of the Our Father see the real meaning of this petition, too, in the temptation which will come about at the end. The noun *peirasmos* is in fact often used as a designation of the eschatological terrors associated with it. Certainly this perspective needs to be taken into account, in so far as the eschatological framework is present as the background to the Our Father. But just as an eschatological constriction is not exclusively determinative for the other petitions, so it is not appropriate as an interpretation of this word with its many meanings either.

Two other meanings of the Greek verb *peirazein* above all need to be taken into account. First, temptation with the aim of leading people astray to evil; secondly, temptation with the aim of putting people to the test, examining and strengthening their stamina, their power to resist.[164] In the first case the subject is the devil:[165] he takes the initiative to evil by attacking all human beings. In the second case, which I mention on pp. 27f. above, God is the subject: out of love, in individual instances he can test people, but here too the devil is at work, albeit under God's command. As this use of the verb occurs often in the Bible, it must not be given a subordinate role.[166]

We find it often in the Old Testament, for example in the book of Job, especially in the narrative framework (Job 1–2.13; 42.7–17). Here it is disaster caused by evil which is to lead Job to forsake God. In the story of the sacrifice of Isaac (Gen.22.1ff.), God does not make use of the devil to test Abraham's obedience (only in the book of Jubilees, Mastemas, 17.15ff.).[167] Not only individuals but also the people are 'tempted' by God.[168]

Thus God and at the same time the devil are at work in temptation as testing, but God is the real subject and the devil is his instrument[169]. This meaning of temptation – and, I would want to say, this meaning in particular – needs the causative explanation: God allows us through the devil to enter into temptation as a test. He leads us into it; not, however, himself but the devil. Although the devil is the one who acts, God's omnipotence is preserved.

Moreover it is not excluded even if, as I said above, the devil himself tempts all human beings, using a freedom which has been put at his disposal. The omnipotence of God does not manifest itself here as it does in the case of the testing of individuals, but it is not absent. Even then God exercises control.[170] God can intervene. This is important for understanding the petition in the Our Father, 'Lead us not into temptation.'

The New Testament, and especially also Jesus himself, does not know any real dualism, but only a relative, 'chronologically' determined, dualism. The devil has been conquered and yet he is still at work, and will be destroyed only at the end. Again I must point here to the 'already' and 'not yet'. The devil still has a certain freedom to exercise his power in the pursuit of his aim, which is to lead human beings to evil through temptation.[171]

Some explanation of the tension between God's omnipotence and the way in which God allows another power than his to be at work, which is undeniably present throughout the New Testament and cannot be resolved rationally, is offered in connection with Rev.20.3 by the image of the binding of the devil, which I supplement with that of the 'line' that can be sometimes shorter and sometimes longer.[172]

If God's omnipotence over the evil reality which still exists remains, then those temptations for which the devil has the initiative towards all human beings is not removed from it. As the omnipotence of God cannot be separated from his love, we could extend the concept of 'testing' – with the necessary proviso and indirectly – to all temptations.

If God's omnipotence is to be presupposed wherever tempting by the devil is mentioned,[173] the distinction between temptation as testing and temptation generally, which should be noted in principle, loses its importance. This applies all the more to prayer, since we cannot know what special significance temptation has for us in God's unfathomable loving will.

After this unavoidable deviation, in order to make more precise the relationship of tension between divine omnipotence and the power of evil, we return to the wording of this petition in the Our Father.

Here I am anticipating a thesis which I shall explain in more detail later, which takes into account both the Greek wording and the use of the causative which is frequent in Aramaic. With a minority of exegetes I infer from the petition the meaning 'spare us temptation', i.e. not primarily 'spare us succumbing to temptation', but 'spare us temptation as such'. Temptation here is at the same time both the divine testing (by the devil as God's instrument) in the narrower sense and the testing provoked by the devil. God can spare us this latter if he hears the petition to spare us by not leading us into a situation where the devil can activate the temptation with which he threatens all human beings, each in his or her own way. In both cases, because of our weakness we find ourselves in the dangerous situation between resisting and succumbing. The two kinds of temptation are therefore not separated in the petition. Both times we ask God that we shall not be confronted with the devil.

To do justice to the causative usage of the verb, I would make the petition more precise: 'do not cause us to enter into temptation by the devil'.

In the testing, God as the transcendent subject is not the one who himself tempts us to evil, but he takes the devil into his service and makes him as a subordinate subject carry out the temptation as a test (causative).[174]

I oppose the formula given above to that suggested by Carmignac at the end of his very long chapter, which is accepted by many exegetes: 'cause me not to enter into temptation by yielding to it'.[175]

If we understand being spared temptation as the object of the petition, a conclusion follows which most exegetes fight shy of, namely that it is in God's omnipotence to lead us or not to lead us into temptation. But I do not take offence at the fact that in the temptation of Jesus it is unambiguously said that the Spirit, i.e. in the end God, drove Jesus into the 'wilderness' (Mark 1.12); Jesus is said to have been 'carried into the wilderness to be tempted of the devil' (Matt.4.1); he was 'led around' by the Spirit in the wilderness (Luke 4.1).[176]

The exegesis proposed here was already rejected in antiquity, for the first time by Origen.[177] We cannot, he argued, ask God to spare us temptation, since it is impossible for human beings not to be tempted. From the list of church fathers after him I need mention only Cyril, Jerome, Augustine and Thomas Aquinas. With the church fathers, Luther and Calvin also speak out against the interpretation mentioned;[178] Bucer (1536) is less resolute.[179]

The vast majority of present-day interpreters energetically contest the reference of the petition to 'being spared' temptation with the same argument, which is repeated almost automatically. However (in contrast to Carmignac), they content themselves with a summary rejection, as though this explanation were too absurd to be discussed. Given the almost universal consensus, there is no need to make a list.

I shall limit myself to citing some of the few exceptions, above all P.Fiebig,[180] who understands the petition in a similar way to me in the sense of not being brought into the situation in which because of our weakness we are in danger of succumbing to evil. The French ecumenical translation 'ne nous soumets pas à la tentation' comes close to this explanation and is not all that remote from the translation of the Greek text which used to be customary.[181] Grelot also puts it well in a precise way: 'do not expose us to the test which consists in temptation'.[182] Carmignac cites P.Dausch[183] and H.Schürmann[184] as earlier representatives of the interpretation which he rejects. I would mention

H.W.Schröder,[185] who with reference to F.Rittelmeyer[186] explains sparing from temptation on the basis of the specially close bond between the suppliant and God.

The main counter-argument about the inevitability of temptation, which goes back to Origen, certainly begins from the correct assertion that the devil tempts all human beings; the associated assumption that (in a way which we cannot fathom in detail) temptation is included in God's plan of salvation is also correct. But does this mean that we have no right to pray that temptations will not come our way? We all know what particular temptations threaten us. We also know the situations which are a particularly dangerous for us, in which the devil has an easy time. Shouldn't the disciples, for whom Jesus formulates this petition, have been able to bring before God the human wish not to find themselves in such situations, like any other concern, and to say 'do not lead us into them', 'do not lead us into this danger'?

In view of the weaknesses of which we are aware, certain situations of temptation are a special danger to us. We may also pray to God to keep the dangers away from us, even though we know that he allows the dangers, that he can lead us into them, but that on the other hand he also has power over them (Mark 14.36 par.).

If we think of testing in the narrower sense, the objection to a prayer to be spared temptation could seem illuminating, given that God thinks it healthy for certain people to be tempted by the devil. Isn't it meaningless, people ask, to pray that God may not carry out his plan which aims at human salvation? Thus we read in the Kittel *Theological Dictionary of the New Testament*[187] that the petition of the Our Father (assuming that it relates to divine testing) should read precisely the opposite: 'lead us into temptation'

If it is the case that not only the divine testing of individuals but also the temptation of all human beings caused by the devil does not come from God, but is not outside his power and his loving will (see above, 62), in other words that the two kinds of temptation should not be separated sharply, then the objection mentioned also applies to the latter one. But in that case the same answer to the objection, namely that our knowledge of the possibility that God can use evil – the evil one – as an instrument in its service should not prevent us from asking God that we should not come into contact with evil,[188] also applies here. For fear of a temptation which especially threatens us, we may pray that the union of God that we seek in every prayer may be so close that temptation is spared us, although it is part of the divine plan that we should be tempted.

With this petition of the Our Father, Jesus gives the disciples the courage to pray to God in childlike trust that he will accept a human wish into his plan, even though the details of this plan are unfathomable to them. Nowadays this trust – 'unless you become as children' – is often regarded as a sign of a human immaturity which needs to be overcome, even as contempt for the divine majesty.

But this is precisely the trust which Jesus calls for in the Gospels; even more, it is the trust that he himself shows us in Gethsemane. Here once again we must return to his own prayer. In it he expresses his wish (which God will not fulfil) that the 'cup' may pass from him (Mark 14.35ff. par.). Certainly this does not accord with being spared temptation, but it also does not accord with being spared an event which belongs in God's plan. Jesus brings this wish before the Father in the certainty that 'all things are possible' for him, in other words that God can incorporate a wish expressed in prayer into a plan which is nevertheless unalterable, albeit with the addition 'if it is possible'.

In expressing the purely human wish that the cup may pass from him, Jesus (true man) by his example indirectly authorizes us in the Our Father to pray that temptation may also pass us by.

God wants us to pray to him, though he does not need our prayer. This will includes the possibility that we may even turn to him with a wish which perhaps cannot be fulfilled, just as a child in hopeful trust makes a request to parents without being sure whether it will be granted.

Thus this petition of the Our Father, like any prayer, requires the words 'but not what I will', 'thy will be done', and thus the possibility of non-fulfilment to be included in the prayer for deliverance from temptation.

In that case – but only in the background, and only in connection with the concluding petition, 'but deliver us from evil', which is to be discussed later – the petition for the power to resist *in* temptation comes into view.

With this perspective I do not want as it were after the event to twist 'not leading into temptation' round into a 'not leading into a situation in which one succumbs'. But I do find, in taking note of the other

Synoptic statements about prayer, as in the case of the explanation of the Our Father as a whole, that the idea that the petition to be spared temptation might not be fulfilled a transition to the subordinate clause 'but deliver us from evil'.[189] For with it the petition to be delivered from the temptation which leads us into the sphere of evil is expanded into the petition to be delivered from evil generally. Moreover in its absoluteness this also includes the petition for support *in* temptation.

The subordinate clause expands the petition 'lead us not into temptation'. So the view that these closing words are a subordinate clause which goes with the sixth petition will be the topic of the next section, to be discussed in more detail.

(g) But deliver us from evil

First of all we must ask: is this really an addition to the sixth petition or an independent seventh petition?

To arrive at the number seven (in Matthew), many exegetes regard the subordinate clause as a new petition. The grammatical construction in Greek really only allows the possibility that the petition is a subordinate clause in the sixth petition, which supplements it.[190]

At the same time it expands the sixth petition: but deliver us *in any case* from evil. The avoidance of any contact with evil is asked for.[191] For contact with evil is possible in two ways: on the one hand it also takes place in testing, and if our explanation of the sixth petition is correct, this is the immediate sense. But on the other hand the expansion probably means to convey that even if we are not spared temptation and are directly subjected to it, we need God's help to resist and so be delivered from evil.

There has been much discussion since antiquity as to whether what is meant in the petition is deliverance from the evil one, masculine, i.e. the devil, or evil, neuter. The Greek genitive which appears here can mean either.

The philological investigation of the use of the Greek *poneros* or *poneron* does not arrive at any completely clear result. However, in the New Testament the masculine is attested as a designation for the devil: in Jesus' parable in Matt.13.19 (at the same point Mark 4.14 has 'Satan' and Luke 8.12 'the devil'). Outside the Synoptic Gospels special mention should be made of Eph.6.16; I John 2.13; 3.12;

5.18. By comparison, the passages which are especially cited for the neuter (John 17.15; II Thess.3.3) do not carry so much weight.[192]

But apart from this, throughout the Synoptic preaching of Jesus evil is so often personified as a matter of course that the explanation that the genitive refers to the evil one rather than to evil is to be preferred.[193]

> The masculine interpretation is quite common, particularly in the Greek fathers. Augustine decides for the neuter (*De sermone in montagna* II.4), and this is the rule for all the Latin fathers and to the present day for most Catholic exegetes. By contrast, Carmignac (306ff.) argues very energetically for a reference to the devil.
>
> Of the Reformers, Luther (in several writings) follows the Latin fathers in assuming the neuter. By contrast, Martin Bucer (*In sacra quattuor evangeliorum enarrationes perpetuae*, 1536, 64) argues for the masculine, as do most more recent Protestant exegetes, in contrast to Luther,[194] e.g. Lohmeyer, *Lord's Prayer*, 217ff.; Brown, *New Testament Essays*, 1965, 251ff.; Bonnard, *Commentary*, ad loc, 87).

The rejection (or acceptance) of belief in the devil should not be a factor in any decision. Calvin writes well in his *Concordance des trois evangelistes* (1555), 142, that the question is fundamentally unimportant and should not give rise to discussion, since whether one means sin or the devil amounts to the same thing.

(h) The doxology: for the kingdom, the power and the glory are yours, for ever

The doxology is absent from the good ancient manuscripts of the New Testament. It occurs in the collection of liturgies in the Didache (beginning of the second century, 8.2), but only in a two-member form: power and glory. That could explain the custom of the Catholic Church of saying the Our Father without the doxology and making it end with the petition 'deliver us from evil', following the old church fathers, who either omit it or with Irenaeus regard it as a liturgical appendix added to a prayer of Jesus. However, here the historical question whether the earliest community of disciples (and

Jesus himself) ever said the Our Father without the words of the doxology cannot be answered from the literary evidence. For Jewish prayers show that there were prayers with a firmly fixed conclusion and alongside them prayers, especially unofficial prayers, the category to which the Our Father belongs (see above, 38, 40), which ended with a freely formulated 'seal'.[195] Generally speaking, however, prayers had to end in a doxology,[196] so we should certainly agree with the assumption of Schlatter[197] and Jeremias[198] that the Our Father also had such a conclusion from the start. It has also rightly been pointed out that the prayer taught by Jesus would hardly have ended with the words 'from evil' in the Matthaean version and 'into temptation' in the Lukan version.

The reason why the old manuscripts omit the doxology may be that Jesus did not have to add it, since it was more or less a matter of course. The question of the Amen, which is also attached to the Our Father only in late manuscripts, is different. The loanword, taken over from Hebrew and probably going back to Egyptian, was originally used as a secular ending and then as a liturgical response in Jewish liturgy; in early Christianity, too, it simply served as confirmation by the community. Only rarely, and at a late stage, was it spoken as a wish for fulfilment by the person praying.[199]

As for the wording, first it should be remarked that doxologies occur not only in prayers but also in other texts in the Old and New Testaments.[200] They appear particularly frequently in the letters of Paul. At some points in describing the knowledge granted to him, which for him issues in praise of God, the apostle feels the need to cite doxological formulae.

To explain the origin of the tripartite doxology which has become customary, Matthew Black,[201] following earlier works by J.J.Wettstein[202] and F.H.Chase,[203] has made a detailed survey of all the relevant passages. Taking special note of the formula in I Chron.29.10f. which is regularly cited, and the Aramaic Targum, he demonstrates the occurrence of one-member and multi-member doxologies in which *doxa*, glory, is always present as a constant: two-member and then three-member doxologies subsequently became established.

Theologically, the doxology, in the framework of the whole of the Our Father, has the deep significance of containing the liturgical response to the first three petitions, so that the circle is closed harmoniously.[204] At this point it expresses the confidence that the fundamental petitions at the beginning will be heard. By directly following the petition for deliverance from the devil, it can also be regarded as a reference to the omnipotence of God over evil which, though not destroyed, has already been overcome.[205]

That glory (*doxa*) also has its fixed place in this conclusion is, as Lochman shows,[206] theologically significant:[207] thanks to its addition the Our Father is not only an intercession but also a hymn of praise.

II. Prayer in Paul (the Pauline corpus)

After mature consideration, I have decided to introduce the whole Pauline corpus, i.e. all the letters attributed to Paul, here, although all the passages relevant to the apostle's view of prayer are contained in the so-called undisputed letters. The question of the authenticity or inauthenticity of the others can be left out of account here; in any case, no consensus can be reached over a solution, even with the use of the same philological and historical criteria. I have therefore cited relevant verses from 'disputed' writings for investigating prayer in Paul. For they are so manifestly in line with the passages to be used from the undisputed letters that we may assume that some disciples of Paul faithfully carried on the master's practice and views of prayer. Whether they come from Paul or his disciples, the disputed letters at any rate help to fill out the picture.

1. Introduction. The general distribution of prayers

In all general studies of prayer, the letters of Paul occupy a particularly large amount of space,[208] even more in those limited to the New Testament.[209] More recently, many monographs have appeared on the prayer of the apostle. From the wealth of them I would select that by G.Harder,[210] along with the most recent, a dissertation by R.Gebauer.[211] The latter offers a good and complete survey of all the relevant literature.[212]

In contrast to the texts of the Synoptic Gospels discussed above, which contain basic instructions on prayer, but apart from the Our Father and the Gethsemane prayer only report Jesus' own prayers addressed to the Father by way of exception, in general, while Paul does not give the wording of his own prayers, he does very often report their content.

We find a list of different prayers in I Tim.2.1.[213] In Paul, too, the most important distinction is that between intercessions and thanksgivings. Whereas the intercessions are more numerous in the Synoptics, in Paul the thanksgivings predominate:[214]

Apart from this distinction, the use of the different Greek verbs and nouns to denote prayer does not indicate any really fundamental characteristics. In what follows, here too, as for the Synoptic and the Johannine writings, I draw on the work by A.Hamman, using Kittel, to list and describe them:

eucharistia, prayer of thanksgiving (especially characteristic of Paul):

deomai, deesis for intercessions, but also used for other prayers, especially in respect of his apostolic calling (Rom.1.10; I Thess.3.10);

aitema occurs only once and relates to the subject of prayer (Phil.4.6);

proseuchesthai, proseuche, prayer in general, but in accordance with ancient usage, especially intercession;[215]

latreuein, latreia (like *eulogein*) (common in Luke, not Mark and Matthew) originally relates to the worship introduced by Moses; in Rom.1.9 to the spiritual worship which Paul offers through his apostolate; in Phil.3.3; II Tim.1.3 to the Christian life.

kauchasthai, kauchema, thanksgiving and praise of God.

krazein in the Septuagint translation of *qara*; used in the important passages Rom.8.15; Gal.4; see p. 74 below.

In addition, the prayers mentioned in the letters of Paul are to be divided into spontaneous and liturgical. The apostle probably said his own spontaneous prayers 'in secret', to use Jesus' expression. But spontaneous prayers also had a place in worship. They could also take the form of speaking with tongues outside and within worship, but in that case for Paul to allow them they had to be interpreted, in accordance with his demand, in language which all could understand (see below, 77ff.)

Paul uses fixed liturgical prayers, which he probably took over from the earliest community, especially at the end of his letters: he knows that these letters will be read aloud to the community gathered for worship. In the Spirit he sees the community before him. The conclusion 'the grace of our Lord Jesus Christ be with you', and in the expanded trinitarian form of II Cor.13.13, 'the grace of our Lord Jesus Christ and the love of God and the fellowship of the Holy Spirit be with you all', probably formed part of the earliest liturgies. At the end of I Corinthians (16.23), the thought of the community assembled for the breaking of the bread suggests to the apostle old and already fixed liturgical and eucharistic ingredients with the prayer cry 'Marantha' (not indicative, but imperative: 'Come, Lord', see Rev.22.20).[216] The original Aramaic form, like the address 'Abba', was respected from earliest times even in the Hellenistic language area.

Liturgical prayer assumes a special form in the 'spiritual' hymns, which go back to Judaism, to the Old Testament psalms, but also include new Christian creations, some of which are taken up into the book of Revelation. With these the community thanks and praises God (Col.3.16; Eph.5.19).

According to II Cor.4.15 all the prayers spoken in the community, whether spontaneous or liturgical, have the greater effect, the more members of the community there are.[217]

As has already been mentioned, in his letters Paul does not give the wording of his prayers, but he does report their content. In careful works on the Jewish background[218] and especially Hellenistic 'letter formulae', it has been demonstrated that in these remarks in the opening verses Paul follows epistolary conventions.[219] Careful attention should be paid to these investigations. However, the important results at which they arrive should not be overestimated. For as we shall see, Paul's doctrine of prayer is so intensively and so closely connected with awareness of possessing the Spirit and with belief in the work of Christ that although what he says in his letters is influenced by traditional forms, it breaks apart this framework.[220]

The prayers which the apostle addresses to God before any important decision and in which he spends whole nights interceding for the communities (I Thess.3.10) are untouched by conventions. We can pick up the resonance of these prayers, the wording of which we do not know, in the reports already mentioned at the beginning of the letters. These indicate to us that he attributes them to inspiration by the Holy Spirit, of whose activity he is aware throughout his life and especially in his apostolic activity.

2. Prayer and the Holy Spirit

In order to understand better Paul's view of the deep significance of prayer in its different concerns, we begin from the indissoluble link which exists for him between prayer and the Holy Spirit. Every aspect of prayer has its foundation here: the need to persist in prayer, union with the will of God, the subject of prayer, being heard. Therefore we shall take the exegesis of the most important part of Romans, 8.12–27, as a starting point.

Before that, however, I shall mention some other passages which show that for Paul prayer is not possible without the Holy Spirit. What he writes of confessing in I Cor.12.3 also applies to praying: 'No one can say "Jesus is Lord" except by the Holy Spirit.' Indeed, confessing is a form of praise.

For Paul, the Holy Spirit can be experienced in a quite concrete way. He describes its effect as power – miraculous power (Greek *dynamis*). His experience is that it comes to full development in our 'weakness' (in illness) as an answer to his prayer in II Cor.12.9, a passage to which we shall return below (pp. 85f.). In Eph.6.18 the readers are invited 'to pray at all times in the Spirit'. According to Eph.3.20 we receive from God through the power of the Spirit 'infinitely more than we ask and know'. In Rom.15.30 Paul asks the community to struggle for him in their prayers to God 'through Christ and through the love of the Spirit'. There is mention of the 'love of the Spirit' here in connection with prayer, since all intercession presupposes the love given through the Spirit. In Col.3.16 and Eph.5.19 the psalms, hymns and songs mentioned there, which are also prayers, are 'spiritual' (*pneumatikoi*), inspired by the Spirit. Psalms inspired by the Spirit are also mentioned in I Cor.14.15.

However, the theological foundation of the relationship between prayer and the Holy Spirit is to be inferred from Rom.8.12–27, to be supplemented by Gal.4.6. To demonstrate that we are no longer slaves but sons, in both passages Paul cites prayer to the Father, and both times as proof he cites the address 'Father' in Aramaic, which goes back to Jesus. Gal.4.6: 'And because you are sons, God has sent the Spirit of his Son into our hearts, crying "Abba! Father!" '; Rom.8.15: '. . . For you did not receive the spirit of slavery to fall back into fear, but you have received the spirit of sonship.'

But how can our prayer to the Father be a sign that God makes us sons? This conclusion by Paul is possible only because he is convinced that the Spirit speaks in our prayers. That the Spirit inspires the name Father in prayer means that God proclaims us his children. That the Holy Spirit as the one who speaks is the subject in our prayer clearly emerges from both passages: in Gal.4.6 God has sent the spirit of the Son into our hearts, who cries 'Abba, Father'. In Rom.8.15 we are the subject who prays: 'in the Spirit (through him) we cry Abba, Father'. However, this distinction is only a superficial one.[221] For of course the Spirit has to make use of our human language. Here we find a similar paradoxical unity to that in Gal.2.20, where Paul says: 'it is no longer I who live, but Christ lives in me'. The apostle is not claiming that he no longer has any 'I' in the anthropological sense; but he does note a dynamic indwelling of Christ which permeates and gives life to his own existence, and which can no longer be forced into anthropological categories. We now also find the same thing in praying according to Rom.8.12ff. 'The Spirit itself' (Rom.8.16)[222] is at work here, but also 'our spirit'.[223] The Spirit itself is the Spirit (the transcendent Spirit) outside us. 'Our spirit' is so permeated and enlivened by this ('it dwells in us', Rom.8.11; 'in our heart', Gal.4.6), that the two form a unity.[224] It is the Holy Spirit which speaks in prayer.[225]

This is the deep truth about prayer which we owe to the apostle. The fact that it occurs twice in two different letters shows how important it is for him. Its significance should not be devalued by the correct indication that both times it is used as a proof in statements about our being children of God. Certainly the theme is being children, sons, but specifically it is the proclamation of this sonship through the Spirit in prayer, and this specific feature permeates the whole section and gives it its unity. Being children and praying to our Father belong very closely together in Rom.8.12ff., and should not be separated. For all prayer has a meaning only if we pray as children to the Father. We pray because we are children of God and, conversely, we are children of God because we pray to God as our Father.

Nor may it be claimed that the utterance of the Holy Spirit when we cry 'Father' does not apply to prayer generally but only to so-called acclamations which consist in liturgical exclamations to God in the original Aramaic form 'Abba'.[226] Even if here the reference is exclusively to such a custom (and that is by no means certain), such acclamations are also a cry of prayer.[227] Just as later (see below, 78f.) Paul cites speaking with tongues only because it is a particularly clear expression of the utterance of the Spirit in all prayers, so here too there is reference to such a cry of prayer only because it is particularly impressive testimony to the Father as a proclamation of the Spirit.

The Greek verb *krazein* used for prayer here does not justify the assumption of such a restriction, excluding prayer in general. The Hebrew equivalent *qara* occurs often in the Old Testament Psalms, and the Greek verb also occurs in I Clement 22.7 to denote all prayer. Because of its reference to any authoritative prophetic proclamation, it is used for ardent prayer.[228]

The address 'Abba' is characteristic of all prayer. Its original Aramaic form has been preserved even in Greek terminology with such a reference because throughout earliest Christianity the recollection remained alive that Jesus' special consciousness of being Son was expressed in the address 'Abba' (see above, 41). Because this term had a unique significance for Jesus, in Gal.4.6 Paul calls the Holy Spirit the 'Spirit of the Son' which is sent into our hearts and cries 'Abba'. Through the Son we become sons.

Although the section which follows in Rom.8, as we shall see, includes in vv.26f. so-called 'speaking with tongues' as a special form of prayer in which the Spirit uses its own language, it is probably wrong to regard 'Abba' in v.15 as a sound which comes about through speaking with tongues. For the whole context shows that it is presupposed that all members of the community can understand what the word means. But one can ask whether the apostle does not have in view the beginning of the Our Father (in Luke's version). However, this is not certain.[229]

It does not conflict with this that according to Paul's view of prayer presented here that on the one hand it is the Spirit which speaks in us and on the other it is our duty to pray.[230] We saw above (p. 73) that in

Gal.4.6 the Spirit utters 'Abba', and that in the parallel passage Rom.8.15 we also pray in the Spirit and in the next verse the Spirit is the subject.

A saying of Jesus handed down in Matt.10.20 clearly states that there is a kind of human discourse in which it is the Spirit who speaks. Granted, the saying is not about prayer but about the disciples confessing before the court: 'When they deliver you up, do not be anxious how you are to speak or what you are to say; for what you say will be given to you in that hour; for it is not you who speak, but the Spirit of your Father speaking through you.' But the statement about confessing and the Spirit in I Cor.12.3, 'No one can say Jesus is Lord except by the Holy Spirit', which comes very close to the view of prayer presupposed in Gal.4.6 and Rom.8.15f., belongs in the same context. Confessing also belongs in the sphere of praise.

So it is clear that human discourse does not exclude the utterance of the Spirit, and conversely the utterance of the Spirit does not exclude human discourse. The urgent calls to persist in prayer which we shall find in Paul remain meaningful, since the Spirit makes use of prayer, for which we must be ready. The tension that we note here pervades the whole Bible. It is the tension between the indicative of faith and the imperative of ethics: 'You are holy', 'You should be holy'. The indicative 'the Spirit prays in us' does not release us from the imperative 'pray without ceasing'. Because the Holy Spirit attests its presence through its utterance we are to pray. According to Paul, as according to Jesus, God wants us to pray, 'asking and thanking', although he is Lord of our prayers and although he knows what we need before we pray to him. The presence of the Holy Spirit in prayer means two things: the Spirit makes known its presence to us; and we may and should seek the answer to our prayer in this presence. Pascal experienced this when he heard God saying, 'You would not seek me unless you had already found me.'[231]

As understood by Paul in this way, prayer is more valuable than all other human discourse. It is the only human discourse in which we transcend our humanity. A transcending of the 'not yet' is indicated: prayer is eschatological discourse.[232] Praying and being like children are both anticipations of the future. The identification of son and heir[233] attested in prayer, which occurs in both Rom.8.17 and Gal.4.7, makes this connection clear. 'If we are sons, we are heirs.'

This concept of being heirs refers the whole section to the future. Our elevation to being children and heirs is indeed proclaimed in prayer through the Spirit, which for Paul is the future that now already breaks into our era: it is a 'pledge',[234] as he calls it in II Cor.1.22; 5.5. In Eph.1.14 it is called the 'guarantee of our inheritance'.[235]

On the other hand, however, the Spirit, even in prayer, is only a pledge, and that means that the dignity of being heirs is first brought about by 'suffering with' Christ before 'being glorified with him' (Rom.8.17). The tension between 'already' and 'not yet' affects the whole existence of believers, and thus, as we shall see in v.26, also prayer, which as the language of the Spirit leads them to experience at the same time the highest pinnacle attainable to human beings, though this is still only a stammering that indicates remoteness from the goal of glorification. Only at the end will the 'redemption of the body' (v.23) which is guaranteed in being children take place. Only then will the Spirit who is 'already dwelling in us' bring our mortal bodies to life. This occurs in the same chapter of Romans, 8.11, immediately before the proclamation in prayer that we are children and heirs.

Verses 24ff. directly connect hope for the future, which we still do not see but expect, with human prayer. Thus the apostle is not as it were introducing a new theme, but continuing the theme of v.15. The whole section vv.12-27 forms a unity. So first v.26 has to be connected with v.15: 'We do not know how to pray as we ought, but the Spirit himself intercedes for us with sighs too deep for words.' This remark in v.26 precisely picks up the fundamental notion of prayer as the utterance of the Spirit in saying 'Abba' in v.15.[236] However, there the positive side is envisaged, whereas here we have the negative, limiting side, the intercession of the Spirit, sighing. This double experience pervades the whole argument.

Verse 26, quoted above, is clearly about all prayer.[237] What had been cited in v.15 as a proof of sonship here becomes a topic. Prayer constantly stands in the background and is not lost sight of. It is the connection with v.15 which first allows us to understand v.26 rightly. That 'we do not know how to pray as we ought'[238] and that the Spirit itself has to intercede for us[239] is the natural presupposition, consequence and explanation of the statement in v.15 that 'the Spirit itself' speaks in us when we pray. If further proof is needed that the two verses are to be taken together, the quite remarkable fact should be cited that the designation 'the Spirit itself' for the transcendent Spirit of God who speaks in our prayers appears both in v.16 ('the Spirit himself bears witness to the Spirit in us') which is connected with v.15 (and interprets it) and in v.26 ('the Spirit itself intercedes for us . . .').

Nor, as we shall see, is the interlude about the sighing of creation in vv.19–23, too, in any way a real interruption. Rather, the double experience of the working of the Spirit is demonstrated even in creation, in so far as in it the painful groaning of the unredeemed weakness of the present (the 'not yet') bears witness to the presence of the 'already' of the fulfilled redemption (which is therefore expected). First of all, we should note that this juxtaposition makes itself known in prayer: the attainment of the highest stage of human discourse and the experience of the boundary which still cannot be crossed because of our inadequacy. Despite everything there is only a stammering, a sighing.[240]

In order to have a complete grasp of the view of prayer as the utterance of the Spirit, however, we must also take into account the important role played in earliest Christianity by the special form of prayer in which the Spirit seeks to break through by means of human organs, but comes up against their inadequacy . . . This is the prayer which in the New Testament is called 'speaking with tongues' (glossolalia), a language which is not akin to any human language and expresses itself in sounds, which is accessible only to those who are seized by a kind of holy ecstasy. To others it is incomprehensible, and can seem to be a meaningless utterance (sighing), indeed a sign of madness (I Cor.14.23).

Whether or not we feel drawn to this overflowing ecstatic phenomenon, which also appears today in so-called charismatic circles, greater attention should be paid to it in the historical accounts of earliest Christianity than is usually the case.[241] It should be recognized that it was a very important form of prayer for the first Christians.[242] It is not by chance that Paul discusses it as such length in I Cor.12 and 13, and especially 14. However, his concern, out of Christian love and his own sense of preserving a balance, is to give it the right place in worship and warn against an overvaluation of it by comparison with comprehensible prayer. Still, with the whole of earliest Christianity he regards it as a quite legitimate gift of the Spirit and he thanks God that he himself has this charisma to a greater degree than any others (I Cor.14.18). (He evidently practises it in his prayer life outside the liturgical assembly.) Only in worship does he prefer, as he writes in the next verse (v.19), 'five words with my mind to ten thousand in tongues'. For he deals with these questions, like all the questions affecting the social life of the members of the community (for example his attitude to the 'weak in the faith' when it comes to ritual prohibitions), with respect for the unity of the community, in this case for those brothers who have not been given the gift of speaking in tongues. Certainly he also allows this form of prayer in worship, but only on condition that someone is present who interprets the content in language which all can understand.

It should not be forgotten that the celebrated praise of love in I Cor.13 was written by the apostle in this precise connection: 'If I speak with the tongues of men and angels and have not love'. 'Speaking in the tongues of angels' denotes the speaking in tongues which in the next chapter the apostle wants to see subject to this love. Bohren, *Predigtlehre* (n.241), 335, refers directly to Lavater's speculation (in *Aussichten in die Ewigkeit*, Letter 16, 1821, in *Ausgewählte Werke*, ed. E.Staehelin), but mentions a 'language in heaven which makes all learned language that is purely direct speech superfluous . . .' (see also Barth's definition of speaking with tongues, 171 n.249 below).

However, it remains important that Paul explicitly calls speaking in tongues prayer: 'If I pray in tongues, my spirit prays[243] (the Spirit in me)' (I Cor.14.14). In the following verse (v.15) he puts both forms of prayer side by side as legitimate: 'What then? I shall pray in the Spirit, and I shall also pray with the understanding.'

This division underlies what Paul says in Rom.8.12ff., to which, after this necessary reference to the great significance of glossolalia for him, we now return. Above all, the utmost importance should be attached to the fact that speaking with tongues is put among the legitimate forms of prayer. For it allows us to assume that when Paul is talking about the Spirit interceding for us with 'sighs which cannot be uttered', he is thinking of glossolalia.[244]

The word 'sighing' is an appropriate term for speaking with tongues, for although it is felt as a blessing from the Spirit by those to who it is granted, it amounts to glossolalia, which to rational minds gives the impression of being incomprehensible stammering, inexpressible sighing. The adjective 'inexpressible'[245] is not to be understood as 'wordless', 'dumb',[246] but rather as being like the 'words which man may not utter'[247] of II Cor 12.4, which Paul also heard in a state of ecstasy when he was transported into the third heaven, into paradise.

So it is not as if here Paul had only speaking with tongues in view: the Our Father from which he begins comprises words which can in fact be understood, and all that is said here concerns all prayer generally.[248] But speaking with tongues stands in the foreground in v.26 because the utterance of the Spirit which takes place in all prayers in this case makes itself known particularly clearly by excluding the human understanding.

But speaking with tongues is also, like all prayer, only sighing. The Spirit is tied to the inadequacy of our human body which is not yet redeemed: 'We do not know how to pray as we ought'. With our human language we can say everything that we have to communicate to our fellow human beings. But praying means speaking with God. Our language is not capable of that. Therefore the Holy Spirit must speak in us if prayer is to be possible at all, as the whole section shows. Verse 26 repeats this, but with an allusion to speaking in tongues: the Spirit supports us and intercedes for us with sighs which cannot be uttered.[249]

The key word 'sigh' links what is said about prayer with what is said about creation in vv.19–23. According to Paul, this sighing takes place wherever, in what God has destined for perfection, in the incomplete framework of the still unredeemed aeon, at the same time the divine fulfilment and the remoteness of its realization are dimly sensed. It can be perceived in the divine creation which waits for the new creation, freed from its present corruption. The Greek word[250] which Paul uses here (v.19) expresses a quite particularly intense longing. Throughout creation he perceives as it were a 'symphony' of sighing, a 'sighing together'[251] which binds all creatures (v.22), and in the same verse he adds another verb: 'travailing together',[252] which at the same time refers to the glorious eschatological transformation of all things by the Holy Spirit in the new creation, when the human bodies of the children of God will be freed (v.21).

The solidarity between human beings and the extra-human creation will become manifest in the eschatological redemption, as it was at the beginning. The whole creation has been drawn into corruption through the sin of Adam,[253] 'for the sake of him who subjected it', as we read in v.20. The preposition *dia*, 'because of', probably does not relate to God, as is usually assumed, but to Adam.[254] It points to Gen.3.17: 'for your sake the earth will be cursed'. But it also points to solidarity in sighing, though this is grounded in hope (vv.19-26), in 'waiting', in the 'already' of the Holy Spirit, which we have as the 'firstfruit of the Spirit' (v.23). By sighing together the creation shares in the embrace of the Spirit which is already ours. Although we are already further on, the creation, too, finds itself in the sphere of the Holy Spirit. There is a 'Good Friday Magic' of creation, and in the light of the whole section we can even say that this is to be found in the sphere of the Spirit.

That the creation is indirectly in contact with the Holy Spirit is a bold notion which should be pursued further by theologians.[255] The verses of Romans discussed here are all the more important since apart from the words of Jesus about the 'birds of the heaven fed by the heavenly Father' and 'the lilies of the field' which 'Solomon in all his glory' could not match (Matt.6.26ff.), the divine elements still present in the fallen creation appear less in the New Testament than they do in the Old. So all the more attention should be paid to this section, because in Christianity the non-human creation is drawn less into the religious sphere than in other religions. Francis of Assisi is an exception here.

I have spent some time on the way in which Paul links prayer with the Holy Spirit, and above all on his view of prayer as an expression of the Spirit, because, as I have already mentioned, it seems to me to form the foundation of the aspects which will be dealt with in the next sections.

3. The need to persist in prayer

We have seen (above, 77) that the fact that the Spirit speaks in us does not mean that we are uninvolved; on the contrary, it is precisely for this reason that we should seek conversation with God. For the fact that the Holy Spirit now already renews us 'from day to day' (II

Cor. 4.16) does not excuse us from making our own contribution, so that all our thought and action is influenced by it.

Thus it is only natural that particularly because he roots prayer so deeply in the Spirit, Paul never wearies of admonishing his readers to persist in prayer, and that he himself gives the example of a life wholly shaped by prayer. More than anyone else he shows that prayer does not exclude action, but makes it fruitful in a unique way. In all his concerns Paul's bond with God does not break off for a moment. Because he is convinced that the Spirit speaks in prayer, he seeks to be continually inspired by the Holy Spirit.

Thus it is more than rhetorical emphasis when in I Thess.3.10 he mentions that he is praying 'day and night' that he may see the Thessalonians face to face, 'to establish what is still lacking in our faith', or when he writes in II Tim.1.3 that he is thinking of Timothy in his 'prayers day and night', also with the desire to see him. It is striking how in Paul's accounts of his intercessions and especially thanksgivings the words 'always', 'without ceasing'[256] recur (Rom.1.9; I Thess.1.2; II Thess.1.11; 2.13; Phil.1.3; Col.1.3; II Tim.1.3). In Col.1.9 we read: 'We do not cease to pray for you.' He also admonishes his readers to persist in the same way: Rom.12.12, 'persist in prayer'; I Thess.5.17, 'pray without ceasing', 'give thanks on every occasion'. The call to persist is also combined with thanksgiving in Col.4.2. The Ephesians are to use their sleepless nights to pray for all the brethren and also for the apostle (Eph.6.18).

Paul knows how much neglect and forgetfulness lead people to stop praying. He also knows that thanksgiving in particular is neglected. Therefore he adds this particularly often in his admonition to pray, as also in Phil.4.6, where he calls for prayer 'in all things'. The almost stereotyped use of the verb 'thank' (*eucharistein*) at the beginning of letters certainly corresponds to Hellenistic usage, as has already been mentioned above, but in Paul it also stems from his inner need to thank God.

The fact that here he is not just following a convention is shown by the absence of thanksgiving at the beginning of Galatians, since he has so much to complain about in these communities. So here instead of the thanks which he usually gives to God he writes: 'I am astonished that you are so quickly deserting him who called you in the grace of Christ and turning to a different gospel' (Gal.1.6). Precisely because in the openings to other letters the thanksgiving is formally adapted to the letter style, he continues to stress the sincerity of his thanksgiving. He calls God as witness to this in Rom.1.9. As this is a conversation with God, God alone can be summoned as witness (see also Phil.1.8).

Paul is certain that God wants us to pray to him, and again that we should also thank him (I Thess.5.18): 'in all things give thanks, for this is the will of God'. We are to thank God for the saving event which, as we shall see, is such an important subject of prayer for him. If we thank God for this, we are given the only possibility of participating in God's saving action through God's grace.

The praise which comes so close to thanksgiving is also participation in God's glory (*doxa*), despite the preservation of the infinite distance. Through the multiplication of thanksgivings the grace of many will 'overflow to the glory of God' (II Cor.4.15). Prayer is the only possibility we have in our weakness of venturing to approach this goal, now already, from afar. In Rom.1.21 the apostle attributes the corruption of all Gentile thought to the fact that despite the theoretical 'knowledge' of God 'they have not glorified him as God or given thanks to him'. Knowledge of God is not possible without prayer to God. God speaks in prayer. In both knowing and praying, the active of our action proceeds from the passive brought about by God: 'now I know in part, then I shall know as I *have been* known' (I Cor.13.12).

4. Uniting with God's will

All prayer is conversation with God, and since God has made human beings in his communication of himself for love, he wants them to participate in his loving will. Thus prayer in itself is already union with God's will. In addition, in all situations of life Paul seeks to discover God's will. He is convinced that he experiences this in prayer in which the Spirit speaks. He seeks to carry out God's will down to planning the details of his journeys. So he prays 'through God's will' that he will find it possible to visit the Romans (Rom.1.10). The Romans for their part are to struggle in prayer with him so that after all the dangers he may 'come to you with joy and be refreshed with your company' (Rom.15.32). His readers are also in this way to unite in prayer with God's will. It is the object of his prayer in Col.1.9 that the Colossians may be filled with the knowledge of the divine will, and he adds: 'in all wisdom and understanding of the Spirit'.[257] For the Spirit bestows this knowledge. Epaphras, the apostle's companion, prays that the Colossians may be enriched with every will of God (Col.4.12). Even if Paul cannot carry out his planned journeys, he submits to the restrictions imposed on him. However, he does not say in Rom.15.22 that in the case of the journey to Rome this happens in prayer,[258] and in I Thess.2.18 he suggests that 'Satan' brought his plans to grief, whereas in Acts 16.6 Luke attributes the impossibility of the apostle getting to Asia to his being 'prevented by the Holy Spirit'.[259]

Through intercession, whether that of the apostle for the communities or of the communities for him, those for whom prayers are offered are united in the divine will with those who pray.

5. The subject of Pauline prayers

Although we shall note that the main subject of prayers in Paul's letters is the saving event of God in Christ, it must first of all be said that according to Paul nothing is to be excluded from prayer, not even personal concerns. 'In all things' the Philippians are to bring their requests to God (Phil.4.6), and the Thessalonians are to give thanks 'on every occasion' (I Thess.5.18). Colossians 3.17 says 'Whatever you do, in word or deed, do everything in the name of the Lord Jesus, giving thanks to God the Father through him.' Here personal concerns are bound up with the saving event.

In connection with the content of the letters in which the apostle discusses all the problems of the communities in the light of theological instruction, of course the work of Christ stands in the forefront of his prayer. In his prayers he includes his own missionary activity, through which he is aware of decisively carrying forward God's plan of salvation, 'that the word of the Lord may go forth and be glorified' (II Thess.3.1). Of course he mentions thanksgiving in connection with the saving event. Formally, as we have seen, he follows the conventions of antiquity in his letters, but their content is the *unique* saving event in Christ. Thus he prays for the communities which he has founded or which are in his care, the rooting and progress of which in faith is part of the divine work of salvation in

Christ. He gives thanks that 'the news of the faith of the Christians in Rome (their conversion and their behaviour) is proclaimed in all the world' (Rom.1.8), that the Corinthians have been given the grace of God in Christ, that they have 'been enriched in him with all speech and all knowledge . . . so that you are not lacking in any spiritual gift' (I Cor.1.4ff.). Thanksgiving is present even in the short letter to Philemon, 'for his love and his faith to God and all the saints' (vv.4f.). At the beginning of I Thessalonians, the faith, love and hope of the members of the community are the object of thanksgiving (vv.2f.), and in II Thessalonians the progress of the faith of the community and the mutual love of all its members (II Thess.1.3; also their election, II Thess.2.13ff.).

The apostle prays especially for the progress of the communities, for the saving event also belongs in intercession: in Phil.1.9, thanksgiving for the community for which he has so much to give thanks is followed by the prayer that their love may grow more and more. In II Corinthians he prays for the strengthening of the community (13.9). When he prays so ardently day and night in I Thessalonians that he may visit this community, it is because he wants to establish what is lacking in their faith (I Thess.3.10). In II Thess.1.11 he prays that God will make its members worthy of the calling which has gone out through him to them.

Paul knows every community very well: its strengths and its weaknesses. He does not need any 'files'; his prayers always relate to the special situation of each one of them. Prayer creates a particularly close bond between him and the communities. It unites them because it unites them with God. Therefore Paul's prayer for the communities must be matched by their prayer for him. For he is the instrument of the saving event. 'Pray for us', he writes to the Thessalonians (5.14), and in II Thess.3.1, 'Pray for us that the word may go forth and be glorifed among you'; similarly to the Colossians, 'that God may open a door to us, to declare the mystery of Christ' (Col.4.3). For the Ephesians, to whom he addresses the same admonition, he adds: 'that utterance may be given me in opening my mouth boldly[260] to proclaim the mystery of the gospel' (Eph.6.18).

Paul needs others to pray for him. He often reports how his work was endangered, how Satan prevented him from visiting the Thessalonian community not just once but twice (I Thess.2.18). But even more it was jeopardized by the dangers to which he refers in II

Corinthians (11.23ff.; also 6.4f.). In Romans (15.30ff.) he prays to the community to struggle with him in prayer that he may be freed from the hands of the unbelievers in Judaea and thus that his collection may be accepted by the community in Jerusalem. For all this is connected with the progress of the saving event, and in particular the collection for the earliest community, which was not just humanitarian aid but was meant to be a bond of unity between the two missions, one to Jewish Christians (through Peter) and one to Gentile Christians (through Paul) (Gal.2.10). Without this unity the work of Paul would have been destroyed.

However, not only Christians but all men and women are drawn into Paul's prayer: primarily the people of Israel, for whom he prays that it may attain salvation (Rom.10.1), and also kings and all in authority (I Tim.2.1ff.). So even the persecuted disciple of Christ still remains bound through prayer to the hostile Gentile state which transgresses the order appointed for it by God.

The prayers relating to Paul's own person are only indirectly connected with his missionary work. That such prayers also occur in Paul's writings is suggested by the passage in Phil.4.6 that has already been mentioned: prayer is to be offered in all things. Here we should think of II Cor.12.5ff. In answer to the charge made by his opponents that he boasts, he mentions his sickness and an experience of prayer connected with it. He wants to boast only of this experience connected with his weakness, not of an ecstatic state which had been granted to him at one moment of his life (v.6).[261] He will boast only of his 'weakness' – and the Greek word for weakness[262] at the same time means illness – and the answer that he received from Christ in prayer. Contrary to more far-fetched explanations, the 'thorn in the flesh' with which the 'angel of Satan' tormented him is probably a chronic illness[263] which is impossible to define more closely – not that that matters.[264]

The petition for healing, which was the subject of this prayer, was not heard. This brings us to the question of prayers being heard.

6. The hearing of prayer

The threefold prayer in II Cor 12.8 was not heard. But a miracle took place at that moment. Paul evidently heard Christ's voice (as he did, according to Acts 9.3, at his conversion) giving an answer: 'My grace is *sufficient* for you.' 'Sufficient', that means that no more is promised to him: 'the miraculous power (*dynamis*) of the Spirit[265] is made perfect in weakness (in the illness)'. That means that the illness remains, but the healing power of the Spirit has its effect despite and in the illness. While the prayer has not been heard, it has been listened to, and that hearing has taken place through the presence of Christ in the very fact that it has not been heard. The life-giving Holy Spirit is present in the sick body, devoted to death. This is 'sufficient'.[266] The section II Cor.6.1-10 introduced by the quotation from Isa.49.8 points in the same direction: being heard in weakness.[267] We can go beyond this unique event reported in II Cor.12.5ff. Paul's view of all prayer as the utterance of the Holy Spirit implies an answer which need not be tied to a miraculous hearing of the voice of Christ as in II Cor.12.9. The divine presence through the Holy Spirit amounts to being heard.[268]

7. Prayer to Christ. Prayer through Christ

In II Cor.12.8 Paul prays to Christ (Kyrios). This is the only passage in whch he does not pray to God, as he usually does. However, there are indirect, if not very clear, indications that he could pray to Christ. In Rom.10.12 the expression 'those who call upon Christ' is a designation for Christians. Paul does not usually use the verb 'call upon'[269] for 'pray'. On the basis of the earliest Christian confession in Phil.2.9ff. of the Kyrios Jesus Christ who is given the name which is above every name (the name of God, Adonai, Kyrios), Paul can in principle pray without distinction to God or to Christ. The Aramaic 'Maranatha', 'Come, Lord', which was probably a fixed element of the earliest eucharistic liturgy and was taken over by Paul (I Cor.16.23, see above, 71), is a (liturgical) prayer to Christ.

But we can understand why a personal prayer to Christ is clearly retained by Paul only in II Cor.12.8 if with most exegetes we accept that the 'thorn in the flesh' refers to an illness: the apostle may have thought of Jesus' healing of the sick.[270]

But what is the meaning of the term 'through Christ' used by Paul, and not only in prayer? We shall see that in the Gospel of John decisive significance is attached to the present role of Christ as mediator in connection with prayer 'in the name of Christ' (see below, 101f.) Is this the meaning of 'through Christ' in Paul? In Col.3.17 the words 'in the name of Christ' and 'through Christ' are used in parallel: 'Do all in the name of the Lord Jesus, giving thanks to God through Christ.' In Paul, in addition to the reference to the present Christ as mediator in prayer, a second relationship must be taken into account. If we remember that the main subject of Paul's prayers, especially the prayers of thanksgiving, is the saving event in Christ, the expression probably relates primarily to this. But the presence of Christ in our prayers – as the exalted one, through his Spirit he stands as it were alongside us – may not be excluded, all the less so if we remember that according to Paul the Holy Spirit speaks in our prayers (see 73 above).

This presence is suggested outside the prayer texts by Rom.8.34, where it is said that 'Christ intervenes for us at the right hand of God'. Here we should probably – at least also – think of our prayers,[271] as is certainly the case in Col.3.17.[272] The two meanings are linked by the notion that through Christ we are taken up into his fellowship with the God who is present.

8. The attitude of prayer

We make a distinction between external gestures of prayer and inner disposition. Not much can be said about the former. We have seen (above, 26) that in the Synoptic Gospels (as in the Gospel of John), Jesus is said to look towards heaven. We can find this presupposed in I Tim.2.8, which speaks of hands raised to God. But the occurrence of 'bowing the knee' in Eph.3.14 is certain. However, for both Jesus and Paul this question was hardly a significant one.

More important is the spiritual attitude of those who pray. In I Tim.2.8, mentioned above, it is said that men should raise 'holy hands to God without anger or quarrelling'. This recalls Mark 11.25 and Matt.5.25: one is to be reconciled with one's brother when praying, before bringing an offering to the altar.[273]

However, prayer should be offered above all joyfully. At the beginning of Philippians Paul already mentions the joy which is a Leitmotif throughout the letter to this community. It accompanies all the prayer which Paul offers for the believers of Philippi, who have a special link with him (1.5). In his letter to the Thessalonians, too (I Thess.5.17), Paul adds to his request to 'pray without ceasing' an admonition constantly to be joyful ('always'[274]). Where the Holy Spirit is at work in those who pray, joy is present.

> In the second century, in an otherwise somewhat mediocre letter, the 'Pastor', Hermas will stress the need for joy in praying very much along the same lines as Paul, when he writes that the prayer of the sorrowful person does not get to God, because sorrow is incompatible with the Holy Spirit.

On the other hand, however, Paul does not forget that prayer can be a struggle. So he asks the Romans 'through our Lord Jesus Christ and the love of the Holy Spirit' to struggle with him in their prayers for him (Rom.15.30). Here the struggle is particularly necessary, since it is one to preserve him from 'unbelief'. According to Col.4.12, Epaphras also 'struggles' in his prayers for the Colossians. The description of the spiritual armour which is needed to ward off the attacks of the devil and the powers of darknes (Eph.6.12ff.) is followed in v.18 by the invitation to 'watch in persistent prayer'.

Prayer as a struggle is also known from the Old Testament, though not entirely in the same sense: Abraham (Gen.18.23ff.); Jacob (Gen.32.23ff.); Moses (Exod.32.11ff.).

Although the Greek word for confidence (joyful, bold confidence: *parrhesia*, etymologically = saying everything) which Luke in Acts describes as a special characteristic of the behaviour of the first Christians, is often used by Paul,[275] but (perhaps by chance) does not appear directly in connection with prayer, it is a good description not only of his preaching and self-defence, but also of the way in which he quietly turns to God in the certainty of being heard, aware that as he is being led by the Holy Spirit he can say 'anything': a certainty which he also offers as encouragement to his readers. In II Cor.3.12; Phil.1.20; Eph.3.12; I Tim.3.13 the word refers above all to the attitude towards God.

III. Prayer in the Gospel of John and the Johannine Letters

1. Introduction

The comment that I made before the investigation of prayer in Paul, about including the whole of the Pauline corpus, applies to an even greater degree to the Johannine writings. Even if we are to assume that they have several authors, despite their different attitudes they share a basic attitude, especially to prayer. The end of John 21 clearly contains the words of a redactor who is different from the real author. So it is more than a hypothesis that a redactor 'edited' the Gospel and in so doing revised it. We therefore have to suppose that there was a group of disciples who were concerned to develop an understanding of Christ which bore the stamp of the strong personality of the evangelist, who came from a special Jewish group.

Here I must refer to my book *The Johannine Circle*. The countless attempts to distinguish in the Gospel of John between the texts which come from the evangelist and those which come from the redactor or redactors often disintegrate completely. Not only do we need to remember that they are hypothetical, but we are justified in discussing the 'Johannine' view of prayer as the common property of the whole circle, leaving aside the literary problem.[276] The evangelist, who on the basis of personal experiences (in Judaea) and under the influence of particular Jewish views (current in Palestine, and not just in the Diaspora) took the initiative in writing a life of Jesus, was inspired by the awareness that the Holy Spirit which was leading him 'into all truth' (John 16.13) had disclosed to him the deep significance of 'all that Jesus said' (14.26). This conviction allows us to draw the lines further.

The farewell discourses (chs.14–16) are so to speak the justification for the special character of his account of the life of Jesus. What we could call his awareness as an evangelist is contained in the verse about the Holy Spirit (the Paraclete) in these chapters: 'the Holy Spirit whom the Father will send in my name, he will teach you all things, and bring to your remembrance all that I have said to you' (14.26). In the Gospel of John 'bring to rememberance' is more than just 'remind'; at the same time it refers to the revelation of a deeper meaning.[277] 'I have yet many things to say to you, but you cannot bear them now. When the Spirit of truth comes, he will guide you into all the truth' (16.12f.). The evangelist knows that his account of the life of Jesus is inspired by this truth.

The aim of his description of the actions and teaching of Jesus, with its orientation, is to show that the Christ who is now exalted and present in his church is already at work in any saying spoken by the incarnate Jesus. The whole circle of his disciples took over this view of the evangelist's.

Whatever the relationship may be between the Gospel of John and the Johannine epistles, certain divergences are not fundamental for the question of prayer. Although there are indisputable similarities between the Revelation of John and the rest of the Johannine works, and perhaps we can assume a later connection with the same circle, in view of the theme which is connected with the different literary genre they will be discussed only in the next chapter.

We shall now go on to discuss the Johannine view of prayer in the next three sections: 1. Worship in spirit and in truth (the conversation with the woman of Samaria, 4.20–24); 2. Prayer in the name of Jesus Christ (the farewell discourses, chs.14-16); 3. The high-priestly prayer of Jesus (ch.17).

2. Prayer in spirit and in truth (John 4.20–24)

The conversation between Jesus and the woman of Samaria by the well of Jacob is primarily about cultic worship. But Jesus' answer is fundamental to prayer generally.

The woman uses the opportunity provided by her meeting with Jesus to learn from him what he has to say about the question of the worship of God which divides Jews and Samaritans. Should it be in Jerusalem or on Mount Gerizim? The Samaritans had replaced the temple in Jerusalem, which they did not regard as legitimate, with the sanctuary on Gerizim above Nablus.[278] Jesus replies to the woman: 'The hour is coming when you will not worship the Father either on this mountain or in Jerusalem (v.21) . . . the hour is coming and now is when the true worshippers will worship the Father in Spirit and in truth' (v.23).

(a) Neither on this mountain nor in Jerusalem

In order to understand the roots of Jesus' remark in John properly, we must first of all refer back to the attitude of Jesus to the temple in the Synoptic Gospels and investigate both this and the attitude of the circle around Stephen in relation to the Qumran community and that of the Samaritans.

We have seen that for the Jesus of the Synoptic Gospels the place of prayer does not play any decisive role. As in Judaism, one can pray anywhere. But Jesus respects the temple as the house of God, which is to be a house of prayer (Mark 11.17 par. Isa.56.7). Therefore it is important for him not to abolish it (see also Matt.5.23), but to purify it and prevent its being made a 'den of thieves' (Mark 11.17; Jer.7.11). Nevertheless he relativizes its significance. Not only does he say in connection with the healing on the sabbath that 'something greater than the temple is here' (Matt.12.6), but taking up the Jewish expectation that in the end the temple will disappear and a new one will take its place (Ezek.40–44; Ethiopian Enoch 90.28ff.; Tobit 13.15f.), and that the Messiah is at work here, he speaks of the destruction of the temple and its rebuilding. This saying is one of the two main reasons for his accusation before the high priest. However, according to Mark 14.57f.; Matt.26.59, it was false witnesses who brought these charges and, as we shall see, Mark emphasized why the witness was false. That special importance was attached to this charge in the condemnation by the Jewish authorities is confirmed by the fact that the mocking passers-by under the cross quoted it: 'Aha! You who would destroy the temple and build it in three days, save yourself, and come down from the cross!' (Mark 15.29f.).

So the false witness was not completely plucked out of thin air. But how was the saying of Jesus twisted by the false witnesses? It is the variant in which the Gospel of John associates the saying as a saying of Jesus in connection with the cleansing of the temple, placed by the author at the beginning of his Gospel,[279] which allows us to answer the question which the Synoptists leave open. According to Mark 14.57, in the hearing of the witnesses the testimonies differ; however, the account then continues: 'And some stood up and bore false witness against him, saying, "I will destroy this temple that is made with hands, and in three days I will build another not made with hands"' (v.57). By contrast, the prophecy cited as a real saying of Jesus in John 2.19 runs: 'Destroy this temple, and I will raise it up in three days (= in a short time).' In this Johannine variation the imperative is not of course to be regarded as an actual invitation but as a conditional: 'If the temple is torn down, I will erect it again.' In that case, the false witness in Mark 14.57 consists in the fact that the imperative 'destroy' is turned into the first person singular, 'I will destroy'.

Mark emphasizes this 'I' with *ego*, 'I myself will destroy', whereas Matthew 26.61 writes 'I can destroy.' Luke omits the saying completely in his account of the trial (22.66ff.). This Synoptic comparison clearly shows that the saying was spoken by Jesus in the Johannine form and that the first three Gospels, each in its own way, take pains to exclude any misunderstanding in the sense of false witness, Mark in particular by emphasizing with *ego* how this witness was false.

So in what sense did Jesus utter the saying which has been correctly transmitted in the Gospel of John? The first part, 'If the temple is destroyed', relates to the stone temple in Jerusalem, the destruction of which Jesus probably often prophesied after the manner of the political prophecies of the prophets (Micah 3.12; Jer.7.14; 26,18): 'Do you see this mighty building? Hardly one stone will be left upon another' (Mark 13.2; cf. Matt.24.2; Luke 2.6; Matt.23.38; Luke 13.35).[280] The second part, which was probably quoted correctly by the false witnesses (Mark 14.58), is harder to explain on the lips of Jesus, '. . . I will build another not made with human hands.' Usually it is interpreted in terms of the coming community, and in fact this assumption is possible, given the image of a building for the community which was current later. It has also been assumed that the Qumran sect regarded them-selves as a spiritual temple.[281] However, in his thoroughly documented article, 'Qumran et le Temple (Essai de Synthèse)', *RHPR* 1991, which makes use of the most recent texts,[282] A.Caquot has disputed this, nor is it completely certain that Jesus meant the temple not made by human hands as a reference to it. However, at all events, like Rev.2.22 he does not foresee any material temple for the coming Jerusalem, though for the moment he still accepts it in purified form.

Stephen argues much more radically, in his speech in his defence (Acts 7.2ff.), in a survey of the history of Israel and with reference to the Old Testament, especially Isa.66.1 ('the temple is my throne'), that the building of the temple is a great apostasy. Accordingly, like Jesus, for the future he does not think in terms of a temple. This contrasts with the Qumran sect, in whose texts, along with the new temple which they are to build themselves, a temple appears which has been erected in the end time by God.[283] It also contrasts with the Samaritans, who replaced the temple in Jerusalem which they repudiated with a specific place of worship on Mount Gerizim.[284]

After this lengthy excursus, which was necessary in order to understand the link between what the incarnate Jesus says about the temple and the way in which this is made more profound in the Johannine writings after Easter, we return to the Gospel of John, to the narrative of the encounter of Jesus with the woman of Samaria. Conscious of being called and inspired by the Holy Spirit (the Paraclete), who leads into all truth, to reveal the deep sense of the words of Jesus in the light of the exalted Christ and his church (see p. 90 above), the evangelist finds that the saying about the temple on the one hand relates to the crucified and risen body of Jesus (2.21) and on the other hand gives Jesus' answer to the Samaritan woman's question about the place of worship.

The identification of the destroyed and rebuilt temple with Jesus' body (2.21) is the Johannine development of the prophecy of building a temple not made with human hands, which Jesus does not make more specific. This interpretation given in the Gospel of John at the end of the narrative about the cleansing of the temple, 'he spoke of the temple of his body' (2.21), is expressly said in the next verse (v.22) to have been disclosed later: 'when he was risen from the dead, the disciples remembered . . .'[285] Paul also uses the image of the temple for the body in I Cor.6.19. This Johannine explanation corresponds to the notion in the prologue of John that Christ replaces the temple. The divine glory (Greek *doxa*, Hebrew *shekinah*) which had previously been attached to the temple had detached itself from it and is now manifest in the incarnate Logos, in Jesus Christ: 'he tabernacled among us' (see the tent as God's abode in Stephen's speech, Acts 7.44) 'and we have seen his glory (*doxa*), glory as of the only-begotten of the Father' (John 1.14). The same Johannine view of Jesus as the place of worship forms the conclusion to Jesus' conversation with Nathanael: 'you will see the heavens open and the angels of God ascending and descending on the Son of Man' (John 1.51). Here the evangelist is developing the narrative of the erection of the monument at Bethel and Jacob's ladder in Gen.28.12: now the angels no longer go up and down the ladder at the sanctuary at Bethel but on the Son of Man. The bond between heaven and earth is Christ himself, Jesus the true place of worship. Jesus' answer, 'in spirit and in truth', to the question 'Temple or Gerizim?' (John 4.21), clarifies this christocentric notion, and it should not be left out of account in any explanation. The limitation of the validity of the temple as a place of worship by Jesus as the incarnate one leads to the Johannine view that the temple has been replaced by the exalted Christ himself: in him we encounter God when we pray.

'The hour is coming and now is' (v.23). The view of time given with the coming of Christ involving a tension between future and present which we can see throughout the New Testament, is also expressed here.[286] At the moment when Jesus himself is present, speaking by Jacob's well, the 'now' must be put alongside the coming of the hour. The tension between 'already' and 'not yet' is not absent from the Gospel of John either, but in accordance with the whole Johannine perspective there is stronger stress on the 'already', for the life of the incarnate Jesus is seen in the light of the exalted Christ (and together with him). What is prophesied in the Synoptic Gospels for the future, the destruction of the temple and its rebuilding, is in the Johannine view already reality. Christ is already the place of worship.

'The Father seeks such worshippers' (v.23). That the Father 'seeks'[287] such worshippers in spirit and in truth corresponds to the view of prayer that we have derived from the Synoptic Gospels (see above, 19f.). God, who does not need the prayers of human beings, wants them, requires them. What is new here in the course of the christological concentration is the emphasis on the manner of the worship which the Father seeks and calls for,[288] 'in spirit and in truth'. Now, when the hour has already come in Christ, it is important that prayer should be offered in this way.

The preposition 'in', which can have both local and instrumental significance ('through'), is here probably to be understood primarily in a local sense, as Jesus' statement is the answer to the question 'where?' – in Jerusalem or on Gerizim?[289] The worship takes place in a different sphere, that of spirit and truth.

(b) In spirit

We must not forget what 'spirit' means throughout the Gospel of John. It is not an anthropological factor, nor is it to be understood in the philosophical sense as the opposite to matter.[290] Rather, the Gospel of John, too, uses spirit to denote the transcendent divine power which enters our world, takes its abode in us and brings about new birth ('from above'): the Spirit blows where it wills, and is not therefore bound to a particular place (see Jesus' conversation with Nicodemus, 3.1ff.). However, it is closely connected with Christ. In the Johannine farewell discourses (14-16) the Spirit is described as the 'Comforter', who now, where Jesus no longer dwells among his own as the incarnate one, represents him, makes him present among them, frees them from the pain of separation; who on the other hand leads them into the 'truth' of the divine revelation in Christ; and who also intercedes for them in prayer. The overcoming of all separation which he achieves, and his intercession, are well expressed in the Greek word '*parakletos*', which has the twofold meaning of 'comforter' and 'advocate'.

The author of the Gospel of John, who has handed down the narrative of the conversation between Jesus and the woman of Samaria, must have understood the saying about worship in spirit and in truth in terms of this view of the Spirit put forward throughout the Gospel. Within the framework of the Gospel of John, here too the christological reference is at least in the background.[291] The Spirit sent by God, which is not confined by space, and in which the true worshippers are to pray to the Father, is connected with Christ. That is also the main motif of the 'praying in the name of Christ' which we shall find in the farewell discourses, chs.14–16.

The christological understanding of worship in the Spirit does not contradict the very next verse, John 4.24, which explains the need for this kind of worship by saying that God himself 'is spirit' and therefore worship is to be offered in spirit (and in truth). This latter statement brings us, without blurring the difference between Johannine and Pauline theology, close to the Pauline view of prayer on which I put so much emphasis, according to which God himself speaks in our prayers through the Spirit which dwells in us: spirit to spirit.

(c) In truth

Spirit and truth are closely connected in the Johannine understanding. I John 5.6 says that 'the Spirit is truth'. In the farewell discourses we even find the expression 'Spirit of truth'[292] (14.17 and 16.13; cf. also I John 4.6). But what is the precise meaning of Johannine truth?[293] Like the word 'spirit', so too 'truth' must not be understood in the sense usual in Greek philosophy, and above all the other passages in the Gospel of John and the Johannine epistles must be taken into account. The Johannine concept of truth implies a relationship, in contrast to an 'objective' detached consideration.[294] Indeed, for John, truth can be communicated to human beings only by God; it cannot be sought as an object separate from them.

For the disciples of Christ, truth then consists in the revelation of God to human beings in Christ. Etymologically, the Greek word for truth, *aletheia*, means not being hidden. This corresponds precisely to the word revelation: in the New Testament it is used to denote both the divine function of self-communication in Christ and the content of this communication which is received by human beings.

In the trial of Jesus before Pilate, the two different concepts of truth stand over against each other: truth as divine revelation, and truth as a separate object to be sought in a detached way. The former is presupposed in Jesus' explanation 'I am come to bear witness to the truth. Whoever is of the truth hears my voice' (John 18.37). Pilate's question 'What is truth?', probably accompanied by a shrug of the shoulders, at all events presupposes the philosophical view of truth. For Pilate, this may have taken the form of philosophical scepticism,[295] but more probably the question implies sheer indifference.[296] But at the same time it probably also expresses a complete lack of understanding of what Jesus says about 'truth', with a touch of contempt for it.

In parallel to John 18.37, 'who is of the truth', in 8.47 Jesus says: 'Whoever is of God hears the voice of God.' So God is identified with the truth. God is the revealer in Christ. We might think of the prologue, John 1.1, 'and the Logos (who becomes flesh in Jesus) was God': God, in so far as he speaks to the world, communicates himself through revelation. 'Your word is the truth,' says Jesus in the high-priestly prayer in John 17.17: the word communicated by God in Christ. Thus Jesus can say in the Gospel of John, 'I am the truth' (John 14.6). That is the answer to Thomas' question about the 'way to God'. Jesus himself is the way. The way and the destination are one: 'He who has seen me has seen the Father' (John 14.9). As Christ is the truth revealed to human beings, it is said at the end of the prologue (1.17), 'Grace and truth have come through Jesus Christ': has not just been preached, but 'become'.[297]

Because the truth consists in the relationship of God to human beings as revelation in Christ, at the same time it includes the capacity of the disciples to receive it: they are 'from God' and therefore hear 'God's voice' (John 8.47; cf. I John 4.6). The Johannine letters, which so strongly emphasize the truth in the battle against the heretics, speak of 'doing the truth' (I John 1.6) and 'walking in the truth' (III John 3).

The disciples 'know' the truth when they 'abide in his word' (John 8.31f.); here 'word' can be identified with truth (John 17.17: 'Your word is truth'). Only abiding in the truth which has been received leads to 'knowledge'.[298] But Johannine knowledge, too, is not to be understood in the Greek sense, but in accordance with the Johannine 'truth' as a 'recognition'. I John 3.19ff. also shows that this is not detached knowledge. It requires the disciples to practise love, so that they may recognize that they are of the truth.

(d) Summary

Thus 'worship in spirit and truth' (John 4.23) means not worshipping the Father in a particular place, but in his spirit, in which he turns to us in Christ, and in his truth, in which he reveals himself to us in Christ. Both spirit and truth belong closely together. Prayer in spirit and in truth is bound up with the revelation in Christ. It is response. In God's spirit given to us, and in his truth given to us through this spirit, we pray to the Father. That is the place where we encounter him. His glory (*doxa*), detached from the tie to the temple, is visible in the Logos, Christ (John 1.14). So the nearness of God which is indispensable for all prayer is given through and in Christ.

With this definition of location we find ourselves close to Revelation 21.22, where the seer sees no temple in the city which descends from heaven to earth: for 'the almighty Lord will be the temple with the Lamb'. 'The hour is coming and now is.' The temple is not yet destroyed and will be purified (John 2.13ff.), but there is already worship in spirit and truth. If we attempt to draw the line further in the Johannine sense with a view to applying it to our time, it has to be maintained that it is important for our cultic worship, too, to be offered in this spirit and this truth, for 'the hour is come'.

3. Prayer in the name of Jesus Christ in the farewell discourses (John 13.31–16.33)

In the Johannine farewell discourses, worship in spirit and truth takes the form of prayer 'in the name of Jesus Christ'. The 'thanksgiving in the name of our Lord Jesus Christ' (which is constantly to be offered) also occurs in Ephesians (5.20), and in Col.3.17 it appears in parallel to the words 'through' Jesus Christ, which are still customary at the end of prayers and are often uttered thoughtlessly. Nowadays this latter addition is often merely formal. That makes it all the more necessary to investigate the invitation which in the Gospel of John the departing Jesus makes with particular emphasis to the disciples, now to pray 'in his name'.

This is one of the various consolations offered by Jesus, which are to convince his disciples that in going away he is not leaving them as 'orphans' (14.18). His perpetual presence is realized in a threefold way. First (13.34f.), through the love that they are to show to one another which is the love with which he has loved them; because of this more specific definition in which the continuation of the bond with him is rooted, he calls this love a 'new commandment'.[299] Secondly (14.16; 15.26; 16.13ff.), by sending the Spirit, the 'Comforter';[300] and thirdly (and in particular), by prayer 'in his name'. The need to couple prayer with his name is repeated several times (14.13; 14.14; 15.16; 16.23f.).

> In this chapter, too, we shall not be going into the different proposals for distinguishing between the original Gospel and later redaction, though they are well worth considering.

In order to grasp the precise significance of the expression 'pray in the name of Christ', we must remember that it denotes one of the decisive consoling promises of the constant abiding presence among his own of the Christ who has left the earth. He leaves the earth behind, but not his own.

However, the words 'in the name of Jesus' need further explanation. They do not occur only in connection with those who pray. Here already it should be noted that they have very varied meanings. Not only does the meaning differ depending on the content, but other meanings are often echoed even where one is dominant.

(a) Name, name of God, name of Christ

What are we to understand primarily by 'name'? We cannot go here into the findings of all the works, including those from the history of religions, about this term in the various religions. Apart from the earlier investigation by W.Heitmüller, *Im Namen Jesu. Eine sprach- und religionsgeschichtliche Untersuchung zum Neuen Testament* (1909), I would refer to the relevant article in the *Theological Dictionary of the New Testament*,[301] and also to Lochman's book, on the first petition of the Our Father.[302] I shall limit myself to a summary relating to prayer in the Gospel of John.

In the world of the New Testament the name denotes everything that characterizes its bearer, his deeper essence and attributes. This explains the listing of names in the 'Book of Life' (Phil.4.3; Rev.3.5). The disciples are to rejoice that their names are written in heaven (Luke 10.20). In John 10, the shepherd calls the sheep by name (v.3), he knows them (v.27).

God's name makes known his presence, his power. In the Old Testament the name of God dwells in the temple (I Kings 8.29). The Hebrew word for name (*shem*) can become a designation of God. To 'hallow God's name' (see p. 44 above) means to keep profanation caused by human sin from God's name.

In the New Testament, the name of God is associated with the work completed by Christ. According to the hymn cited by Paul in Phil.2.6ff., God bestows the 'name' which expresses his own being on Christ by more than exalting him after he has been humbled to death on the cross, bestowing on him 'the name which is above every name, Jesus Christ the Lord'. This name is higher than all other names since it is his own divine name Kyrios = Adonai. So it is said of this name in Acts 4.12 that there is salvation in no other name and that no other name under heaven is given to human beings for their redemption. In the letter to Pergamon in Revelation (ch.2.13), this church is praised for having 'held fast' to the name.

In the Johannine framework, the unity between the Father and the Son (the Logos, God, who communicates himself)[303] is shown specifically in the revelation of his name. It is the same when in John 12.28 Christ, confronted with the imminent 'hour' of death, asks the Father to 'Glorify your name', and when in the high-priestly prayer (17.1), 'he lifted his eyes to heaven and said, "Father, the hour has come; glorify your Son that the Son may glorify you."' Some verses later (v.6), Jesus says that he has revealed the divine name to those whom he has been given. At the end of the prayer (17.26) he repeats: 'I have made known your name, and I will make it known, that the love with which you have loved me may be in them, and I in them.' The name of God, God's innermost being, is love (I John 4.15). It can be identified with Christ: 'The love of God in us' virtually amounts to 'Christ in us'.

'Believing in the name' of the Son (John 1.12; 2.23; I John 3.23; I John 5.13) means believing in his relationship to the Father and in his work. So the expression 'all who call on the name of our Lord Jesus Christ', in which 'call' means both 'pray' and 'confess', is one of the first designations for Christians.[304]

(b)   In the name of someone; in the name of Jesus Christ

What does it mean to act or speak in someone's name? The ambiguity mentioned above, which is produced by the particular context, gives the phrase an indefinite character, and it is not possible always to limit the formula to a particular sense. Very generally, one acts or speaks in another's name if one so to speak replaces this other, takes her or his place as though she or he were themselves present. Thus in Deut.18.19 God says of the prophet like Moses whom he will raise up: 'And whoever will not give heed to my words which he shall speak in my name, I myself will require it of him.'[305] The sense of acting 'on behalf of' God is also echoed here. The words 'in the name' of someone who is invoked can be aimed at the effective working of his power. If this effect is attributed to the utterances of formulae as such, the invocation borders on a magical practice. This is not the case when honoured persons are invoked who are absent or dead – in Israel, for example, the patriarchs – and if by this invocation not only is their ethical responsibility cited as a model, but in addition their real influence on the present is expected. In this case the invocation of the name comes near to a prayer addressed to God.

Membership of Christ or his community is indicated by the expression 'in the name of Jesus Christ'. This is brought about above all in baptism.[306] But according to Matt.7.22, those 'who do not do the will of the Father' (7.21) are wrong to refer to the name of Jesus: 'Did we not prophesy, cast our demons, do many wonders, in your name?'[307] Jesus does not recognize such people. By contrast, in another case (Mark 9.38f.) he grants spiritual membership to those who have cast out demons in his name without belonging to the circle of disciples.

Despite the great differences in the formulae, almost all of them imply the presence of the exalted Christ. This will be important for understanding the Johannine demand to pray in the name of Jesus. Thus in I Cor.5.4f. the condemnation of the person who has committed incest is pronounced 'in the name of the Lord Jesus Christ'. That certainly means that the verdict has been passed in accordance with the commandments of Christ, but also at the same time in his presence. This is also the case in II Thess.3.6 with the admonition 'in the name of the Lord Jesus Christ' that those to whom the letter is addressed should keep away from brothers who are living in idleness. When Paul calls on the Colossians (3.17) 'to do whatever they do, in word or deed, in the name of the Lord Jesus Christ', he is probably expecting them constantly to reflect on Christ's teaching and work, but at the same time also to be united with the exalted Lord. In the saying of Jesus in Matt.18.20 the phrase 'in the name' is quite clearly orientated on his presence among his followers: 'where two or three are gathered together in my name, there am I in the midst of them.'

(c) Prayer in the name of Jesus

After investigating the term 'name' and the phrase 'in the name (of Jesus)', we come to the Johannine 'prayer in the name of Jesus' (14.13f.; 15.16; 16.23f.,26). The variety of meanings of 'in the name' shapes the view of praying in the name of Jesus which is characteristic of John 14.1-6. Certainly we are to think of a reference to the work of Christ. However, what predominates is a reference to the abiding presence of Jesus among the disciples who pray. It is governed by the perspective of the farewell discourses: his exaltation to the Father guarantees them not only the continuation of his earthly presence with them but an even closer link which leads them to 'greater works'. For he is not going just anywhere, but 'to the Father' (14.12).

This 'comforting' is especially needed in prayer after Easter. During the incarnate life of Jesus the disciples needed him to instruct them in their prayer: 'Lord, teach us to pray' (Luke 11.1). In Luke Jesus teaches them the Our Father in response to this request. We have seen that according to Paul 'we do not know how to pray as we ought' (Rom.8.26) and the Spirit intervenes to help us. We shall also note in the Johannine farewell discourses that the Spirit is sent as the Comforter after the death and resurrection of Jesus. But first of all the formula 'pray in the name of Jesus' means that in their prayer the disciples largely continue to need the presence of Jesus as during his earthly life, and that this help will be given them because he will not be absent.

'Hitherto you have asked nothing in my name', says Jesus in 16.24. For as the incarnate one he was always with them with his intercession. From now on, help in prayer must be given to them by calling on his name. The previous v.23 promises: 'If you ask anything of the Father, he will give it you in my name.' Here the Father as the one who hears prayer is the subject of the words 'in my name'. In this verse, at the same time the phrase has the meaning 'at my request'. This indicates the twofold nature of the help in prayer which Jesus offers to the disciples after his resurrection by their calling on his name: on the one hand he is as it were present alongside (in) them while they pray, and on the other he enters heaven to intercede for them with the Father.

In the Gospel of John he already did this as the incarnate one. His intercession brought about the resurrection of Lazarus: 'Now I know,' says Martha to Jesus (11.22), 'that God will grant all that you ask.' And in 11.41 Jesus himself thanks God for hearing him.

The following verse, which probably comes from the redactor, continues, 'I knew that you always heard me', and adds that it was only necessary to express this thanks so that 'the bystanders might attain faith in his divine mission'.[308] The disciples may also be assured of this intercession even after Jesus' death and resurrection, even more so since he will have returned to the Father. The unity of the Son with the Father which has existed since eternity, and his participation in the Father's divine glory (17.5), then gives prayer in the name of Jesus its profound significance. The whole of the high-priestly prayer which follows the farewell discourses (ch.17) is as it were the basis of the need for the disciples to pray in his name after his glorification to God. This intercession of the one who has been exalted to God at the same time means that we need his help to pray, and that on the basis of the presence of the Son with the Father we for our part are directly joined with the Father in our prayer.

Therefore despite all the Johannine christocentricity, the prayers of Jesus to which the texts in the farewell discourses that we have discussed refer are addressed to God the Father. Only in 14.14 (and here not in all manuscripts) are they addressed to Christ. There is no problem here in the framework of the basic Johannine view. Thomas, the doubter, to whom Christ has said 'He who has seen me has seen the Father' (14.9), can say to the risen Christ after the invitation to put his hand into the wound in Christ's side, 'My Lord and my God' (20.28). Thus prayer is addressed to God, but in the name of Jesus, who as Kyrios is glorified through and in his death, and in that way glorifies God's name.

But although Christ is now with God and intercedes there powerfully for him, in the Johannine writings his intercession and thus our prayer in his name is such a special help for us because he has shared his humanity with us (but without sin, as we read in Hebrews). Since the Gospel of John, and especially the Johannine epistles, strongly emphasizes the humanity of Christ to ward off the docetic heresy and its false teaching that Christ's body was not real, this aspect, too, may underlie 'prayer in the name of Jesus'.

(d) Spirit and intercession

Though Christ leaves the earth, he remains present among his own: on the one hand on earth, in those who pray, and on the other hand with God, through his intercession. This twofold activity is made known and intensified by the sending of the Holy Spirit, whose presence will also take further the earthly work of Christ. He too will help the disciples to get over their parting from the incarnate Jesus. He will free them from all sorrow about being forsaken. He will 'comfort' them, and so he is called the 'Comforter'. That is the etymological meaning of the Greek word 'Paraclete'.[309] 'I will pray the Father, and he will give you another Comforter, to be with you for ever . . . He dwells with you, and will be in you' (14.16f.).

Jesus also calls him the Paraclete, the Comforter, in 14.26. He too makes his presence known, like Christ himself as the exalted Lord, on the one hand on earth in us (14.17b, 'he will be in you'), and on the other hand with God as intercessor. For as so often the Gospel of John deliberately chooses an ambiguous word, 'Paraclete', to denote the Spirit:[310] in Greek it not only means 'comforter', but is also the legal term for 'intercessor' (and in the Vulgate is translated into Latin as *advocatus*).

The Spirit is closely connected with Christ. According to 14.26 the Father sends the Spirit in his [Christ's] name. According to 15.26 Christ himself (*ergo*) will sent him 'from the Father'; ''he proceeds from the Father', but 'he will bear witness to me [Christ]'. The unity between Christ and Spirit[311] is further emphasized in 16.13f.: 'He [the Spirit] will not speak on his own authority, but whatever he hears he will speak, and he will declare to you the things that are to come.'

As the duration of the presence of Christ among the disciples and that of the Spirit belong together, in I John 2.1 Christ is described in the same way as the spirit as 'comforter' and 'advocate'; granted, this is not in respect of prayer but in respect of the forgiveness of sins, but this can be the subject of prayer. Even if the Spirit bestowed by the Father at Christ's request is called '*another* comforter (advocate)' in 14.16, it is presupposed that Christ himself is a Paraclete. Throughout the ' "high-priestly prayer' (John 17), Christ speaks as 'advocate'.

The Paraclete is called 'Spirit of *truth*' (14.17; 15.26; 16.13). Spirit and truth are closely connected. The Spirit 'leads into all truth (6.13); he will 'teach you all things and bring to your remembrance all that I have said to you' (14.26). Here we have confirmation of what we noted in the explanation of Jesus' reply to the Samaritan woman about the place of worship ('in spirit and in truth', see above, 95ff.): on the one hand Johannine truth is the revelation communicated by

God to human beings in Christ; on the other hand, spirit and truth belong together.

In the conversation with the woman of Samaria both are concerned with prayer. Is that also the case in the farewell discourses? The question must be raised, since in the texts cited the Spirit is not mentioned in connection with prayer. But in the framework of the remarks of this chapter which are centred so emphatically on prayer, it must be assumed that what is said about the Holy Spirit also belongs in this perspective.[312] This is confirmed in ch.14 by the sequence of vv.14 (prayer) and 16 (sending of the Spirit).[313]

(e) The hearing of prayer

In the farewell discourses and in the letters of John it is promised unconditionally that prayer will be heard: 14.13f.: 'Whatever you ask in my name I will do'; 15.7: 'If you abide in me, and my words abide in you, ask whatever you will, and it shall be done for you'; 15.16: 'Whatever you ask the Father in my name, he will give you'; 16.24: 'Ask, and you will receive'; I John 3.22: 'What we receive, we receive from him'; I John 5.14: 'If we ask something in his name, he hears us.'

That Jesus repeats the promise so often in the Fourth Gospel shows that it probably goes back to a common early tradition.[314]

In most of the Johannine texts, hearing is combined with the addition 'in my name'. Where this is not the case, it is presupposed – thus especially in 15.7: the abiding of the disciples in Jesus and his abiding in them, which is clarified in vv.4ff. by the image of the branches that wither if they are detached from the vine, is here mentioned as a condition of hearing. The union with Christ which is designated in this image means the same thing as the formula 'pray in my name'.

The faith that prayers will be heard, which is called for with such emphasis in the Synoptic Gospels, appears less urgent, but is nevertheless implied in the 'abiding in him'.[315] In I John 5.13f. confidence that God will hear prayers is explicitly based on 'belief in the name of the Son of God',[316] and even more clearly so in I John 3.21, 23. In addition to faith, here a further condition that needs to be fulfilled is that those who pray should exercise mutual love – the new commandment, according to 13.34 (see above, 98). This recalls the request of Jesus in the Synoptic Gospels to practise love, and in particular the forgiveness of sins (Mark 1.25; Matt.5.23) before praying. When the author of I John (5.14) attaches to the hearing of prayer the condition that that prayer should be 'according to his will', he may also be thinking of the forgiveness of sins, especially as the next verse, v.16, is an invitation to 'pray for a brother whom he sees committing a sin'.[317]

In investigating prayer in the Synoptic Gospels, I put a good deal of emphasis on prayers which were not heard and on submission to the will of God, especially in the prayer struggle in Gethsemane. However, this does not come within the horizon of the Johannine writings. It is unconditionally promised that prayer will be heard.

> Going beyond the framework of exegesis, one could find in the equation of the verbs 'hear' and 'listen to'[318] in I John 5.14f (if we ask something he 'hears us') the idea that the encounter with God as such is already hearing.

It is as though the union with Christ in Johannnine prayer was experienced so intensely that there was no problem in leaving all individual wishes out of account.

A last question. Who hears prayer? We have seen that prayer in the name of Christ is usually addressed to the Father and only exceptionally to the Son. By contrast, Christ is sometimes denoted as the one who hears. In John 14.13, 14, Jesus promises that he will fulfil the petition;[319] in v.14 this is even emphasized by the addition of *ego*. In I John 5.15 it is probably Christ who hears, but in John 1.16; 16.23 and I John 3.21 it is God. The question whether God or Christ hears is not of fundamental significance in the Johannine writings, which so strongly emphasize the unity of the Son with the Father. John 15.7 does not say who hears prayer; all we have is 'it shall be done for you'.[320]

4. The high-priestly prayer

We have seen that in the Johannine instructions which the departing Christ gives to the disciples for their prayer, above all for praying in his name, special importance is attached to his intercession for them.

In this respect the long prayer which since the sixteenth-century Lutheran theologian D.Chrytraeus has been called the 'high-priestly prayer'[321] is significant. Here Christ appears as 'intercessor' for the disciples. This prayer shows us the special nature of the intercession which Christ promises to his own when he invites them to pray in his name. Without going into any of the exegetical details of ch.17, we shall therefore concentrate on this aspect.

> Certainly here, too, we have a further development of the preaching of the incarnate Jesus. In v.3 it is clearly the evangelist who is speaking. For the Jesus who still lives on earth could not designate himself as 'the one whom you have sent, Jesus Christ'. As I remarked above (pp. 89f.), the overall perspective of the Gospel of John embraces both the incarnate Jesus and the exalted Christ, the Lord who is present in his community. On the basis of 'being led into all truth' (16.13), the evangelist feels that he has been 'instructed in all the things' that the incarnate Jesus said (14.26). We may find this confirmed in certain echoes of the Our Father in the Johannine prayer.[322]

Whether ch.17 has its place at the end of the farewell discourses, where it stands in the manuscripts, or rather, as various exegetes assume, it belongs at the beginning,[323] there is certainly an internal connection between this prayer and the preceding chapter. They have a common theme: the hearts of the disciples should not be filled with sorrow because of Christ's departure from the earth: their sorrow will be turned to joy (17.13; cf. 15.11; 16.20).

No logical sequence of statements, each built on the one before, should be looked for in this prayer, no progression without repetition. Rather, the presentation of ideas, as generally in the Johannine writings, is a cyclical one. Nevertheless we can go on to emphasize the basic notions.

The relationship of the disciples to the world runs through the whole high-priestly prayer as a Leitmotif which in this respect is of particular importance and even topicality, although, as we shall see, the prayer is spoken as an intercession for the disciples who have lived with Jesus on earth.[324]

In this context, at first v.9 sounds offensive: 'I am not praying for the world but for those whom you have given me.' Does that mean that the world is abandoned to corruption? Verses 21 and 23 give precisely the opposite as the final aim: 'that the world may believe (or know) that you have sent me', and in v.26 Jesus prays for those who will believe because of the preaching of the disciples. This goal accords with John 3.16f.: 'God so loved the world that he gave his only-begotten Son that all who believe in him should not perish . . . God did not send the Son into the world to judge the world, but that it might be saved.' According to John 17, the disciples are to enter into this work of salvation, and in respect of this mighty task with which the world presents them, they are the object of this petition. That is how the limitation of the prayer to the disciples must be understood. Jesus has 'chosen' them (15.16) that they may 'bear fruit', i.e. that they may carry out a world-wide mission.[325] This is the election of a minority to lead all to salvation. It is the pattern of all the salvation history in the Bible,[326] and it is the special mission of the small group of disciples in the time when Jesus returns to the Father. They are the ones who are to ensure the development of the work which Jesus was sent into the world to carry out. That is how the concentration of the high-priestly prayer on them is to be understood.

The perspective of the petitions relating to the life of the disciples in the world is a twofold one: on the one hand the task to be fulfilled by the disciples in the world (vv.18f.), and on the other their preservation from the world, from the evil in which the world is deeply entangled (vv.11,15).

Not only the petitions themselves but the presupposition on which they are based, their starting point, relates to the relationship of the disciples to the world. What is their situation? In the time after his death and resurrection Jesus is 'no longer in the world', but 'the disciples are in the world' (v.11). Because of this apparent aloneness in the world it is necessary for them to be preserved from it at this time, as Jesus preserved them from it when he was living with them on earth (v.12a), and 'none of them is lost but the son of perdition [Judas]' (17.12b).

On the other hand, they who are largely in the world are not 'of the world',[327] just as Jesus himself is not of the world' (vv.14,16). Therefore the 'world hates them' (v.14). While they are in the world they must continue to be preserved in this state of not being of the world. Therefore Christ must pray to God, whom he here deliber-ately addresses as 'holy Father', to 'keep' those whom God has given him 'in his name' (v.11b). The term 'keep', 'separate' is expressed in v.17 in the words of the petition 'sanctify them in the (by the) truth', and again the participation of the disciples in what marks out Christ himself is added: 'and for their sake I consecrate myself, that they also may be consecrated in the truth' (v.19).

They are to be sanctified by 'the truth', which is truth in the Johannine sense (see above, 96f.), i.e. the revelation of God in Christ. Jesus has revealed the truth, or what amounts to the same thing, the 'name' of God, to his own (v.6). He has 'made known to them this name and will continue to make it known' (v.26), and v.25 again indicates that the content of the truth and name which are to be known on the basis of this revelation is that Christ is sent by God. Already according to the first part of the prayer the disciples have 'known' that Christ has 'come forth' from God; they have believed that God has sent him (v.8).

The verb 'send' keeps recurring throughout the prayer. Not only is God known in the fact that he has sent Christ, but sending generally is the principle of all revelation: Christ too sends the disciples: 'As you sent me into the world, so I have sent them into the world'. He expressly prays to God 'not that you should take them out of the world, but that you should keep them from the evil one' (v.15). For Christ has sent them in particular into the world. And what is the aim of this sending? That the world may know that Christ has 'sent' them (v.23). The world is to survey as it were the whole course of the divine sending, which ends in its own knowledge and thus brings it to God, in the knowledge that God has sent Christ. For this whole process of sending, the sending of Christ by God, of the disciples by Christ, culminates in the attainment of the world to knowledge; God's communication of himself is evident in this saving course of the sending.

But in this prayer, 'being sent by God' belongs with 'being loved by him'. God's self-communication is a self-communication of his love. According to v.23, which has already been quoted, the world is to know 'that you have sent me and that you have loved it as you have loved me'. The belief that God is love, as the author of I John writes (I John 4.16), underlies the whole of Johannine theology. Its christ-ocentricity is grounded in this: God has loved Christ 'from the beginning of the world' (v.24b). The same love runs through every saving event like a stream: the same love binds God with Christ, Christ with his own, his own with Christ and God. The love of the disciples for one another is also grounded in this love in which God communicates himself. That is the sole foundation of the new commandment to love as Christ gives it and defines it in John 13.34 ('as I have loved you'), the commandment on the fulfilment of which according to I John 3.21–23 (see above, 105) the 'confidence' that our prayer will be heard is based. Johannine prayer is utterly grounded in God's communication of himself as love and from love, and its climax is God's communication of himself in Christ.

Now this is also the special feature of the petition for unity in v.21 'that they may all be one', which is closely connected with this commandment. It is constantly and rightly cited in ecumenical gatherings, but wrongly, without the continuation[328] which alone gives it its depth: 'I in them and you in me, that they may become perfectly one, so that the world may know that you have sent me.' And again in v.23: 'I in them and you in me, that they may be perfectly one, so that the world may know that you have sent me and have loved them even as you have loved me.'

For the world, the unity of the disciples among themselves is the foundation of the knowledge of God. In it they are to know the stream of love which stems from the same source of love: God, Christ, disciples, world; what is important is not only the chronological sequence but also the inner bond of love. The world will follow the way of knowing as it were in the reverse order: it see the bond of love in the unity realized among the disciples and come to know and believe that God sent Christ into the world for love of the world: 'God so loved the world . . .' (John 3.16).

Therefore the departing Christ must pray for the unity of Christians and 'those who come to believe on the preaching of the disciples' (v.20). Hence the concluding prayer in the last verse (v.26) applies to the disciples, 'that the love with which you have loved may be in them, and I in them'.

5. Summary (Prayer in the Johannine writings)

We have investigated the Johannine view of prayer in connection with three different sections of the Gospel of John: 1. the conversation between Jesus and the woman of Samaria (4.20ff.), worship in spirit and truth; 2. the farewell discourses (chs.14-16), praying in the name of Jesus, the Spirit as Paraclete, being heard; 3. the high-priestly prayer (ch.7): Jesus' intercession for his own.

The same basic view links all three sections together. It is characterized by the consistently christocentric orientation of prayer. Its great contribution to the understanding of prayer consists in the fact that it connects the help which according to the whole of the New Testament (especially Rom.8.26) we need to pray with the support of Jesus Christ. Our prayer certainly remains orientated on God the Father, but it is rooted in the work of the incarnate and exalted Lord Jesus Christ. The Johannine preaching according to which we know God through Christ – 'he who has seen me has seen the Father' (John 14.9) – also applies to prayer. The way to the goal of any prayer, encounter with God, is opened to us through Jesus, the incarnate one, in whom God turns towards humankind.

Jesus tells the woman of Samaria that in the end time, which is ushered in by his coming, the worship of God will no longer be tied to a particular place but will seek encounter with him, who is himself Spirit – in the Spirit who reveals God to us in Christ, who leads us into truth and therefore is closely bound up with the truth.

So in the time which dawns after Christ's death and resurrection, i.e. the time to which the farewell discourses relate, Jesus will be present not only in the memory of the disciples, but really among them as a living reality, if they pray to God in his name. This prayer unites them with him. They see him as it were alongside them in their prayer and thus gain the confidence that he is praying with them, but on the other hand bring their petitions before God in intercession.

The high-priestly prayer teaches us what this intercession consists of: it is intercession for the disciples to be preserved in the world into which they have been sent to fulfil their task, to lead the world to know the love of God; intercession for them to be preserved from the world, by their sanctification in the love which is the nature of God and which binds them and the world to Christ and to God.

IV. Prayer in the Other New Testament Writings: A Survey

As I remarked at the beginning of this book, its aim is not to cover all the New Testament passages in which prayer is mentioned, like a lexicon.[329] Rather, it aims to develop a theology of prayer from the New Testament as a whole on the basis of the testimony of its key theological statements. Such a theology in fact seems to me already to follow from the preceding chapters: the Synoptic Gospels, Paul and the Johannine writings. Each of these three biblical complexes offers a special aspect, and in the last part of the book I shall attempt a synthesis of the many and varied expressions. The fact that now, in contrast to the preceding chapters, which were quite long, I shall be dealing more briefly with the other writings (Acts, I Peter, James, Hebrews, Revelation) is not meant to indicate that they are unimportant for our question, but rather that they merely endorse the views which have already been established. I have already brought in some of the passages they contain in passing.

1. Acts

Acts comes from the same author as the Gospel of Luke. However, we did not have to discuss the two works together in the present book, since Acts is not concerned with the prayer of Jesus according to the Synoptic Gospels, which was the subject of the earlier chapter. But in the account of the life of the earliest community we find features in common with those of the life of Jesus by the same author. It is important for our question that in Acts, too, we note that among the different expressions of the life of the first Christians Luke puts particular emphasis on prayer, which corresponds to the numerous mentions of the prayer of Jesus in his Gospel (Luke as the 'evangelist of prayer').

Just as Luke is the only one of the Synoptic evangelists to report in his Gospel that Jesus spent the whole night in prayer before choosing the twelve apostles (6.12ff.), so at the beginning of Acts (1.24ff.) he reports the prayer which Peter speaks with the assembled brethren before the election of Matthias, the apostle who replaces Judas. Certainly the matter is later decided by lot (v.26), but the prayer removes the choice from the sphere of chance and derives it from God.[330]

In the summary description of the life of the earliest community (2.42ff.) 'perseverance' in prayer (see above, 3f., 80f. and below,

124) and 'praise of God' (v.47) are not forgotten alongside 'instruction in the teaching of the apostles and the breaking of the bread'.

It is theologically relevant that Luke, like Paul, grounds prayer in the Holy Spirit. This, too, is in accord with his Gospel, in which the Holy Spirit is brought so strongly into the foreground. After the account of the prayer spoken by the assembled community after the liberation of Peter and John (3.24ff.)[331] it is said in v.31 that while they were praying the place where they were meeting shook, thus making known the presence of the Holy Spirit with which they were filled, just as at Pentecost the mighty wind from heaven which filled the whole house accompanied the miracle of the Spirit (2.2ff.). The vision of heaven and Christ was also granted to Stephen (7.55ff.) at the moment when – 'filled with the Holy Spirit and looking towards heaven' (v.55) – he began to pray, while his enemies rushed on him 'grinding their teeth' after his speech, just as immediately afterwards he continued to pray during the stoning (vv.59,60).[332] The whole of Luke's narrative (Acts 10.1ff.) of Peter's vision of the laid table as an invitation to him 'not to regard as impure what God has made pure' takes place in the sphere of the influence of the Spirit which comes about through prayer ('ecstasy', v.10), when he goes up to the roof where the vision takes place 'to pray' (v.9).[333]

2. I Peter

In I Peter 3.7 at the end of a long enumeration of the duties of wives and husbands, husbands are told that the aim of all this is 'that your prayers are not hindered'. This is probably not a reference, as some exegetes suppose, to the short-term continence commended to married couples by Paul in I Cor.7.5 so that they can concentrate on prayer; rather, moral conduct is seen as a precondition for prayer. The idea is probably that where this is lacking, the disposition needed for true praying is not present, just as in the Synoptic Gospels and other writings the need to show love is emphasized. Similarly 4.7 states, 'be reasonable and moderate in respect of prayer', and in the next verse 'mutual love' is called for 'above all'. Otherwise in 5.7 the author calls on readers to 'cast all your cares on God', since God cares for them. As for Jesus (see above, 54f.) and for Paul, Phil.4.6, here too prayer is meant to exclude all anxiety.

3. James

Prayer occupies a good deal of space in the Letter of James. Taking up Jesus' promises in the Synoptic Gospels that prayer will be heard, 'Pray and it will be given you', right at the beginning the author writes: 'If any of you lacks wisdom, let him ask God, who gives to all men generously and without reproaching, and it will be given him' (1.5). Further on, as in Matt.21.21, we read: 'Let him ask in faith with no doubting, for he who doubts is like a wave of the sea that is driven and tossed by the wind' (1.6). In 4.3 the author criticizes the disputatious for not receiving 'because you ask wrongly'. The context shows that this refers to their immoral conduct, just as in the Synoptic Gospels Jesus requires forgiveness of sins as a precondition for prayer, and I Peter (see above) above all the practice of love in respect of prayer (see above, 113).

In James, the requirement of a moral life may be connected with the letter's strong emphasis on righteousness. In 5.16 the author writes that 'the prayer of a righteous man has great power in its effects'. We have just noted in 1.6, where it is said that wisdom is to be prayed for in faith, that faith is also needed here, and in 5.15 there is mention of the 'prayer of faith'[334] which is to save the sick.

As in Phil.4.6, so also according to James 5.13 prayer is to be offered in every situation: 'Is anyone among you suffering? Let him pray. Is any cheerful? Let him sing praise. Is any among you sick? Let him call for the elders of the church, and let them pray over him, anointing him with oil in the name of the Lord.'

All life moves in the direction of prayer. The link with God must not be broken off at any moment, whether in intercession or thanksgiving.

4. Hebrews

Hebrews is relevant for our problem, less through direct instructions than through its basic theological notions, which can be regarded as a preupposition for prayer. Certainly – rather indirectly – in 13.18 there is the imperative 'pray for us', and in 5.7 there is mention of the 'prayers and supplications' of Jesus[335] in Gethsemane, even with details which go beyond the accounts in the Gospels. But important as these are for the picture of Jesus, the real, albeit more indirect, contribution of Hebrews to the New Testament view of prayer is the concept of the high priest which stands in the foreground.

We have met this in the Gospel of John and in the New Testament generally in connection with the intercession of Jesus, although the term 'high priest' for Jesus first occurs in Hebrews. In contrast to the petitionary texts in the Gospel of John (with which the letter in other respects shows some affinity), the concept of high priest in Hebrews is not connected with prayer. Only the remarks about the superiority of the new priesthood to the old, the Old Testament terminology for which is taken over, remarks which dominate the whole argument, indicate lines which lead to prayer.

Approach to God has been made possible in a unique way by the sacrifice offered *once* by Christ. Access to the sanctuary is open (10.19). According to 9.14 the blood shed by Christ offers the possibility for our 'conscience' to serve the living God, not by dead works. The expression for 'serve'[336] here embraces our whole life, but the orignial cultic meaning is probably included. This certainly underlies the statement of 12.28 about the grace through which we serve God 'acceptably, with reverence and awe'.

The new access to God opened up by Christ is denoted by the verb 'approach',[337] which is repeated on a number of occasions, and if the goal of all prayer is encounter with God, this basic notion of Hebrews brings us to an important aspect of our theme. The possibility created by the 'great priest' to 'approach' the 'throne of grace' in 4.16 and the 'access to the sanctuary' in 10.19 give us the 'confidence'[338] mentioned in both passages, which in other New Testament texts is related to the certainty that prayer will be heard. In both 4.16 and 10.22 the priestly work of Christ, which has given us access to God and thus confidence, this indicative of grace ('we have access') leads to the imperative 'let us approach'. The new priesthood obliges us to 'offer the sacrifice' which according to 13.15 consists in the praise of God and is more closely defined as the 'fruit of lips which confess his name'. So here the author invites readers to pray. This is praise in which the 'confessing of lips' can be included.[339]

5. Revelation

Although – to a limited degree – a certain affinity can be demonstrated between the Revelation of John and the other Johannine
writings, I have not discussed it with them, since it belongs to a very
different and quite special literary genre. Moreover it differs from
them in that we cannot infer any information from it about
individual prayer, but only about liturgical prayers. Apart from the
cry of prayer 'Come, Lord', it does not contain petitionary prayer,
but praise and thanksgiving.

This is not uttered by human beings on earth, but in heaven and
at the end. Nevertheless it can be considered a source for the praise
and thanksgiving, the doxologies, which are offered in the community. Indeed the whole framework presents a liturgical service in
heaven. The seer hears prayers in heaven which are familiar to him
from the worship of the community, especially as this is regarded as
an anticipation of future worship.[340] On this assumption we may
draw conclusions about early Christian liturgical prayers from the
hymns contained in the Revelation of John.[341]

At the beginning (1.5f.) there is a doxology addressed to Christ,
which in a short summary glorifies his person and his work. With
the threefold 'Holy' from Isa.6.3 (*trishagion*, see above, 45) praise
is sung in 4.8 by the winged creatures to the 'almighty'[342] God who
'was and is and is to come', and subsequently it is reported that in
accordance with monarchical custom the twenty-four elders cast
their crowns at the feet of the one who sits on the throne and utter
the typical formula of homage: 'You are worthy to receive glory,
honour and power . . .' (vv.10f.).[343]

In contrast to the great majority of the prayers that we encounter
in the other New Testament writings (including the Johannines),
almost all of which are addressed to God, several hymns in
Revelation are in praise of Christ, 'the one who was slain'. Thus in
5.8 'the four living creatures and the twenty-four elders fell down
before the Lamb, each holding a harp, and with golden bowls full
of incense, which are the prayers of the saints,[344] and they sang a
new[345] song . . .'; myriads of angels joined in the song of praise in
the third person, 'worthy is the Lamb . . .' (5.12). The homage
offered by a countless multitude from all nations, peoples, tribes
and tongues in 7.10 is addressed simultaneously to both God and

Christ: 'Salvation to our God who sits on the throne and to the Lamb.'

In a long hymn of praise in 11.17f., the twenty-four elders thank[346] God the almighty for taking power, exercising lordship and judgment. The 'hymn of Moses' and that of the Lamb are also addressed to almighty God (15.3).

After the fall of Babylon, the seer in 19.11ff. hears 'a loud voice like a great multitude in heaven', a cry of jubilation introduced with Hallelujah which praises God in the third person for his righteous judgments, and immediately afterwards he hears three more times the Hallelujah, which derives from Old Testament worship and has been taken over by Christians.

Thus hymns pervade the whole of Revelation. It is significant for its view of prayer that the future unfolds in the form of a tremendous liturgical service with songs of praise and thanksgiving to God and Christ the sacrificial Lamb.

Only at the end, in 22.17, is there an intercession, one which – in Aramaic garb – is part of the earliest religious liturgy:[347] 'The Spirit and the Bride say, "Come", and let him who hears say, "Come".' And the seer ends his book (v.20) with the same prayer that he has heard: 'Amen, come Lord Jesus.'[348] It is the prayer for the coming of the glorious future which Jesus himself has taught the disciples in the first part of the Our Father, 'Your kingdom come', the prayer in which we so to speak hear the prayer of Jesus.

The great significance of Revelation for understanding New Testament prayer lies in two things: on the one hand the emphasis on 'hearing' the heavenly voice, the utterance of the Spirit which governs our prayers, and on the other, connected with this, the eschatological character of prayer which anticipates the future.

'Hearing' plays a prominent role in Revelation.[349] The 'seer' not only sees, but in particular hears. He hears the 'voice' of those who strike up the songs of praise in the texts I have cited. But hearing is also one of the main features of all New Testament prayers. We might recall the view of prayer in Paul (see above) according to which the Spirit of God speaks in our prayers, and in which we clothe in imperfect human forms what we 'hear' from the Spirit. In the Revelation of John the relationship between the utterance of the Spirit and our prayer is clearly expressed in the closing prayer mentioned above, where it is said that the Spirit (and the Bride) say 'come' and the one 'who hears' is invited to utter the same word, 'come'.

> Listening to the utterance of the Spirit in prayer is an obligation which affects more than prayer. Thus at the end of the seven letters (chs. 2–3) the churches are admonished: 'He who has an ear, let him hear what the Spirit says to the churches.'

That all worship and thus all prayer must be a response to hearing is also expressed in the words of Christ at the end of the letter to the church in Laodicea, which is firmly rebuked for its lukewarmness (3.20): 'Behold, I stand at the door and knock; if anyone hears my voice and opens the door, I will come in to him and eat with him, and he with me.' There is probably a reminiscence here of early Christian worship with the breaking of the bread. It does not make any difference that here it is Christ and not the Spirit whose voice must be heard. In prayer, Christ and the Spirit are present.

The parallel which has been noted between the prayer of the early Christian community and the eschatological worship which the seer hears in heaven is grounded in the fact that our prayer involves listening to the Holy Spirit; for its effect among us is an anticipation of the end ('pledge', see above). Thus all our prayer is an anticipation of the end: an eschatological action. When we pray, we already transcend the limits of our existence. That is the most noble aspect of prayer.

Part Three

Synthesis. What Answer does the New Testament give to Today's Questions?

Introduction

In this last part I shall attempt a synthesis of the various New Testament aspects of prayer and at the same time return to the beginning of this book, which contains a survey of the objections to prayer or to particular forms of prayer. As I said at the beginning (xivf. above), the main object of the book is not to refute objections but to give an account of the New Testament view of prayer. It may have become evident from the way in which this topic has been discussed in the previous chapters that I have carried out this investigation independently of the questions underlying the objections, although here and there answers implicitly emerged of their own accord. This independence was all the more necessary since there were already such objections in the world of the New Testament; however, they have emerged in a more specific form only relatively recently, and were not a special challenge to the New Testament authors. Nevertheless it is possible and desirable as a subsidiary aim, at the end of the New Testament section, now to go into the objections in the light of the New Testament.

I would emphasize that here only those answers will be given which can be derived from the New Testament view of prayer. I shall not aim at a comprehensive, overall treatment which takes all the philosophical problems into account. However, in the course of investigating the significance of the New Testament writings for prayer I was surprised to note how pertinently many challenges to prayer can be countered precisely from this standpoint. So it seems to me appropriate to find in the conclusions which arise from the purely exegetical work an answer to the argument of those who regard prayer as nonsensical, and also to the arguments of those who allow only a certain degree of prayer. It seems to me all the more urgent to ask whether such a reduction is justified, when authors of modern monographs suppose that they can rely on the New Testament to combat the kind of prayer which rests on a 'theistic' belief in God. Whether it is right to refer to the New Testament in this way can be investigated only on the basis of the New Testament itself.

Given the importance of prayer, which is stressed by almost all systematic theologians, the concluding part of the present book can be classified both as New Testament research and at the same time as that theological discipline which in Protestant faculties is termed 'dogmatics' and in Catholic theologies fundamental theology. In the introductory part we saw that both the claim that prayer is meaningless and the New Testament view of prayer are rooted in attitudes to belief in God. Here we find ourselves at the heart of systematic theology. In the end, a synthesis of the theology of the New Testament is a foundation for any Christian dogmatics.

But is it the exclusive task of dogmatics to offer such a synthesis of the many different theologies contained in the New Testament (the theology of the Synoptics, of Paul, of John, and so on)? Must such an attempt be excluded from the sphere of the work of exegetes as such? Many New Testament scholars are inclined to answer this question in the affirmative, as they see the real task of exegesis as that of emphasizing the different views in the texts concerned. I recall that my former teacher and later colleague in Paris, Maurice Goguel, energetically disputed the possibility of writing a 'New Testament theology' in so far as it presupposes a synthesis.

Without going as far as this, many New Testament scholars think a quest for agreements between Jesus and Paul, Paul and John, suspect. They see this as manifest or concealed 'integralist fundamentalism'. But isn't the establishment of common features between New Testament texts *alongside* the differences also the task of the exegete? Certainly the desire to produce connecting links must not be the starting point for an explanation. At first each New Testament author must be interpreted on his own terms. The very multiplicity of the New Testament comprises its wealth;

and not only its wealth, but also the unity which stems from the same root which is to be uncovered, just as – to use Paul's well-known image from I Cor.12 – the human body is a unitary organism by virtue of the difference of its members.

On the basis of the account of the distinctive stamp of each New Testament author which I attempted in the previous chapters, without violently bringing together what are certainly differences I shall attempt to demonstrate exegetically the common tendencies and thus venture a brief outline of a New Testament theology of prayer. The common Christian nucleus which underlies the whole apostolic practice of prayer should become visible in this way. To anticipate an unjustified criticism, I would emphasize that where I drawn the lines further in order to understand this nucleus, I do so deliberately, but attempt to remain loyal to the faith of the earliest Christian authors.

I. The Difficulty of Praying

Praying is difficult. Can we human beings pray to God at all? Can a weak human being presume to speak with God? On the other hand, can one talk of conversation if the forms of expression of the partners are so fundamentally different? After all, a conversation involves exchanges.

This difficulty innate to all prayer, which is often an occasion for claiming the impossibility, the nonsensical character of all praying, is recognized by the New Testament. 'We do not know how to pray as we ought,' writes Paul in Romans, and in the Gospel of Luke we heard that the disciples had to ask Jesus, 'Teach us to pray.' He has to give them an example. Prayer has to be learned, but the New Testament offers us help: the Holy Spirit prays in us. Only when the Spirit speaks in us is talk with God possible: the Spirit brings us nearer to the divine mode of expression. This is what Paul writes in the same chapter, in which he mentions our human inability to speak with God. However, the Spirit has to make use of our imperfect language, and comes up against limits which speaking in tongues attempts to transcend. But in all prayer it is the Spirit which speaks in us. Spirit speaks to Spirit. We are also taught that by the Gospel of

John when in his meeting with the woman of Samaria Jesus explains his preaching that a time is coming when prayer will be offered 'in the spirit' by saying that God himself is Spirit. And in the Johannine 'farewell discourses', too, Christ calls the Spirit the 'helper', by naming him 'comforter' and 'advocate'.

If the very Spirit of God speaks in our prayer, it can be and has been objected: am I then responsible for not praying if the Spirit does not speak in me?[1] The assurance of help is certainly not meant in this way. Otherwise the many New Testament admonitions to pray would make no sense. Rather, the imperative, 'Pray', follows from the indicative 'the Spirit prays in us, help is offered to us in him'. It is our task to be ready to allow ourselves to be helped. Because this help is offered us, because praying is possible, we must pray. Prayer is one of the great gifts which God gives out of love for his creatures. To scorn this gift is human arrogance. The Spirit is not reserved for anyone, though it is also expressed in different forms: in languages accessible to all or, in special cases, also in speaking in tongues.

The difficulty of praying is also indirectly recognized in the New Testament, and help is offered in yet another way. We have seen that, with very few exceptions, prayers in the New Testament are addressed to God, not to Christ, even in the Gospel of John, which emphazizes the unity between the Father and the Son so strongly. In the Johannine 'farewell discourses' Jesus admonishes the disciples to pray to God 'in his name'. The addition of these words could on the one hand be a help to prayer and on the other make it more difficult. They are thought of as a help to prayer in the Johannine circle and probably in earliest Christianity generally, in so far as they lessen the distance between the Creator and the creature, and remove inhibitions by showing us that by communicating himself in his love God has turned to us in the incarnation of Christ and in his work. Thus our prayer is a response to the love with which 'he first loved us'. The incarnation makes it easier for us to pray to God. In the incarnate Christ, God with whom we speak in prayer has come close to us. This is meant to be the meaning of the words 'in the name of Christ' or 'through Jesus Christ our Lord', which are often thoughtlessly added at the end of our prayers.

Today, however, on the other hand they may represent a further burden for those who want to exclude Jesus Christ completely from prayer. However, just as Jesus on earth taught the disciples to pray (the Our Father), so now he wants to support them as they pray.

But even this help, which is meant to make it easier for us to pray, does not spare us the real effort that we must make to overcome the difficulty inherent in any prayer and also to fight our own weaknesses which keep us from prayer through our faults. To these we now turn.

II. Human Weaknesses and Prayer

1. The wrong kind of prayer

The New Testament also knows the human weaknesses which lead to a wrong kind of prayer. This false prayer which is contested by the New Testament itself is often cited – in complete ignorance of the Bible and against Christian prayer and all prayer, as though these weaknesses were part of praying itself. It is enough to quote the relevant passages of the New Testament to counter such charges.[2] Thus the magical prayer which consists in using many words is censured by Jesus with a remark to which we shall return, since it is important in another connection, namely that God knows what we need before we ask. All the thoughtless prayer which is so often uttered is also part of such 'babbling'. Furthermore, Jesus is particularly sharp about the prayer of the hypocritical Pharisee who thinks that he is in contact with God in his prayers, but in reality wants to be admired by his fellow men and women and pleases himself in his supposed righteousness. With unforgettable pictures Jesus described those who prayed at street corners or in the temple. It might seem that this sort of thing no longer exists, and in that particular form it certainly does not. But some of the prayers spoken in church gatherings in which people give the impression of talking with God but are pursuing other aims come under this wrong kind of prayer. Certainly prayer should also be offered in public worship, but on the other hand all prayer also requires a degree of religious awe. This should be observed both in the congregation and in the secret room in which Jesus tells the disciples to pray. A failure to follow the example given by Jesus, who seeks solitude for prayer, also occurs here in different ways. The wrong kind of prayer is worse than no prayer at all. However, it should not be identified with prayer generally.

2. Ceasing to pray

In contrast to the wrong kind of prayer, ceasing to pray, giving it up, is not contested directly in the New Testament; however, it is opposed indirectly. I have mentioned that today, in addition to the main objections, to which we shall be coming later, human weaknesses like laziness, stress, forgetfulness and impatience generate a reluctance to pray or lead to prayer being abandoned altogether. Although such weaknesses are not explicitly combatted, they can implicitly be inferred as obstacles to prayer from the admonitions to pray and the examples of the right way to pray which can be found in the New Testament. The fact that throughout the New Testament hearers and readers are constantly called on to pray shows that even then there were already weaknesses which completely dissuaded people from praying.

That is why 'persistence'[3] in prayer is called for so often. That is why Paul uses words like 'always'[4] or 'unceasingly'[5] so often in his admonitions to pray. The parable of the widow fighting for her rights (Luke 18.5ff.), like that of the friend who asks for bread (Luke 11.25ff.), is certainly intended to assure that unceasing prayer will be heard, but 18.1 mentions explicitly that with it Jesus wants to inculcate the duty to 'pray always'. The continuity of the life of prayer gives all prayers the power that they need. Paul writes to the Thessalonians that prayer should be offered 'on every occasion', and the Philippians are to bring their cares before God 'in all things'. We have seen the demand for the same continuity in James, whether we are in a good or a bad mood. In addition to the other expressions of life in the earliest community produced by the Spirit, Acts emphasizes 'continuing' in the temple in daily prayer.

Persistence in prayer is simultaneously both a demand and a means of help for overcoming the human temptation to neglect prayer. Certainly prayer should not be a mechanical routine, but on the other hand regular prayer makes uniting with God easier – that is the purpose of observing hours of prayer in monasteries. In always praying before meals[6] Jesus was not just observing a rite but showing his interrupted bond with his Father. So for us, too, grace at meals could also encourage the continuity of a life of prayer. I mentioned above (pp. 4f.) that the real concentration which is needed here is made very difficult by the external framework. A further complicating factor is that the religious communication which is needed is not possible with a nunber of guests, and that makes prayer on this occasion merely an external folding of hands out of courtesy, which must come up against passive resistance and tacit disapproval. In this case giving testimony by praying before non-believers could also be questionable. If grace before meals is said only as a thoughtless custom, it cannot be described as prayer, since the intention of speaking with God which makes a prayer a prayer is absent. Only if grace is said in true gratitude and intercession for all those who do not have enough to eat does it further the consciousness of owing God thanks 'in all things', as Paul says (Phil.4.6).

It is particularly necessary to persist in prayer when we are in great distress. Persistence is needed here, and also courage to pray. Certainly 'necessity teaches prayer', as the well-known saying has it. But the difficulty of continuing to pray in really serious distress should also be conceded. Who has not experienced that precisely in this situation we often lack the courage to pray, the courage to fight against the despair which paralyses and sometimes strangles any attempt to pray; the courage not to let doubt in deliverance from distress become despair about God.

The episode from Brecht's play *Mother Courage*, quoted so often, in which the peasants only pray in a great emergency while the dumb Kathrin acts and so averts disaster, should not lead to a dismissal of prayer in distress as such. Certainly all prayer is to be condemned which fails to engage in action when action is still possible. That is the wrong kind of prayer. According to the New Testament, by contrast the right kind of prayer leads us to act. If that is the case, we can say 'We act because we pray.'[7] Certainly Jesus puts us 'on the road'.[8] But he also sends us to our rooms (Matt.6.6). Certainly the Good Samaritan in the parable acted at the moment when action was necessary, in contrast to the priest and the Levite, but the consequence of that is only that the prayers of the 'pious' priest and the 'pious' Levite were of the wrong kind. It does not follow that the Samaritan who was excluded from official Judaism and proved to be the neighbour did not pray on Gerizim. Brecht's episode presupposes that action is still possible. The peasants would have been in no way to blame for their action had it been a stimulus for them to act. For this is the significance of courageous prayer in distress: it is meant to keep us from the despair which paralyses action in emergencies. But there are emergencies where action is not possible as it is in Brecht's incident. Would prayer have been condemned if neither drumming nor any kind of active intervention had been possible? On the contrary, prayer would have been an action which required courage. This is also particularly true of the other story about the storm, mentioned above, which Dorothee Sölle puts at the beginning of her discussion of prayer. Certainly those who pray only when they are in distress are to be condemned. In that case God really does become a *deus ex machina*.[9] But the same verdict should not be passed on praying in distress as such. The fictitious story could be supplemented by a story from Acts (27.14ff.) about a shipwreck caused by a storm which lasted for days. When all hope of rescue was lost, Paul encouraged the crew (vv.21ff.) with the divine assurance which had been granted him the night before as an answer to his prayer for deliverance by an angel of the God whom, as he said, he 'served in prayer'.[10]

Action in distress must not be played off against prayer. The Benedictine slogan *ora et labora*, 'pray and work', also applies in distress and must not be mutilated into a mere *labora*. When *laborare* is no longer possible, *orare* may and should remain.[11]

Jesus prayed in Gethsemane in deepest distress. He also prayed on the cross. Although according to the New Testament we may not put Christ's redeeming work on the same level as our human suffering, we may recall that during his earthly humanity, in this incomparable distress he gave the greatest example of the courage to pray. Though the cry 'My God, my God, why have you forsaken me?', which forms the beginning of Psalm 22, expresses the pain of physical torment and forsakenness to the edge of despair, Jesus did not go over this edge. For with his tormented complaint about the remoteness of God, paradoxically he maintained the conversation with God which had never been interrupted during his lifetime, and still prayed with the Psalmist.[12] Here already we may find an answer to the sad question which is put so often today and which is humanly so understandable, 'How can we still pray after Auschwitz?', even if it is a provisional and inadequate one. We shall be returning to it.[13] Throughout this chapter it has been my sole concern to show that necessity not only teaches us to pray but also, on the contrary, tests the overcoming of despair which makes prayer impossible and therefore requires the greatest courage to pray.

Courage needs to be shown to conquer not only despair but also the doubt associated with it which inhibits prayer. In the Synoptic Gospels on the lips of Jesus, and also in the letter of James, we have found the need not to doubt mentioned as a presupposition of the faith called for by prayer. But how can we have such a bold faith which quenches all doubt when so many prayers are not heard? This brings us to the main section of this concluding part, to the doctrine of prayer in the New Testament, in which we shall be looking for an answer to some of the objections against prayer in principle.

III. The Idea of God and Prayer

The question of God governs attitudes to prayer: not only negative ones of repudiation, but also positive ones. How do those who pray imagine God?[14] The many different forms of prayer correspond to the many different views of God.

However, it would be a mistake to think that praying must be preceded by reflection on the question of God. For as we have seen (above, 21), conversely – as Luther points out – knowledge of God arises from the experience of prayer. It is implicitly contained in prayer. So we are justified in asking: to what God is prayer offered in the New Testament? This investigation is all the more necessary, as it allows us to judge for which forms of prayer reference may be made to the New Testament.

Here a preliminary comment is necessary which applies not only to the discussion of this topic but to the application of the New Testament to the solution of present-day problems generally. To show that the biblical passages on which the answer of the New Testament is based must not be chosen on the basis of views which have been already established by some other means and without noting other passages, I begin from the story of the temptation, which both Matthew 4.1ff. and Luke 4.11ff narrate (in a rather different order). In the dialogue between the devil and Jesus, the tempter suggests to Jesus that in awareness of being the Son of God he should cast himself from the pinnacle of the temple. To prove that God's angels would have to protect him as Son of God, the devil quotes the Bible, Psalm 91.11: 'God will command his angels to preserve you to bear you in their hands . . .' But Jesus answers with another passage, Deut.6.16: 'You shall not tempt the Lord your God.'

The term 'heresy' comes from the Greek verb *hairesthai*, which means 'choose'. In this case it is a matter of choosing biblical passages. Certainly we can find texts in the New Testament for some of our favourite ideas which derive from elsewhere, but if we select only these and cite them in isolation, the doctrinal view which arises may not be claimed as a New Testament view. For isolating a statement distorts it, and in the story mentioned it is a means of temptation. This temptation has to be resisted, above all if we consider the view of God on which it is based.[15]

In the Bible, both Old and New Testaments, we find a juxtaposition of different pictures of God, some of a God who is near and some of a God who is remote; some of a God who is immanent and some of a God who is transcendent; some of a loving merciful father and some of a judge. When faced with this juxtaposition of biblical texts we should remember what was said earlier and not over-simplify by taking only one of them as an example of the biblical view. So we must not follow Marcion (in the second century) in playing off the New Testament against the Old Testament, which he radically rejected, the 'good' God against the 'just' God. And even if the Old Testament is taken together with the New, against Marcion and with the early church, within each of the two Testaments we must allow both sides to stand. So we may not see in the New Testament only the God who is near and present in the world and who acts; we must not leave out of account the God also attested in it who is remote and hidden, the 'eternal being'. Oppositions which by human logic cannot be reconciled may not be transferred to God.

In now going on to show that the transcendent God is not done away with by the God of love and mercy, I do not want to play off the 'being' of God against his saving action. That would be a contradiction of my salvation-historical conception of the theology of the New Testament. God's action, God's continual communication of his innermost being as love first brought about in the creation, comes to a climax in the sending of Christ into the world, in the incarnation and his redeeming work 'when the time was fulfilled'. In this sense it may said that 'God becomes', 'happens'. But it is the transcendent God who acts in this event in his communication of himself to the world. Christ certainly 'emptied' himself, as the Christ hymn in Philippians (2.7) confesses.[16] According to the prologue of the Gospel of John the Logos of God became flesh. But it is the 'God in heaven' who in the 'humbling of Christ' 'even to the cross' reveals his eternal being, his love. The movement takes place from above downwards, and not vice versa.[17]

It is correct to understand the God of the Bible as the God not of philosophical ontology but of experienced relationship.[18] In full accord with the Bible, Pascal writes 'not the God of the philosophers but the God of Abraham, Isaac and Jacob'. The whole Bible is in fact about the action of the transcendent God in the world. That is also the case in the New Testament. But in two important places there is mention of God's being: in the beginning as the 'Word' (though there is an indication of action, John 1.1 and 2) and at the end (I Cor.15.28). The New Testament revelation is framed by these two brief passages. The prologue of John begins with the imperfect[19] ('in the beginning *was* the Word and the Word *was* with God and the word *was* God') and then goes over into the Greek historical tense, the aorist;[20] and the whole long main part of the Johannine narrative (like that of the Synoptics) remains on the historical level of the divine activity in the world. But in I Cor.15.28 Paul writes that at the end of the whole event, when all has been subjected to the Son, he himself will be subject to the God who has subjected all things to him, 'that God may be all in all'.

Without doing away with the tension between the action and the being of God, the two may not be contrasted as contradictory opposites. Certainly it may be said with an allusion to the parable of the Good Samaritan that God may be found 'on the road from Jerusalem to Jericho'.[21] But we must not forget that God is also present in secret, in our room, where he 'who is in secret' (thus Matt.6.6 according to the best textual evidence) sees those who pray in secret. It is in keeping with the inner relationship between the hidden God and the God who reveals himself in the world that human prayer in a private room leads to action 'on the road'.

Transcendence and immanence stand side by side, but not as opposites.[22] Divine transcendence does not mean a remoteness of God which is felt by human beings as forsakenness in the sense of that absence from great disasters and fearful catastrophes which human beings experience so painfully, and which for many people put God's goodness, power or existence in question.[23] I shall be discussing this difficult problem in the last section of this book.[24] Here by transcendence of God I understand only his being beyond the earth. This is not as such to be equated with the absence of God. On the contrary, it is the positive basis of God's immanence. Because God is the almighty God, he awakens trust in us: trust which can be illustrated by the trust of a child in its parents, which rests on awareness of its own weakness as compared with the loving superiority of its parents.

Jesus envisages this childlike trust in his sayings about children conscious of their dependence: 'Unless you repent and become like children you will not enter the kingdom of heaven' (Matt.18.3, see also Mark 10.15 par.: 'Whoever does not accept the kingdom of God as a child will not enter into it'). Our model is not to be the immaturity of a child, which Jesus does not commend for imitation (Matt.11.16; Luke 7.33), but this childlike trust,[25] a model also for the faith of those who have come of age in a God who is infinitely superior to us and only for that reason can help.

Because God is the transcendent God, God can help us, and because God's transcendent nature is love, God will help us. For, as I John says, 'God is love'. Love cannot be alone, but must communicate itself. But it must have an author who brings about this communication. The nature of God shows itself in the combination of transcendence and immanence. On the one hand God's love must communicate itself, but on the other it must be combined with the divine power in order to be able to communicate itself. Both these things happen in God's communication of himself in the creation of the world and also in the incarnation of the Logos.

The divine love produces a stream of love, as the Johannine high-priestly prayer describes it. God loved his 'Word', 'Christ', 'I in you and you in me', and only from this love rooted in the Trinity does the love of human beings who live in the world emerge: 'God is love, and whoever abides in love abides in God and God in him.' The stream of love is constantly nurtured by the transcendent source of divine love, from which human beings on earth draw this power of love, and not only in a unique act of self-communication.

That is what the love of God can be in us. It is always outside us and within us. The nearness of the God who is at the same time in heaven finds its expression in the combination 'God in us, Christ in us', which often occurs. The statements 'we in God' or 'we in Christ' are always synonymous with 'God in us', 'Christ in us'. This close connection ('he abides in God and God in him', I John 4.16) again points to the fact that immanence derives from transcendence.

We hear that God is in us, not only in the Johannine writings but also in Romans, where God is said to speak in us in our prayer through the Spirit (8.15). 'The Spirit of God dwells in us' (Rom.8.11). More frequently we read 'Christ in us', with special emphasis in Gal.2.20: 'It is no longer I who live, but Christ lives in me.'

. So all our prayers are addressed to God who is within us and outside us. When we pray the Our Father with the Matthaean text, 'in heaven' (transcendence), we may and must add 'and in us' (immanence: Father). This contemporaneity of 'God in us' and 'God outside us' clarifies the divine omnipresence which is denoted in theology by the Latin technical term 'ubiquity'. Thus God can hear our prayers and the prayers of others which may be the opposite of ours at the same time.

In the light of the New Testament view of God which has been described here, we shall now discuss the answer to individual questions of prayer implicit in it, moving to that within the framework of the summary of the results of the preceding chapters. Here we shall find confirmation that the answers to different problems to be inferred from the New Testament presuppose faith in God who is in heaven and yet at the same time is near and cares for us. This is the 'theistic God' who nowadays is often tabu, the God who, as the hymn puts it 'gives way and course to clouds, air and winds, and who helps us in all distress',[26] but has no trace of magic about him; it is the God without whom, on the other hand, 'no sparrow falls from the rooftop' (Matt.10.29), by whom all the hairs of our heads are numbered, as Jesus impresses on his disciples in deliberately exaggerated imagery to indicate the sureness of providence. That is the God of the Bible, the God who appears in the pillar of cloud in his majestic glory at the entrance to the tent speaks with Moses 'face to face, as a man speaks with his friend' (Exod.33.11). The God of the Old Testament is also the God of the New and vice versa. The almighty God and the loving God both belong to the indispensable biblical nucleus, and it is not posisble to push one of these aspects to the periphery as 'historically conditioned' or to let it drop.

IV. God's Foreknowledge and God's Will that We Should Nevertheless Pray to Him

Transcendence involves not only omnipresence but also omniscience. In the New Testament this takes the form of knowing our needs in advance: 'Your Father knows what you need before you ask him.' Jesus twice gives this explanation in the Sermon on the Mount, in Matt.6.8 specifically in connection with prayer. It is particularly important to him. Prayer of praise and thanksgiving is compatible with this divine foreknowledge and raises no problems. But petitionary prayer does, since in this light it could seem superfluous and even absurd, and indeed this objection has been raised. If God knows everything that we have to ask of him in advance, then why pray, especially as the divine knowledge also includes the divine decision? And yet in the New Testament, alongside the clear and repeated proclamation of the divine providence as divinely willed stands the equally emphatic invitation to the disciples to pray.

Again it is too simple to deal with this juxtaposition by maintaining only one side and dropping the other. What is contradiction, paradox, when applied to inter-personal human relations assumes another character for the relationship between God and human beings. How then is the conclusion which follows from the New Testament evidence, that God does not need our prayers, but wants them,[27] to be explained?

Within the biblical message this formula, which from a human perspective must seem paradoxical, is brought into the light of its view of God. We have seen that the immanence of God proceeds from God's transcendence, is an emanation of God's transcendence, namely in the self-communication rooted in the divine being of which I have spoken, and in which omnipotence and love are combined. From the perspective of God' communication of himself, God's foreknowledge and God's will that people should pray to him are not opposites, but condition each other.

Out of love, God has created free men and women in order that they should enter into his love, participate in the outflowing of his love. This participation is expressed in loving actions towards fellow human beings, in the action of the 'Good Samaritan' – 'what you have done to the least of these you have done to me' (Matt.25.40), but in addition we show our love to God in prayer. This is the natural, direct response to the love of God out of which God created us. In his love for his creatures, God gave them the possibility of prayer, that great gift which allows us to share in his love. Prayer is the loving inclination towards God in which we bring our needs before him, as a child brings them before its parents.[28]

Here it is part of childlike love that we should ask in prayer for the fulfilment of wishes which we are not sure whether God will hear.[29] Jesus' prayer in Gethsemane which, as we have seen, brings clarification in so many respects, should also be a model for us here. 'If it is possible, let this cup pass from me,' Jesus dares to pray, although he knows of God's purpose of redemption. The words 'if it is possible' do not indicate a lack of faith; they do not include any fundamental doubt, but rather are a sign of his certainty: 'all things are possible for you' (Mark 14.36). We shall be looking at this 'possibility' in the next chapter in connection with the divine plan. Jesus reckons that God could incorporate even such a human wish to be spared the 'cup' into his plan. Even the prayer in Gethsemane which is not heard by God is divinely willed.

No prayer inspired by honest concern for union with God is excluded from God's will that we should pray to him: not only thanksgiving and praise but also intercession, provided that it does not contradict Jesus' instructions.[30]

That applies in particular to intercessory prayer, of which the New Testament gives us so many examples. If we pray for our fellow human beings, we come close to entering into God's loving will particularly clearly. For God equally loves those for whom we pray, and does so far more than we are capable of. God's will is that by our intercession (made possible to us through him) our love shall unite with his, and thus we shall contribute to the bulwark of love with which God surrounds our fellow men and women.[31]

So God's foreknowledge of our needs is bound up with his love for his creatures, and therefore his foreknowledge and his wish that we should pray to him are not opposites. They are not opposites in so far as the foreknowledge of God is to be understood in the New Testament intrinsically as the loving care of the caring Father'; in other words, 'foreknowledge' becomes 'providence': 'the hairs on your head are numbered'. The prayer which God wants, thanksgiving and praise, and also intercession, should be our response as participation in his love.

In terms of content, intercession is a prayer that our wishes shall be heard. The question arises, and has been raised, how such a prayer required by God is compatible with God's eternal plan. We shall now go on to see whether an answer can be derived from the witness of the New Testament as a whole, and if so, what this answer is.

V. The Immutability of the Divine Plan and the Divine Freedom to Hear Prayers

All prayer presupposes that God can hear human prayers. Is such an expectation compatible with God's eternal plan, in which according to James (1.17) there is no 'changing' in God? Doesn't this make prayer meaningless, or at any rate a lack of reverence for God's sovereignty? We have seen that great theologians of the nineteenth century therefore recognized only prayer of thanksgiving and praise as legitimate,[32] though this view is indisputably incompatible with the New Testament, which calls for uninhibited intercession.

The immutability of God and thus of God's plan should be combined with other biblical views which seem to contradict it, for example the possibility that God hears human prayers; again we have a juxtaposition. Here we should first of all recall that the whole Bible bears witness to a progression of salvation history within the divine plan of salvation, which does not always follow a straight line. In this connection I would refer to my book *Salvation as History*, and above all to the chapter 'Constant and Contingency'.[33] Salvation history is constantly crossed by a history of disaster caused by human sin. Time and again this necessitates a new event which nevertheless develops in the direction of a goal that remains the same. Taking up a Portuguese saying ('God writes straight, but in crooked lines'),[34] I have used the term 'wave' to characterize the movement of salvation history. It may suffice here to cite the development in salvation history from the Old Testament to the New with the work of Christ which atones for sin: the development of a divine plan which aims at the same goal.

Within the Old Testament, freedom of God integrated into this plan is expressed by the concept of the 'repentance of God' which occurs there; this implies that even the divine will does not develop in a straight line.

It follows from the biblical juxtaposition of the unalterable divine plan and divine freedom that God's plan itself foresees the acceptance of human requests. Certainly we find no theory about this in the New Testament. But Jesus' prayer in Gethsemane attests belief in the possibility that God will integrate into his plan a human request which he may or may not hear: 'If it is possible, let this cup pass from me.' 'All things are possible for you.' It is important that the New Testament reports this request. It is a prayer which was not heard. God said 'no' to the condition 'if it is possible' contained within the request. But the issue here is the possibility which is presupposed that God could have combined the fulfilment of the human wish with his plan. Otherwise Jesus' prayer would not have made sense, and this is confirmed by the fact that immediately after the condition the confession follows: all things are possible for you. Without this certainty, all prayer loses its meaning.[35]

That brings us to the question what requirements for our prayer follow from our recognition, derived from the New Testament, that God has the possibility of incorporating the hearing of prayer into his plan. We saw in the previous chapter that even prayers that are not heard are willed by God as an answer to his love. In the light of the divine plan they become the occasion for submission to the will of God in our prayer.

This can then even become a condition of prayers being heard, if we regard the ultimate aim of prayer as union with God. Even if a specific request is not granted, it can still guarantee that this goal is achieved. In prayer, to union with God's love must be added that union with God's will which is required by reverence for God's omnipotence.

In his instructions for prayer, Jesus makes the promise that prayers will be heard dependent on the need for faith. His own prayers lead us to make this point more specific, and say that this faith must include submission to God's will in prayer. Already in the first part of the Our Father Jesus taught the disciples to pray 'Your will be done on earth as it is in heaven', and in Gethsemane – in this form only according to the Gospel of Matthew – he added to the request 'if it is possible' and the confession 'all things are possible for you' a humble declaration of readiness to submit to God's will: 'If it is not possible, your will be done.'

However, it takes great courage to follow Jesus' example and to add the statement 'your will be done' to the fulfilment of our most ardent prayers. The need for such an attitude can provoke the objection, 'Why then pray at all, if both the hearing of the prayer and the failure to hear it are objects of our petition? Aren't we conceding that it makes no difference whether or not we pray?' Here first of all it must be repeated that at all events God wants our prayer as an entering into his love. But in particular we need to remember the sense of all prayer: to enter into union with God. That happens not only by uniting with his love but also by uniting with his will, which is a loving will.

This union with God will not be broken off, even if our wishes are not granted, if we succeed in struggling through the addition 'Your will be done'. We are told of a prayer which was not heard in II Cor.12.8f., where Paul says that he called on the Lord three times to make the 'angel of Satan' (probably as the author of an illness) depart from him. Evidently he was not granted healing, but he did hear God's answer 'My grace is sufficient for you; my power (*dynamis*) is made perfect in the illness[36] (which remains)'. Accepting this 'sufficiency', the apostle finds that his prayer is heard in not being heard. In this connection we return once again to the prayer in Gethsemane, a prayer of Jesus himself which is not heard. It does not destroy the union with the Father which Jesus experienced all through his life. Even the words of the psalm spoken on the cross, the cry of pain 'Why have you forsaken me?', are a question to God. Conversation with God is not broken off.

It is possible for human beings to fall in with God's will only if the faith which Jesus requires of them is unshakable, is faith that God's goodness is so infinitely greater than that of human beings that if even human beings will not give stones to those who ask for bread, far more will God give only good gifts. Only then can we struggle through to the prayer which Job utters after the severest blows of fate:

The Lord gave
and the Lord has taken away
blessed be the name of the Lord (Job 1.21).

Does this divine will for good prevail even over the attacks of evil? This leads us to the last and perhaps most difficult question, which also underlies the main objection to prayer.

VI. Prayer and the Question of God's Omnipotence over Evil

According to both the Old and the New Testaments, God is exalted above evil, which is personified in the 'devil', 'Satan', the 'demons', the 'powers'. This is particularly evident in the cases in which he uses temptation by the devil to test individuals (Abraham and Job are examples in the Old Testament and Jesus in the New). If the attacks carried out by the devil on God's initiative which threaten all human beings are tolerated by God, this too can ultimately be seen as testing by God.[37] In this second case the attack of the devil can be so terrible that its toleration by God seems hardly compatible with his undisputed goodness. The question then arises: can the God of love make use of such cruel instruments, even if they do not come from him but from the devil?

Paul probably knew such an objection or a similar one when he replied in I Cor.10.13: 'God is faithful, and he will not let you be tempted beyond your strength, but with the temptation will also provide the way of escape, that you may be able to endure it.' For Paul, God's goodness is certain, despite the presence of evil; thus also in Rom.3.5ff., where he explains how God can bring good out of evil without this being an excuse or an encouragement for human sin. God's omnipotence remains undisputed by Paul, however evil may work out. Is there a more terrible torment than that of the suffering and cross of Jesus caused by evil, from which, according to the New Testament, redemption derives?[38]

By contrast, nowadays God's omnipotence is doubted because of the terrible character of the events provoked by evil, for example in the question which is often heard whether it is still possible to pray after Auschwitz. This cites just one of the many examples in which evil so often establishes itself with boundless force despite all prayers, and thus conquers, raising the question whether in such instances God can hear at all the prayers of the victims affected by evil and the intercessions of their fellow men and women. Isn't God's power limited? Not only the omnipotence but the very existence of God is then put in question, and in both instances prayer seems meaningless. We have seen that according to the New Testament, even prayers which are not heard are divinely willed if they include a readiness to be united with God's will. However, if the feeling that evil has conquered shatters the belief that a will of the good God, albeit unfathomable to us, is at work in the fact that the prayer is not heard (see above, 35ff.), then the addition 'Your will be done' to the prayer is no longer possible.

Although this objection lies outside the New Testament sphere, and thus is not given a direct answer at any point, I shall now go on to investigate whether a solution can be inferred from New Testament theology as a whole. I believe that this possibility can be affirmed only with another reference to the tension between 'already' and 'not yet' which in all my works I have found to be a key to understanding the Christian situation. The decision has already been made, but it will be effective only at the end of time. Again I would recall the image of the decisive battle which may have taken place in a war at a point well before the cease-fire, so that after that battles continue in an interim period of indeterminate duration.

Here I shall apply this image which I have used to the problem of the omnipotence of God, especially as this relates to a battle, namely the battle against evil. The question whether God can hear our prayers to avert evil must be discussed with the question of divine omnipotence.

To help us to understand this better, I shall anticipate the result of the subsequent investigation: the salvation history which points to the end demonstrates God's omnipotence over evil, in the victory over evil 'already' won by Christ and in the annihilation of evil at the end. This eschatological, salvation-historical view of the New Testament does not allow any dualistic Manichaean solution of the problem to arise. By contrast, in the interim between Christ's victory and the end time in which we live, according to the New Testament the omnipotence of God is limited (through God's own plan), to the degree that evil, though conquered, bound, can for a time be free, can for a time conquer, and has to be fought against by God: a paradox which, however, is to be seen in the light to the victory that has already been won and is still to come, yet certain. I shall now demonstrate this by relating the tension between 'already' and 'not yet' to the occurrence of evil in the different stages of salvation and history, and especially to the exercise of power by evil in the intermediate period.

The following passages show that in the New Testament it is said – sometimes with the same words – on the one hand that the subjection of the powers has already taken place and on the other that it will take place at the end.

Already: according to the saying in Luke 10.18, the authenticity of which is rarely disputed, Jesus has seen 'Satan falling from heaven like lightning', and yet he continues to fight against him and his host, the demons.

Throughout the New Testament there is mention of the minions of the devil: the 'powers' of evil, which are designated as 'elements', 'lords', 'thrones', 'authorities', 'powers'. [39]

In the sphere of early Christianity they are identified with the 'enemies' who are mentioned in the royal psalm 110.1. In this psalm, which was later applied to the Messiah, the king receives the honourable summons, 'Sit at my right hand until I have made your foes your footstool.' This passage from Ps.110 is the most-quoted text in the New Testament and the apostolic fathers for proclaiming the conquest of the invisible powers of evil by Christ. [40]

It is important for our problem that this host of evil powers, which according to Eph.6.12 are disastrously at work on earth, [41] has already been subjected by Christ, yet nevertheless continues its evil work until it is destroyed at the end. It clearly emerges from I Peter 3.22 that the victory over the demonic powers has already been won: 'Jesus Christ, who has gone into heaven and is at the right hand of God, with angels, authorities, and powers subject to him.' In Eph.1.20, too, in connection with his sitting at the right hand of God, mention is made of his rule over the powers, again with a reference to Ps.110: 'he has put all things under his feet.'

This victory which has already been won is so important for early Christianity that the beginning of Ps.110, 'sit at my right hand', has found its way into the creed. Already according to the preliminary stages leading to the later creed, [42] e.g. in what is perhaps an earlier hymn to Christ cited by Paul, 'all things in heaven and on earth and under the earth bow the knee to him and confess that Jesus Christ is Lord (Kyrios)', with the short confessional formula which is developed further in the hymn. In Col.2.10 Christ is called the 'head of all power and might',[43] and some verses later we even read that the 'bond' has been destroyed by the death of Christ, 'nailed to the cross', and that the 'powers have been disarmed and made a public example' in a 'triumph'. The victory over the powers which has already been won could not be depicted more vividly.

Not yet: but equally clearly, their defeat is prophesied only for the end, also with a quotation from Ps.110, as in I Cor.15.25; Heb.10.13. The latter passage even emphasizes that since sitting on the right hand of God Christ 'still continues to wait until his enemies are made his footstool'.

It is interesting that in I Cor.15.26 the same Greek verb, *katargein*, is used to denote the final annihilation of the last enemy, namely death, as in II Tim.1.10, where there is mention of the subjection of death which has unambiguously already taken place. In order to mark the difference of meaning Luther translated II Tim 1.10: 'he has robbed death of its power', but the Greek verb which in I Cor.15.26 means '(death) is destroyed' is the same.[44] This philological observation[45] clearly expresses the theological state of the 'already' and the 'not yet'.

In this way the New Testament assumes an intermediate period, whatever its duration,[46] during which evil, though conquered, continues to be at work. The question which is so burning, namely why there is still this intermediate period in which the fight against evil has to go on, is not raised in the New Testament and therefore not answered. According to Mark 13.32, no one knows the time of the end, 'not the angels in heaven nor even the Son, but only the Father'. Thus the temporal course of the saving event also belongs in God's unfathomable counsel.

However, the New Testament does contain a pointer from which we can infer the role that it attributes to the evil which still exists in this interim period and the way in which God counters it. How can the devil, who has already been defeated, have such a free rein in the intermediate period without the omnipotence of God which is assumed in the New Testament being put in question? One could refer to what I said in explanation of the sixth petition of the Our

Father, 'let us not be led into temptation': the executive author of evil is the devil, albeit tolerated by God, and not God. But that does not do away with the stumbling block to the omnipotence of God still presented by the devil.

Here an image used in Revelation is much more important to me: according to 20.2, Satan is 'bound' for a time (for a thousand years) and is then freed for a time for the final annihilation (20.7). This image corresponds to the one used in the passages discussed above of the subjection of the hostile powers and their destruction, which will take place only at the end. If we apply the binding of Satan, which in Revelation takes place for the duration of the thousand-year kingdom, to the whole interim period between the work of Christ and the end, an answer to our question about God's omnipotence in the face of evil can emerge. In my previous works I have allowed myself to expand the image of the binding of Satan for only a limited duration and – after it, but still before the end – then being freed, leaving aside the insertion in v.3. The devil is bound to a line which can be lengthened, even to the point where for a while Satan can make himself independent and has to be fought against by God.

Going slightly beyond the Revelation of John, this means that the whole fearful character is to be attributed to the evil which temporarily looses itself from these bonds. If this event is taking place in accordance with the divine plan, then God himself has limited his omnipotence for this interim period, without giving it up in the long term. We cannot go any further, because to do so would be to take us into speculations which would remove us too far from the New Testament, and I have tried to avoid doing this, given the topic of this book.

However, there is one thing we can say in summary: it is confirmed that while in the New Testament the omnipotence of God is not put in question, for unfathomable reasons the power of evil is still at work alongside it in the interim period and has to be fought against by God.

What conclusion is to be drawn from the preceding remarks for our praying, with which we can attempt an answer to this question? We have seen that it is God's will that we should always pray. But that means that the situation is as it was when in such terrible events as we experienced, say, in the time of Hitler, when we noted the temporary victory of evil and the temporary absence of God and had to have courage to pray. What we know of Dietrich Bonhoeffer's prayers in the last moments before his execution may serve as an example here.

Even then we have to pray. For here prayer has a quite special effect which transcends all the functions that we have illuminated so far. I have said that as creatures of the God who is love we must unite with his loving will in prayer through our praying. But we go almost beyond the bounds of human possibility as we enter into the action in his battle against evil. This happens if, alongside the action that is possible for us, we pray for victory over evil. Given the provisos enjoined by God's sovereignty, we may venture to say that through our prayers we become God's helpers in the battle against evil in the world. All individual and collective prayers for peace belong here. This is the supreme nobility of this human activity, in which with the help of the Holy Spirit we go beyond all other human language.

Conclusion

Now that we have come to the end of this study, I shall formulate some brief key statements which follow from it; however, in doing so I do not want to suggest that the subsidiary statements which also arise from the basic exegetical part are not unimportant. Once again I would ask the reader to reflect on the synthesis only in the light of a careful examination of the main analytical section.

1. In his omnipotence and omnipresence God does not need our prayer, but wants it, thanksgiving and intercession, as the entering of his creatures into his loving will, by which he created human beings in his communication of himself.

2. So the ultimate aim of prayer is encounter with God, entering into his love. Petitionary prayer shows this particularly clearly, since God loves those for whom we pray, infinitely more than we do.

3. We pray to God who is in us and outside us (hence his omnipresence, 'ubiquity').

4. We need divine help to pray, i.e. to be able to speak with God as helpless human beings; we need the help of the Holy Spirit. Prayer is one of God's great gifts of love to human beings.

5. For our prayers to be heard we need to believe at the same time in God's goodness and in God's omnipotence, and we also need to be ready to submit to his will in reverence for his majesty. Difficult though it may be for us, the possibility that specific wishes may not be heard must also be taken up into prayer, so that in this case, too, hearing takes place at a higher level.

6. The possibility that God will hear our prayers does not contradict the immutability of his fixed plan. God's freedom to hear prayers is built into his plan.

7. We should pray in all situations of life in order constantly to

remain in contact with God ('persistence' in prayer). Even prayers which are not heard are willed by God.

8. In the interim period between the conquest of evil by Christ and the annihilation of evil at the end, evil is still at work and must be combatted by Christ. This gives our prayer against evil special significance.

9. Even if evil is victorious in this interim period, we must pray so that through prayer we may be God's helpers in his fight against evil.

10. Almost all New Testament prayers are addressed to God, and only very much by way of exception to Christ, but reference to Christ's word (Paul) or name (John) stamps prayer in the New Testament by emphasizing the fundamental nearness of the God who is distant, yet loves us, in all human prayer. The Our Father and Jesus' own prayers, above all the prayer in Gethsemane and the prayer addressed to God in the forsakenness of the cross, and also the great Johannine prayer (John 17), include all the essential features of Christian prayer.

Notes

Foreword

1. Cf. Gerhard Ebeling, 'Das Gebet', *ZTK* 1973, 206ff., and *Dogmatik des christlichen Glaubens* 1, Tübingen 1979, 192ff., especially 208: prayer is 'not one religious act alongside others; the whole of one's relationship with God is concentrated in it'. But also see already Heinrich Ott, 'Theologie als Gebet und Wissenschaft', *Theologische Zeitschrift* 1958, 123; Hans Urs von Balthasar, *Das betrachtende Gebet*, Einsiedeln 1965, and Hans Schaller, *Das Bittgebet. Eine theologische Skizze*, Einsiedeln 1979, 11f. Gotthold Müller, 'Gebet', *TRE*, 88, exaggerates, but is basically right: 'The decisive question can no longer be "What place does prayer have in dogmatics?" but only "What place does dogmatics have in prayer?".' Luther in particular emphasized that prayer is a means of *knowing God* and ourselves, see below, p. 6.

2. See below, pp. 18f.

3. See Friedrich Heiler, *Prayer*, Oxford 1932, which is still a classic, though in some respects it is outdated.

4. For the first three centuries see the excellent work by A.Hamman, *La Prière*, Vol.II, *Les trois premiers siècles*, Tournai 1963 (the title of the first volume is given in n.7 below). There are also articles in encyclopaedias, like that by Severin in *Antike und Christentum* and especially that by Klaus Berger in *TRE*, 47ff. For the *New Catechism of the Catholic Church* see p.xvii below.

5. *Peri Euches* (*On Prayer*), in P.Koetschau (ed.), *Origenes*, Die griechischen christlichen Schriftsteller, Berlin 1899.

6. It would be a good thing if the Tübingen series Beiträge zur Geschichte der biblischen Exegese were to contain a work on the history of the interpretation of Christian prayer in these centuries. For the Luther texts see the detailed study by Vilmos Vajta, 'Luther als Beter', in Helmar Junghans, *Martin Luther von 1526 bis 1546*, 1983, 279ff.

7. A.Hamman, *La Prière*, Vol. I, *Le Nouveau Testament*, Tournai 1959.

8. C.Senft, *Le courage de prier. La prière dans le Nouveau Testament*, ²1985.

9. E.Lohmeyer, *The Lord's Prayer* (1952), London 1965.

10. J.Carmignac, *Recherches sur le 'Notre Père'*, Paris 1969.

11. J.M.Lochman, *Unser Vater. Auslegung des Vaterunsers*, Gütersloh 1988.

12. G.Harder, *Paulus und das Gebet*, Gütersloh 1936.

13. R.Gebauer, *Das Gebet bei Paulus. Forschungsgeschichtliche und exegetische Studien*, Giessen and Basel 1989.

14. F.Ménégoz, *Le problème de la prière. Principe d'une révision de la méthode théologique*, Strasbourg and Paris 1925, ²1932.

15. There are many references to prayer, and especially the Our Father, in Karl Barth's *Church Dogmatics*, passim.

16. A. de Quervain, *Das Gebet*, Zollikon 1938.

17. H.Mottu, 'La prière et les mouvements théologiques actuels', *Bulletin du Centre protestant d'Études*, 1968.

18. O.Hallesby, *Vom Beten. Deutsch als Taschenbuch*, Wuppertal 1985 (translated from the Norwegian).

19. Ebeling, 'Das Gebet' (n.1), 206ff.

20. R.Leuenberger, *Zeit in der Zeit. Über das Gebet*, Zurich 1988.

21. H.W.Schröder, *Das Gebet. Übung und Erfahrung*, Stuttgart 1963ff., 1977, ³1988.

22. R.Guardini, *Vorschule des Gebets* (1943), Einsiedeln 1952.

23. H.Schaller, *Das Bittgebet. Eine theologische Skizze*, Einsiedeln 1979.

24. W.Bernet, *Gebet*, Stuttgart 1970.

25. Ibid.

26. D.Sölle et al., 'Gebet', in *Theologie für Nichttheologen*, Stuttgart 1966, reprinted also in *Atheistisch an Gott glauben*, Olten and Freiburg 1968, 109ff. (the version quoted here); ead., ' "Wir wissen nicht, was wir beten sollen" ', in *Die Wahrheit ist konkret*, Olten and Freiburg 1967; ead., *Politisches Nachtgebet in Köln*, Stuttgart ²1969.

27. She is right here, in so far as this model conflicts with aspects of prayer which are also condemned by the New Testament. However, at the same time she eliminates other elements which are incompatible with her understanding; these we must examine exegetically to see whether they are not the indispensable presuppositions of all New Testament prayers and statements about prayer. We shall be returning to this later.

Part One: Introduction: Difficulties in Praying and Objections to Prayer

1. However, Gotthold Müller, 'Gebet', *TRE*, 85, also mentions the view of Hermann Schmidt, *Wie betet der heutige Mensch?*, 1972, according to whom the crisis of prayer, like the 'Death of God theology', has had the

opposite effect, with the result that there has never been so much writing and talk about prayer as there is today.

2. See below, 126, 137, 180 n.26.

3. See below, 137ff.

4. See below, 131.

5. R.Guardini, *Vorschule des Gebets*, Einsiedeln 1952, makes some very good remarks on this in his chapter on 'The External Order', 45ff.

6. See the title of Leuenberger's book *Zeit in der Zeit*, Zurich 1988 ('Time in Time').

7. Dr Matthias Stauffacher, one of the editors of the edition of Overbeck currently in preparation, has kindly made available to me this and other texts from the Overbeck archive in the University Library at Basel (A 268B). See this text also in Eberhard Vischer, *Franz Overbeck, Selbstbekenntnisse*, 1941, 122. Overbeck's last wish contradicted this statement, see 149 n.40 below.

8. In this context I must quote a witty and also malicious story, of course apocryphal, which went the rounds in Basel. A member of the Basel aristocracy went to church on Sunday, since years ago this was the thing to do. On one occasion a business friend went with him who had never been into a church before. On the way home he asked: 'What were you doing standing in your place after you got into church, before you sat down?' The reply was: 'I always count to thirty. Some only count to fifteen, but I regard that as hypocrisy.'

9. Leuenberger, *Zeit in der Zeit* (n.6), deals with this in detail.

10. Thus C.Senft entitled his book *Le courage de prier*.

11. D.Bonhoeffer, *Letters and Papers from Prison*, London and New York 1971, 199: '. . . it's true that it needs trouble to shake us up and drive us to prayer'. However, Bonhoeffer finds this 'something to be ashamed of'.

12. Guardini, *Vorschule des Gebets* (n.5), 237, rightly recalls that it sometimes has to be said that 'in distress prayer escapes one'.

13. D.Sölle, *Atheistisch an Gott glauben*, Olten and Freiburg 1988, 109.

14. B.Brecht, *Mother Courage and her Children*, London 1980.

15. For playing off action against prayer see below, 13, 126.

16. WA 32, 219, 100. See above xiv. G.Ebeling, *Dogmatik des christlichen Glaubens* 1, Tübingen 1979, 192ff.; also G.Sauter, *Das Gebet als Wurzel des Redens von Gott*, Glauben und Leben, 1986, 31f.; Gotthold Müller, 'Gebet', *TRE*, 487; U.Eibach, 'Prayer and Conceptions of God', *Concilium* 1990/3, 60–74.

17. See below, 129; 148 n.21; 178 nn.14, 16.

18. For John A.T.Robinson's attitude to prayer see *Honest to God*, London and Philadelphia 1963, 84ff., and Henry Mottu, *La prière et les mouvements théologiques actuels*, Bulletin du Centre protestant d'Études, 1968, 7ff.

19. D.Sölle, *Die Wahrheit ist konkret*, Olten and Freiburg 1967, 106, and *Atheistisch an Gott glauben* (n.13), 53.

20. For monologue and dialogue see 150 n.58 below.

21. See now her book *Thinking about God*, London and Philadelphia 1990, in which she develops her own view of the relationship between God and human beings, in the perspective of feminist theology and liberation theology, more moderately than in her earlier works and with a concern to give a more objective account of the opinions which she rejects. I have only felt able to cite the new book in what follows after already dealing with the most important of the sections in her earlier works devoted to prayer. Although in the new book the author discusses belief in God at greater length, she simply endorses the repudiation of 'theism' that she has already advanced (see below, 131), which underlies an attitude to prayer that she has not abandoned.

22. See above, 1.

23. By contrast, the condemnation of the view of a God as a 'God of the gaps', an 'old magician' (D.Sölle, *Atheistisch an Gott glauben* [n.13], passim), accords with the New Testament when it refers to the notion of an anthropomorphic God which the New Testament also contests as 'pagan' (Matt.6.7ff.). However, this ceases to be the case when at the same time belief in the theistic God who is both remote and near, which is described above and attested by both Old and New Testaments, is repudiated.

24. Contested by Sölle, *Atheistisch an Gott glauben* (n.13), 58. For this hymn see below, 131. I refer to D.Sölle in this connection, although her view is shared by many others, because she is so particularly eloquent and combats the belief that she repudiates with irony and with choice phrases which do not fail to make a mark on the reader (especially in the German-speaking world). For her reference to the New Testament see what she says in the previous note and especially at 179 n.22.

25. E.Jüngel, *Evangelische Kommentare*, 1969, 133ff.

26. See below, 10ff.

27. See below, 35, 134f.

28. Among more recent writers see W.Bernet, *Gebet*, Stuttgart 1970.

29. See also J.Ratzinger's clarificatory letter to the bishops of the Catholic Church, *Some Aspects of Christian Meditation*, Vatican 1989.

30. Leuenberger, *Zeit in der Zeit* (n.6), devotes a relatively large amount of space to them in his book. Although there are points of contact, and meditation leads to prayer, the boundaries between the two do not seem to me always to have been drawn sufficiently sharply.

31. Mention should be made among them especially of L.Feuerbach, who, with his general view of religion as a projection of human wishes and the designation of prayer as 'the absolute relation of the human heart to

itself' which follows from this (*The Essence of Christianity* [1841], reissued New York 1957, 123), has directly or indirectly influenced most objections, probably also the more recent one by Bernet, *Gebet* (n.28 above).

32. F.Ménégoz, *Le problème de la prière. Principe d'une revision de la méthode théologique*, Strasbourg and Paris 1925, ²1932, is therefore concerned in his comprehensive study to detach Protestant theology from Kantian philosophy and to create another basis, particularly with Max Scheler.

33. I.Kant, *Religion within the Limits of Reason Alone* (1794), reissued New York 1960.

34. I.Kant, *Vom Gebet. 7 kleine Aufsätze aus den Jahren 1788–1791*, ed. E.Cassirer, 1912.

35. Guardini, *Vorschule des Gebets* (n.5), 16.

36. Kant, *Religion within the Limits of Reason Alone* (n.33), 183.

37. Ibid., 158f.

38. See above, 5, and below, 12f., 125f.

39. Kant, *Vom Gebet* (n.34), 525.

40. Overbeck mentions the concession made by Kant, 'the value [of prayer] among men, which he [Kant] reecognizes as such, but not otherwise, not outside the effects that are observed from it among men. Kant even says in so many words that prayer is folly . . .' (Univ Bibl.Basel A 223). Contradicting his firmly negative remarks about prayer (see above n.10), Overbeck wanted a prayer to be spoken at his funeral (Erinnerungshaft A 278, 8).

41. F.Nietzsche, *Also Sprach Zarathustra*, Harmondsworth 1961.

42. Ibid., 321.

43. Ibid., 199. It is interesting how the charge of cowardice levelled against those who do not dare to confess that they pray coincides with Kant's remark about 'something of which we should be ashamed' (see above, 8) .

44. Ibid., 200.

45. See above, xivf.

46. See H.Schaller, *Das Bittgebet. Eine theologische Skizze*. Einsiedeln 1979, 19f.

47. J.-J.Rousseau, *Émile* (1762), London 1911 reissued 1992, Book IV, 'The Creed of a Savoyard Priest', 308.

48. F.Schleiermacher, *The Christian Faith*, Edinburgh 1928, §147.

49. Ibid., §147.2.

50. F.Schleiermacher, *Predigtband* 4, 357.

51. Wilhelm Herrmann contested Schleiermacher's position in his book *The Communion of the Christian with God* (²1906), reissued Philadelphia and London 1972, 243f., which is still worth reading.

52. A.Ritschl, *Instruction in the Christian Religion* (1881), in A.T.Swing,

The Theology of Albrecht Ritschl, London and New York 1901, 265 and passim.

53. M.Kähler, *Dogmatische Zeitfragen* 1, 1898, 186.

54. See below, 30.

55. This is not the case even with D.Sölle. But the question does arise whether she does not implicitly devalue this form of prayer. We must wholly agree with her when very much in line with Jesus she emphasizes the right to pray (*Atheistisch an Gott Glauben* [n.13], 113f.). But her polemic against the *beati possidentes*, which is intrinsically justified ('We do not know what we should pray', in *Die Wahrheit ist konkret* [n.19], 111), leads her to speak of thanksgiving only in connection with the tabu piety of the *religiosi* and of Harvest Thanksgiving only by citing one which 'is celebrated without the awareness that two-thirds of humankind do not have enough to eat', which she rightly describes as hypocrisy. But thanksgiving itself is not discredited by an exclusive reference to the misuse of thanksgiving: *abusus non tollit usum*. See S.Hausammann, 'Atheistisch zu Gott beten. Eine Auseinandersetzung mit D.Sölle', in her article in *Evangelische Theologie*, 1971, 414ff., based on the New Testament. In this connection I would also refer here to the criticism by Helmut Gollwitzer, *Von der Stellvertretung Gottes. Zum Gespräch mit Dorothee Sölle*, 1967. See below, 178 nn.14,15.

56. I must anticipate somewhat here in describing these objections as objections to certain *New Testament* prayers, although it will only emerge from the main part of the book that these prayers cannot be cut out of the New Testament.

57. See below, n.58.

58. Thus Sölle impressively puts the important Pauline text Phil.2.6ff. (the 'Christ hymn') at the head of her book (*Atheistisch an Gott glauben* [n.13]). She sees it as the foundation of her main thesis, that God has become secular. But in her view, the 'self-emptying' of Christ in his incarnation implies that God has laid down his transcendent properties in so far as he ceases to be supernatural. Hence her polemic against 'theistic' prayer to God, who 'gives way and course to clouds, air and winds' (ibid., 58) as the hymn puts it. However, this polemic rests not only on her view of the 'worldliness' of God but above all on the 'modern experience of the world which she emphasizes so strongly'. In *Atheistisch an Gott glauben* (n.13), 116, she also finds the worldliness of God expressed in Ex.33.11, where God speaks 'with Moses face to face as one does to his friend', a text which precisely expresses the nature of biblical prayer, namely its character as dialogue. However, she somewhat blurs the distinction between dialogue and monologue in calling prayer 'talking to oneself', and not seeing it as a conversation with 'one who is thought as standing over against one' (ibid., 115; for a degree of contradiction in her so-called 'Political Vespers' in

Cologne see Hausammann, 'Atheistisch zu Gott beten' [n.54], 428f.). I must already emphasize here that all the critical remarks about her polemic which I make here are solely meant to examine within the framework of the present book whether this polemic is compatible with the New Testament, see below, 179 n.22.

59. Thus Sölle denounces prayer to God if God is regarded as an old 'magician' (*Atheistisch an Gott glauben* [n.13], 113); here she can refer to Jesus who rebukes 'empty phrases like the Gentiles' (Matt.6.7f.). But she then goes on to regard even praying to a God imagined 'theistically', to the 'children's father' (ibid., 548), as a sign of immaturity.

60. We saw above (8f.) that in connection with his doctrine of the moral law, Kant repudiates prayer generally in favour of ethical action — apart from the concession mentioned. Dorothee Sölle, who also opposes action to prayer, does not go so far, and in condemning 'only praying' where action is possible and necessary, she can refer to the New Testament; she is particularly fond of referring to the parable of the Good Samaritan (Luke 10.30f.). She also objects to false prayer which does not lead to action, citing repeatedly the incident in Brecht's *Mother Courage* of the peasants who pray and Kattrin who beats the drum and thus sacrifices herself (see 5 above); similarly, she begins her treatise on prayer (*Atheistisch an Gott glauben* [n.13], 109) with the witty story of the pastor and the sea captain. In a great storm the ship's captain says, 'Now we can only pray'. The pastor responds 'Is it that bad?' But the way in which these examples are introduced, without even the slightest hint that the kind of prayer practised in them is offensive only because it does not lead to action which is still possible, inevitably gives the impression that using them implies a devaluation of prayer as opposed to action (for intercession for the persecuted Jews see below, 178 n.11).

Part Two: What the New Testament says about Prayer

1. However, very similar objections can already be found in antiquity among the Stoics and Neoplatonists, for example in the treatise by Maximus of Tyre, Εἰ δεῖ εὔχεσθαι (If it is necessary to pray), ed. H.Hobein 1910, from the end of the second century. There are also traces of a criticism of prayer in the Old Testament (especially in Job and Ecclesiastes).

2. For prayer in the Old Testament see J.Hempel, *Gebet und Frömmigkeit im Alten Testament*, Göttingen 1922.

3. This will be confirmed from these texts by the major commentary on the New Testament which we may happily expect from M.Philonenko and his colleagues. (See also my book on the Pseudo-Clementines, 1930, my articles edited by K.Froelich, O.*Cullmann, Vorträge und Aufsätze*, 1967, 225ff., and my work *The Johannine Circle*, London and Philadelphia 1976.)

4. See Cullmann, *The Johannine Circle* (n.3).

5. ἀπέχει is the formula for receipts.

6. ταμιεῖον.

7. The witnesses to the Western Text (D, Old Latin and Syr) read 'pray in secret to your Father', as they omit the article τῷ before ἐν τῷ κρυπτῷ. With the article, it means 'pray to your Father, who is in secret'.

8. Ubiquity: see Strack-Billerbeck, *Kommentar zum Neuen Testament aus Talmud und Midrasch* 1, 399f.

9. Thus, well, G.Ebeling, *Dogmatik des christlichen Glaubens*, Vol.1, Tübingen 1979, 242.

10. It cannot be concluded from the fact that, for example, the content of the prayer in Gethsemane is reported by the evangelists, that Jesus always prayed aloud.

11. See below, 73ff.

12. βατταλογεῖν.

13. προσευχόμενοι.

14. Jesus gives the same reason as he does here for rejecting 'many words' when admonishing his hearers not to 'be anxious' but to trust in God's providence, in the same chapter, Matt.6.31f.: 'for your heavenly Father knows that you need all these things'. (See below, 54, on the petition in the Lord's Prayer for bread.)

15. *Catechism of the Catholic Church*, no.2560: 'God thirsts for us to be thirsty for him.'

16. C.Senft, *Le courage de prier. La prière dans le Nouveau Testament*, ²1985, emphasizes throughout that prayer is an expression of our creatureliness.

17. ἀναίδεια.

18. Being watchful in prayer, since the end may come 'at any time' (Luke 21.36).

19. See above, 10ff.

20. If we include the doxology (see below, 67f.), the Our Father also includes praise.

21. This is emphasized by Senft, *Le courage de prier* (n.16): D.Sölle, *Atheistisch an Gott glauben*, Olten and Freiburg 1968 (albeit in connection with her exclusive emphasis on the 'worldliness' of prayer); M.Lochman, *Unser Vater. Auslegung des Vaterunsers*, Gütersloh 1988, esp. 71ff.; R.Leuenberger, *Zeit in der Zeit. Über das Gebet*, Zurich 1988, passim.

22. In a book which is well worth reading, H.W.Schröder, *Das Gebet. Übung und Erfahrung*, ³1988, well emphasizes that something happens as one says the petitions of the Lord's Prayer (see below, 45). But he probably goes too far in his discussion of the petition for bread when he ceases to maintain the petitionary character in the 'real' sense and sees 'egoism' here.

Thus he writes: 'If this is a real petition, it is hard to think of anything more trivial'(89), and also refers to God's knowing our needs before we ask. But the fact that God wants us to ask him justifies even 'egoistic' prayers. Here I can agree with Sölle, along New Testament lines (*Atheistisch an Gott glauben* [n.21], 114f., 'in good egoistic fashion').

23. However, the friend's request for three loaves in Luke 11.5ff. can hardly be cited here, since the point of comparison in the parable is not the content of the request but the persistence of the person who prays and the fact that the prayer is heard by God.

24. ἐν παντί.

25. B.Brecht, *Mother Courage and Her Children*, London 1980.

26. Sölle, *Atheistisch an Gott glauben* (n.21), 109.

27. E.Schweizer, *Good News according to Matthew*, 178.

28. Ibid., 179.

29. Following the Gospel of John (18.3,12) I am in agreement with M.Goguel, *Jésus*, ²1950, 363ff., and would emphasize that it was the Roman cohort (χιλίαρχος) which arrested Jesus. See O.Cullmann, *The State in the New Testament*, London 1957, 24ff., and O.Cullmann, *Jesus and the Revolutionaries of his Time*, New York 1970.

30. A degree of priority can be inferred from the saying in Matt.6.33: 'Seek first the kingdom of God and his righteousness, and all these things will be added unto you.'

31. I shall go more closely into my understanding of the New Testament situation as a tension between 'already' and 'not yet', 'already fulfilled' and 'not yet fulfilled', in connection with the petition in the Lord's Prayer and in the last part (138f.).

32. In his thoughtful theological work *Fürbitte*, 1979, Lukas Vischer shows how all the New Testament intercessions have their foundation in the person and work of Christ. He draws a line from the Old Testament view of the intercession of the men of God, the prophets, priests and kings, and especially the suffering sevant, to the 'intercession of the exalted Christ'. Thus he also recalls that the New Testament has no word for 'intercession', but only for 'intercessor' (παράκλητος, 47 n.3).

33. For an explanation of the fact that it still exists, see the section on the goodness of God, 136. 137ff. below.

34. ἐξητήσατο.

35. For its 'authenticity' see above, 24.

36. For the relationship betwen our forgiveness and God's forgiveness see what is said below, 55f., on the fifth petition of the Our Father.

37. Mark 14.36, what (τί); Matt.26.39, as (ὡς).

38. ἀλλά.

39. πλήν.

40. There is special emphasis on this in the Gospel of John: 'My food is to do the will of him who sent me, and to accomplish his work' (4.34).

41. In the repetition of the prayer Matt.26.42a reproduces precisely the wording of the third petition of the Our Father. For the relationship between the Gethsemane prayer and the third petition of the Our Father see below, 48. Luke 22.42 interprets: 'Not my will, but yours, be done.'

42. E.Drewermann also cites the example of the child's request in connection with Mark 11.22ff. in his *Das Markusevangelium*, Olten and Freiburg ³1990. This is a extraordinarily well documented work which refers to the relevant literature, Catholic and Protestant, but makes too one-sided use of depth psychology as a key to exegesis. In his example of the child asking the Christ child for a red ball or a doll (Part II, 211ff.), it is correct that the wish to be loved by the Christ child or by parents plays a decisive role. But that this is fundamentally more important to the child than the red ball does not seem to me to be true to life, and at all events it is not the intention of Jesus to force the petition for material things as such into the background by requiring unconditional trust.

43. However, James 1.17 also calls God the 'Father of lights with whom there is no variation or shadow due to change'.

44. E.g. Jer.13.8; however, here it is attached to penitence. On 'repentance' see the work by Jürg Jeremias, *Die Reue Gottes*, 1974.

45. O.Cullmann, *Salvation in History*, London 1967, 122ff.

46. I can only hint at the connection between this problem and my view of the biblical salvation history; H.Schaller, *Das Bittgebet. Eine theologische Skizze*, Einsiedeln 1979, 139ff., has discussed it comprehensively and philosophically in connection with the solution put forward by Thomas Aquinas.

47. Also the Old Testament (the Suffering Servant in Isa.53).

48. Critics will perhaps accuse me of repeatedly emphasizing this, but for me it really is the key to understanding the basic problems of New Testament theology.

49. Luke 23.34; 43.46. However, he does not have the cry from the cross which refers to Psalm 22.

50. Despite the lesser use of discourse material in the Gospel of Mark, it is amazing that the Our Father does not appear in this Gospel.

51. Unfortunately we do not possess this prayer taught by John the Baptist. Because of the difficulty of surveying the multi-level material contained in the Mandaean texts, it cannot be inferred from them.

52. See above, 19; below, 117f. If we note in Rom.8.15,26; Gal.3.6, that the Spirit of God speaks in prayer, the concluding saying added to each of the letters in the book of Revelation, 'He who has an ear, let him

hear what the Spirit says to the churches' (chs.2–3), could be regarded as a parallel to listening to the utterances of the Spirit in prayer.

53. See J.Jeremias, *New Testament Theology*, London and New York 1971, 197.

54. However, this is uncertain, though it would not be incompatible with his wish to pray to his Father in solitude. Nor is it a certain argument against this that in the Gospels Jesus says 'my' Father and not 'our' Father in his own prayers (see 42f. below).

55. In his interesting book *Jesus als Lehrer*, 1981, 446, which takes up the thesis put forward in B.Gerhardsson, *Memory and Manuscript*, [2]1964, Rainer Riesner assumes that the request of the disciples to Jesus in Luke 11.1 to teach them a prayer envisaged learning a formula for community prayer by heart.

56. However, the invitation in this work to pray the Our Father three times a day, following the Jewish custom of prayer, brings the danger of a 'mechanical' practice which was remote from Jesus (Matt.6.7).

57. Cf. e.g. II Tim.4.18; John 17.15.

58. To go beyond the framework of exegesis for a moment, and refer to present-day practice: it should be thought appropriate that the Lord's Prayer is a main element of Christian worship. It also makes sense to say the Our Father together, in order to give particularly powerful expression to fellowship in prayer. But I would also want to draw attention to a danger which this almost universal custom brings with it: the danger of distraction from the content of the prayer which Jesus intended, so that even in worship it keeps its significance. It may be more difficult to concentrate if, as one can often observe, everyone is trying to avoid those discords which often happen when people are speaking together. Concentration on the content of the prayer is made more difficult by this effort.

59. Thus Cyprian, *De domenica oratione*: '*coelestis doctrina compendium*'.

60. Literature up to 1969 can be found in the index of J.Carmignac, *Recherches sur le 'Notre Père'*, Paris 1969, with its extensive documentation, 469ff.; there is also a complete listing up to 1984 in U.Luz, *Matthäusevangelium*, EKK, [2]1988, 332f.

61. In Matthew, exegetes either count the petition 'but deliver us from evil' as the seventh petition or regard it as a supplement to the sixth. It is completely lacking in Luke, as is the third petition of the text of Matthew ('Thy will be done . . .').

62. For an attempt at a reconstruction of a Q text see J.M.Robinson, 'A Critical Text of the Sayings Gospel Q', *RHPhR* 1992/1, 15ff. (the issue dedicated to me on my ninetieth birthday), see 21f.

63. According to E.Lohmeyer, *The Lord's Prayer* (1952), London 1965,

294f., one, used by Matthew, comes from Galilee, and the other, used by Luke, from Jerusalem. Jeremias, *New Testament Theology* (n.53), 196 (also earlier), puts forward the view that the text of Luke should be regarded as the more original in length, and that of Matthew in general wording. Among recent scholars Carmignac, *Recherches sur le 'Notre Père'* (n.60), consistently regards the Lukan version as an abbreviation of the text of Matthew, and accordingly takes Matthew to be older. In contrast to him, P.Grelot, 'L'arrière-plan araméen du Pater', *Revue Biblique*, 1984, 531ff. (also already in his rather earlier work 'La quatrième demande du Pater', *NTS* 1978/1979, 299f.), equally consistently prefers the Lukan text.

64. In an earlier period G.Dalman, *Die Worte Jesu*, 1898, now Jeremias in the works cited above (most recently in *New Testament Theology* [n.53], 197) and especially Grelot, 'L'arrière-plan araméen du Pater' (n.63), 531ff.

65. Also J.Starcky, 'La quatrième demande du Pater', *HTR* 1971, 401ff.

66. Grelot, 'L'arrière-plan araméen du Pater' (n.63), 531ff.

67. The borderlines between the use of Aramaic and Hebrew are sometimes fluid. For this discussion see also M.Hengel, 'Zur matthäischen Bergpredigt und ihrem jüdischen Hintergrund' (*Theologische Rundschau*, 1987, 387f.); also W.D.Davies and D.C.Allison, *The Gospel according to St Matthew*, 1988, 592.

68. Grelot, 'L'arrière-plan araméen du Pater' (n.63), 554, 556.

69. 'We', 'us' is characteristic of the second part, which begins with the petition for bread. See below, 43.

70. From an earlier period already J.Lightfoot, *Horae hebraicae et talmudicae in quattuor evangelistas*, 1684, 299ff.; J.J.Wettstein, *Novum Testamentum Graecum*, 1781, 323. Among many more recent scholars see especially Jeremias, *New Testament Theology* (n.53), 197ff.

71. Luz, *Matthäusevangelium* (n.60), 351, refers to the decline in the mention of decisive events in the history of Israel. However, I would not play the petition for the coming of the *kingdom of God* off against this. Rather, salvation history is presupposed in it. Otherwise, the remarks of Luz, ibid., 350f., on the question are very well worth noting (apart from his use of the ugly word Jesuanic, though I cannot find any adequate short equivalent).

72. In Mark 14.36 ὁ πατήρ stands as a translation for '*abba*', i.e. the nominative used as a vocative. Matt.26.39 has πάτερ μου, and Luke 22.42 πάτερ.

73. In Matthew and Luke the same verse first has πάτερ and then the second time ὁ πατήρ as a vocative; both of these are first, as in the Our Father (Matthaean version), combined with 'Lord of heaven and earth'.

74. Jeremias, see especially the article 'Abba', in *The Prayers of Jesus*, London and Philadelphia 1967, 11–55, and now *New Testament Theology* (n.53), 193ff.

75. The following remarks on Abba could shed special light on Karl Barth's dogmatic remarks in the last volume of his *Church Dogmatics*, IV.4, *The Christian Life*, Edinburgh 1969, compiled from his papers (with the unfinished exegesis of the second petition of the Our Father). For him, the address to God is particularly important, because he argues that one can really name God only in the vocative. One can only speak *to* God; any talk *about* God in the nominative must be derived from this vocative. In all Barth's remarks, prayer is regarded as a response to God's revelation in Christ. Hence his concern that sufficient justice is done to thanksgiving alongside petition, which is indispensable for him (see below, 180 n.30).

76. Jeremias, 'Abba' (n.74), and now especially *New Testament Theology* (n.53). See also the thorough investigation by G.Schelbert, 'Sprachgeschichtliches zu Abba', in *Mélanges Barthélémy*, 1981, 395ff.

77. P.Grelot, 'Une mention inaperçue de "Abba" dans le Testament araméen de Levi', *Semitica* 1983, 101ff.; J.A.Fitzmyer, 'Abba and Jesus' Relation to God', in *Études offertes au Père Jacques Dupont*, 1985; J.Barr, 'Abba isn't Daddy', *JTS*, 1988, 28ff.; cf. especially E.M.Schuller, 'The Psalm of Q 372, 1 within the Context of Second Temple Prayer', *Catholic Biblical Quarterly*, 1992, 67ff.

78. Jeremias, 'Abba' (n.74).

79. Jeremias had earlier expressed the view that it was a word used by small children (like 'Daddy'), and had been taken over as such by Jesus. But after discovering further attestations of the word used by adults he gave up this assumption (*New Testament Theology* [n.53], 61ff.). See Barr, 'Abba isn't Daddy' (n.77).

80. Jeremias gives this explanation of Jesus' saying in Matt.23.9, 'And call no man your father on earth, for you have one Father, who is in heaven.' Of course the prohibition does not apply to physical fathers, but more to older persons who are held in respect. The address 'Abba' should not be used towards them, since this form of address is to be reserved for God.

81. A possible translation according to Jeremias, 'Abba' (n.74), 54ff.

82. There are many instances, see e.g. Strack-Billerbeck, *Kommentar zum Neuen Testament*, I, *Matthäus*, ad loc.

83. This explanation is given by Lohmeyer, *The Lord's Prayer* (n.63), 34f., and J.M.Lochman, *Unser Vater*, 1988, 26.

84. Against Luz, *Matthäusevangelium* (n.60), 341. The juxtaposition of Abba and heaven comes close to what I said above on p.17 about all prayer: we pray to God who is at the same time both in us and outside us. M.A.Schmidt, 'Thomas von Aquin zu Matthäus 6.9–10', *TZ*, 1992/1, 44ff. (dedicated to J.M.Lochman), shows that Thomas similarly contrasts the words 'Father' and 'in heaven' so that they supplement each other. 'Father': God *wills* to give what the children need; 'in heaven': he *can* give it.

85. A.Schweitzer, *The Quest of the Historical Jesus*, London ³1950, 362.

86. However, in his *New Testament Theology* (n.53), 67, Jeremias remarks that though he emphasizes the unique consciousness of being Son so strongly he does not want to attribute the whole of the later Son of God christology 'in detail' to Jesus himself.

87. See J.Elbogen, *Der jüdische Gottesdienst in seiner geschichtlichen Entwicklung*, ⁴1962, 92ff.

88. See W.Stärk, *Altjüdische liturgische Gebete*, 1910.

89. However, in the Kaddish the will is mentioned in connection with the hallowing of the name, not as a petition but as a statement about the creation of the world 'according to his will'.

90. Thus P.Fiebig, *Das Vaterunser, Ursprung, Sinn und Bedeutung des christlichen Hauptgebets*, 1927, 109. Riesner, *Jesus als Lehrer* (n.56), concludes from the fact that this part, which so closely resembles Jewish liturgical prayers, comes first, that the Our Father was envisaged as a community prayer.

91. ἁγιάζειν and δοξάζειν.

92. See Lohmeyer, *The Lord's Prayer* (n.63), 67; on the basis of many examples from the Old Testament, and with reference to Qumran texts (Rule 10.3; War Rule 12.2), Carmignac, *Recherches sur le 'Notre Père'* (n.60), 85f., confirms that both words are synonymous. Grelot, 'L'arrière-plan araméen du Pater' (n.63), 543, concedes that they are related in content, but emphasizes the philological difference between the two words.

93. Lochman, *Unser Vater* (n.83), 38f. also accords a major place to the ethical understanding of the petition, but puts it under the hallowing of the name by God himself.

94. However, in that case the first petition is no longer completely parallel to the next two.

95. P.Prigent, *Apocalypse et liturgie*, 1964, 56, makes some very good comments on this. He assumes that the 'Trishagion' was used in Jewish liturgies (he refers to Quedduta Joser, see Stärk, *Altjüdische liturgische Gebete* [n.88], 15), and in this way came into the heavenly liturgy spoken by the four living creatures.

96. H.W.Schröder, *Das Gebet. Übung und Erfahrung*, ³1988, 43ff., stresses particularly strongly that something *happens* when one speaks the petitions of the Our Father: 'The reality of what is spoken is created in the speaking . . . As I speak these words, they become reality.' See what is said by G.Müller, 'Gebet', *TRE*, on prayer as sacrament. H.Ott, 'Das universale Gebet', *TZ* 1, 7 (dedicated to J.Lochman), stresses that something 'happens' in prayer in relation to its universality (7).

97. The assumption already mentioned above that the words 'on earth as it is in heaven' relate to all three initial petitions in the text of Matthew could be confirmed here. For this hypothesis see 50f. below.

98. 'Realized eschatology'.

99. In his article 'Luther et Calvin commentateurs du Notre Père' (*RHPR* 1992/1, 73ff., to celebrate my ninetieth birthday), M.Lienhard gives a good account of the agreements and deviations between the Reformers in their explanations of the Our Father. He mentions (78f.) that both agree in speaking of the kingdom which on the one hand constantly grows, and on the other comes only at the end (Luther, WA 30, 1, 200, 25ff.; Calvin, Corpus Reformatorum 34, Vol.6, col.97).

100. The book of Isaiah mentions as eschatological signs the giving of sight to the blind (35.5) and the preaching of the good news to the poor (61.1).

101. Not only the 'Synoptic apocalypse' (Mark 13 par.) but sayings like that before the high priest (Mark 14.62, quoting Dan.7.13) about the coming of the Son of Man on the clouds of heaven.

102. For the use of the historical books of the Old Testament in the New see B.Corsani, *Festschrift A.Soggin*. For the problem of salvation history in the New Testament see K.H.Schlaudraff, *Heil als Geschichte? Die Frage nach dem heilsgeschichtlichen Denken, dargestellt an Hand der Konzeption Oscar Cullmanns, mit einer Vorwort von O.Cullmann*, 1988, and his article, 'Oscar Cullmann. Neutestamentliche Theologie in heilsgeschicht-licher Perspektive', in *Gegen die Gottvergessenheit. Schweizer Theologen im 19. und 20. Jahrhundert*, ed. Stephan Leimgruber and Max Schoch, 1990, 206ff.

103. Given the erroneous understanding of my book *Christ and Time*, I must keep emphasizing that I did not write it to discuss the problem of 'linear time', which I introduced only by way of clarification, but in order to demonstrate that this tension between 'already' and 'not yet' is a fundamental New Testament experience of past, present and future (e.g. against J.Ansaldi, *L'articulation de la foi, de la théologie et des écritures*, Paris 1991, 35 and 202 n.41). The Heidelberg philosopher K.Löwith (Heidegger's successor, *Weltgeschehen und Heilgeschichte*, 1953) rightly saw this intention of my book, in contrast to the philosophers who regarded it as a treatise on the philosophical problem of time.

104. If the second person singular (σοῦ) is to be given special emphasis in the three (or two) petitions, the same is true of this petition: *thy* kingdom. The kingly rule of God replaces all imperfect human rule (Luke 22.25).

105. J.Jeremias, 'The Lord's Prayer in the Light of Recent Research', in *The Prayers of Jesus* (n.74), 82–107. See 38f. above.

106. See above 155f. n. 63.

107. This view is also put forward by M.Philonenko in his article 'La troisième demande du Notre Père et l'hymne de Nabuchodonosor', *RHPR* 1992, 23ff.: 30, to which I shall be returning (see below, n.117), contrary to the view of M.Dibelius, 'Die dritte Bitte des Vaterunsers', *Botschaft und Geschichte*, 1953, 174ff., who by contrast derives the petition of the Our Father which appears only in Matthew (6.10b) from the prayer in Gethsemane.

108. G.Lohfink, 'Der präexistente Heilsplan. Sinn und Hintergrund der 3.Vaterunserbitte', in *FS R.Schnackenburg*, 1989, 110ff.

109. R.Schnackenburg, *Das Matthäusevangelium*, 1985, 65. See also B.Gerhardsson, 'The Matthaean Version of the Lord's Prayer. Some Observations', in *FS B.Reicke*, 1984, I, 207ff.

110. E.g. in the Qumran texts QS 3.15f. Cf. the notion of the heavenly tablets and scrolls in the Testaments of the Twelve Patriarchs (Levi 5.2; Asher 2.18; 7.5) and in IV Esdras 6.20.

111. Lohfink, 'Präexistente Heilsplan' (n.108), 126f., here bases himself on the useful Philonenko-Sayar edition in M.Philonenko, *Die Apokalypse Abrahams, Jüdische Schriften aus hellenistisch-römischer Zeit*, 1982, 421ff.

112. See Philonenko, 'Troisième demande du Notre Père' (n.107).

113. Cullmann, *Salvation in History* (n.45), passim. Thus I find Lohfink's article, although its aim is different, in a sense a confirmation and supplementation of my salvation-historical view.

114. εὐδοκία.

115. See below, 134f.

116. Lohfink, 'Präexistente Heilsplan' (n.108), 131 n.67, does not seem to me to give sufficient reasons for his summary rejection of this explanation, although the third petition of Matthew's version is particularly closely connected with the addition 'as in heaven'.

117. As for the formulation of the petition, careful attention should be paid to Philonenko's proposal that it should be derived from a reminiscence of the hymn of Nebuchadnezzar in Dan. 4.32, which he investigates in the Massoretic Aramaic text and in Theodotion's translation. See id., 'La troisième demande du Notre Père' (n.107).

118. ἐπιούσιος.

119. The Vulgate translates it only in the Gospel of Luke (not in the Gospel of Matthew) with *quotidianus* (see below, 54).

120. Maurice Goguel has pointed out the importance of this question particularly impressively in his works on John the Baptist and Jesus.

121. Matt.6.16f. should also be mentioned here. If Jesus is talking about the right attitude to fasting there, this presupposes that he did not reject fasting in principle.

122. Especially e.g. Lohmeyer, *The Lord's Prayer* (n.63), and R.E. Brown, *New Testament Essays*, 1965.

123. Thus e.g. Jeremias, *New Testament Theology* (n.53), 199f.

124. Among more recent scholars I would mention at random A. Schlatter, *Der Evangelist Matthäus*, 1929, 210; P.Bonnard, *L'Evangile selon S.Matthieu*, ²1962, ad loc.; A.Hamman, *La prière*, I, *Le nouveau Testament*, Tournai 1959; Luz, *Matthäusevangelium* (n.60), ad loc.

125. U.Gabler, 'Das Vaterunser in der Basler Reformation', *ThZ* 1992/1, 118ff.: 122, shows that Oecolampadius did not go along with Luther's phrase and retained the spiritual interpretation of the early Luther. See also below, n.130.

126. See A.Debrunner, *Theologische Literaturzeitung*, 1925, 303f.; A.H.Sayce, in Preisigke, no.5224.

127. Thus e.g. P.Joüon, *L'Evangile de notre Seigneur Jésus-Christ*, 1930, 35; more recently Lochman, *Unser Vater* (n.83), 82.

128. See below.

129. ἐπιτήδειος, ἀναγκαῖος, see Luz, *Matthäusevangelium* (n.60), 346.

130. Sometimes the requirement of daily communion and the prohibition of the chalice to the laity are based on this explanation. Gabler, 'Das Vaterunser' (n.125), 123, mentions that Oecolampadius in his order of service puts the Our Father after the words of institution.

131. This is the Gospel of the Nazareans, which is preserved only in fragments, and was probably translated into Aramaic from the Greek Gospel of Matthew. See P.Vielhauer and G.Strecker, in W.Schneemelcher, *New Testament Apocrypha*, Vol.1, Louisville and Cambridge 1991, 154ff. Here the mistaken opinion is expressed (156) that *mahar* is an 'erroneous' translation of the Greek ἐπιούσιος. Jeremias, *New Testament Theology*, 200, writes, probably correctly, that the translator wrote the word *mahar* in the way that he was accustomed from Aramaic prayers.

132. Among many others e.g. Schlatter, *Der Evangelist Markus* (n.124), 211f.; Lohmeyer, *The Lord's Prayer* (n.83), 142; Brown, *New Testament Essays* (n.122), 299ff.; Bonnard, *L'Evangile selon S.Matthieu* (n.124), 83; Jeremias, *New Testament Theology* (n.53), 199f.; but cf. W.Foerster, ἐπιούσιος, *TDNT* II, 590ff.

133. Accordingly Luke puts the present δίδου instead of Matthew's aorist δός.

134. In Matt.6.11 it translates it *supersubstantialis* (see above, 53).

135. See my article '"Beten und Sorgen". Zur vierten Bitte des Vaterunsers', in *TZ* 1992/1, dedicated to Lochman, who rejects 'tomorrow's' with the same objection. See Lochman, *Unser Vater* (n.83), 81.

136. Carmignac, *Recherches sur le 'Notre Père'* (n.60), 215f., bases this objection, in so far as it refers to the material bread, on this saying of Jesus,

but it is introduced with the imperative 'Do not be anxious' (and not 'Do not pray'). Nor does Jesus' instruction to the disciples to take nothing with them on their journeys (Matt.10.9ff.; Luke 10.4ff.) exclude their praying that they may find hospitality.

137. This affects only the translation of the saying. The sense of the petition is not fundamentally different whether we say 'for tomorrow' or 'daily' or 'necessary (for today)', provided that we leave the material significance for 'bread'.

138. Paul uses precisely the same Greek word, μεριμνᾶν, as Matthew.

139. E.g. R.E.Brown, *ThSt* 1961, 175ff.; Starcky, 'La quatrième demande du Pater' (n.65), 401ff.; Grelot, 'La quatrième demande' (n.63), 291ff.

140. *hoba*.

141. R.Brändle, 'Die 5.Bitte in der Auslegung Gregors von Nyssa', *ThZ*, 1992/1, 70ff., shows that Gregory puts material debts and their remission at the centre of his exegesis of the fifth petition.

142. ὡς.

143. καὶ γάρ.

144. Thus the attempt by Grelot, 'L'arrière-plan araméen du Pater' (n.63), 547. P.Joüon, *L'évangile de notre Seigneur Jésus-Christ*, 1930, approximates Luke to Matthew in also translating the Lukan καὶ γάρ, in the light of the Aramaic, as 'so also' (*aussi bien*).

145. Joüon, *L'évangile de notre Seigneur Jésus-Christ* (n.144), 35.

146. C.Brockelmann, *Hebräische Syntax*, 1956, 40f., cites many examples of this grammatical phenomenon (e.g. Isa.14.22). He describes this perfect well as a (chronological) 'coincidence' between the statement in the present and action performed in the perfect. See also Rudolf Meyer, *Hebräische Grammatik*, ³1972, 54f., and also already P.Joüon, *Grammaire de l'Hébreu biblique*, 298 (also including the future sense).

147. Joüon, *L'évangile de notre Seigneur Jésus-Christ* (n.144), 35: 'as we forgive at this moment'.

148. Jeremias, *New Testament Theology* (n.53), 201.

149. Brockelmann, *Hebräische Syntax* (n.146), 40f., like Joüon, *Grammaire de l'Hébreu biblique* (n.146).

150. Or as in Matt.18.23ff., *does not take place*.

151. Lochman, *Unser Vater* (n.83), 106, but without going into the philological argument discussed here.

152. If we understand the subordinate clause in this way, in other words refer it to the praying itself, the translation of καὶ γάρ in Luke (from the Aramaic) as 'so also' (see n.144 above) takes on special significance.

153. Lienhard, 'Luther et Calvin commentateurs du Notre Père' (n.97), 83, stresses that both Luther and Calvin are agreed in finding in the subordinate clause the notion that our capacity to forgive depends on the

forgiveness of our sins by God and not vice versa (of course still without the modern philological background).

154. Thus many good textual witnesses even connect these verses 14ff. to the preceding Our Father with γάρ, 'for'.

155. For this passage see 164 n.174 below.

156. μὴ εἰσενέγκῃς ἡμᾶς εἰς πειρασμόν.

157. Lienhard, 'Luther et Calvin commentateurs du Notre Père' (n.97), 84, cites Luther, WA 30, 1, 209, a text which shows that the Reformer already emphasized the leading *into* and that (perhaps all too quickly) he understood this as 'make to succumb', when he spoke of 'drowning' (in temptation). Carmignac, *Recherches sur le Notre Père* (n.60), 269ff., makes a philological distinction between εἰσφέρειν with the dative = lead into and εἰσφέρειν εἰς = introduce to. Here he also assumes that 'lead into temptation' amounts to 'make to succumb to temptation (*consentir*)'.

158. εἰσέλθητε: however, according to good manuscripts (B and ℵ) Mark 14.38 has only ἔλθητε (C and D have εἰσέλθητε; according to p.37 Matt.25.41 reads ἔλθητε.

159. Carmignac, *Recherches sur le 'Notre Père'* (n.60), here emphatically refers to an earlier work, J.Heller, 'Die 6.Bitte der Vaterunsers', *Zeitschrift für katholische Theologie*, 1901, 85ff. (in a French translation in ibid., 437ff.), especially to the remarks on the use of negation in Hebrew and Aramaic, which in connection with a verb used causatively does not refer to the causative subject, but to the object, in this case to 'us' (Heller, in ibid., 443fff.).

160. E.Jenni, 'Kausativ und Funktionsverbgefüge. Sprachliche Bemerkungen zur Bitte "Führe uns nicht in Versuchung"', *ThZ* 1992/1, 77ff.

161. H.-J.Heringer, *Die Opposition von kommen und bringen als Funktionsverben*, 1968; R.Lohr, *Neuhochdeutsch. Eine Einführung in die Sprachwissenschaft*, 1986, 102ff.

162. The examples cited by Heller (French, 442f.) and Carmignac, *Recherches sur le 'Notre Père'* (n.60), 272, are not so clear as to necessitate an identification.

163. For the 'wide spectrum of meaning' of the verb in the Old Testament see H.J.Stoebe, 'Überlegungen zur 6.Bitte der Vaterunsers', *TZ* 1992/1, 89ff.

164. That human beings can also lead God astray is certainly important for the meaning 'tempt' = 'test', but it can be left out of account in our understanding of the petition in the Our Father.

165. With the Synoptic Gospels and the New Testament I call the tempting power of evil the devil (Satan).

166. Carmignac, *Recherches sur le 'Notre Père'* (n.60), distinguishes between 'testing', which he finds in the Old Testament, and the temptation to evil in the New Testament (with a transition in the Qumran texts). He

calls the first 'épreuve' and the second 'tentation' (263ff.). He makes a sharp distinction between the two and completely excludes the former ('testing') from the petition in the Our Father. He does not note their inner connection, which I shall attempt to demonstrate in what follows. Luz, *Matthäus-evangelium* (n.60), rejects the meaning 'trial' in Matt.6.13, because in that case the Greek would have to be πεῖρα and not πειρασμός. But as πεῖρα is attested only in the profane sense (Seesemann, πεῖρα, *TDNT* VI, 23, 28) only πειρασμός, from the verb πειράζειν, which means both 'tempt' and 'test', was available for religious use in the New Testament.

167. I.Willi-Plein, 'Die Versuchung stet am Schluss. Inhalt und Ziel der Versuchung Abrahams in der Erzählung in Gen.22', *TZ* 1992/1, 101ff., has written on Gen.22.

168. E.g. Exod.20.20.

169. Certainly Calvin in *Institutes* III.20.45 makes a good distinction between temptation by the devil to evil and temptation by God to strengthen his servants. But he does not define the connection and the relationship between the two. Therefore he must reject the possibility that in the Our Father God is thought of as the one who leads, or does not lead, into temptation.

170. According to Jesus, too, what Paul writes in I Cor.10.13 may apply to all temptations by the devil: (God) 'does not allow' (ἐάσει) human beings to be tempted 'beyond what they can bear'.

171. The tension between God's omnipotence and the power that the devil can exercise appears less in the Old Testament, as it is not accentuated by an 'already' ('Satan fallen from heaven', Luke 10.18). For the question of this tension see 137ff. below.

172. W.Pfendsack, *Das Vaterunser*, 1961, 87, also shows that God's omnipotence is not excluded in either form of temptation.

173. Luz, *Matthäusevangelium* (n.60), 349, rightly emphasizes that in Matthew faith in God's omnipotence is taken for granted. But the conclusion that he draws from this, that therefore 'lead us not into temptation' is not to be seen as a problem, does not seem to me to be justified. The tension mentioned above between God's omnipotence and the power of the devil must be noted.

174. In that case it is not those who are tempted who are primarily the subordinate 'executive subject', as they are for those exegetes who refer the causative to 'not letting people succumb' (see above, 163 n.159); the devil is the one who carries out the temptation. However, he makes use of the human desire of which James 1.14 speaks, and is at work in it. In this context I hope that I may be allowed to put a question about James 1.13, which is always mentioned in connection with the sixth petition of the Our Father. Is the fact that it conflicts with the statement 'God himself does not tempt

anyone' so remote from the understanding of Matt.6.13 proposed above? If the Greek pronoun αὐτός is not only unemphasized, the third person contained in the verb ('he'), but, as seems likely, emphatic ('he himself'), i.e. God himself tempts no one, one could see here an indirect reference to an author of the 'desire' mentioned only in v.14, who is not named here. I merely ask the question. It does not seem to me to be completely unjustified, since at another point (4.7) James summons its readers 'to withstand the devil', and the demons are mentioned in the famous section on faith and works in 2.19. The explanation of the fact that the devil is not mentioned in connection with James 1.13, but only the desire of human beings, could be that the whole section is introduced in v.12 with the beatitude (μακάριος) on the person who 'withstands' temptation.

175. 'Fais que nous n'entrions pas dans la tentation en y consentant', Carmignac, *Recherches sur le 'Notre Père'* (n.60), 292.

176. Even if Carmignac, *Recherches sur le 'Notre Père'* (n.60), 281f., is right in the problematical assumption that in Matt 4.1 after the words 'he was led up by the Spirit into the wilderness' the infinitive πειρασθῆναι ὑπὸ τοῦ διαβόλου does not express the purpose of the Spirit (to be tempted) but the result (and he was tempted), the fact remains that in all three Synoptic Gospels it is the Spirit which leads (or drives (Mark 1.12) Jesus into the wilderness, i.e. the place where he encounters the devil.

177. Origen, *On Prayer* 29.9, Migne PG 10, 530.

178. See Lienhardt, 'Luther et Calvin commentateurs du Notre Père' (n.99), 84.

179. Carmignac, *Recherches sur le 'Notre Père'* (n.60), 291.

180. P.Fiebig, *Das Vaterunser. Ursprung, Sinn und Bedeutung des christlichen Hauptgebets*, 1927, 90.

181. 'Ne nous induis point en tentation.' So the ecumenical translation has already often been criticized.

182. 'Ne nous soumets pas a l'épreuve qui est la tentation.'

183. P.Dausch, 'Die drei ältesten Evangelien', in *Die heiligen Schriften des Neuen Testaments*, 1918, 139.

184. H.Schürmann, *Das Gebet des Herrn*, 1958.

185. Schröder, *Das Gebet* (n.96), 55f., esp.61.

186. F.Rittelmeyer, *Das Vaterunser*, ⁵1985, 124f.

187. Seesemann, πεῖρα, *TDNT* VI, 31.

188. In contrast to similar allusions in the Old Testament, the Gospels contain no revelation on the question where evil comes from and also why it still exists in the interim period, although it has been conquered. See below, 141.

189. We saw above, 28f., that Jesus' admonition to the disciples in Gethsemane to pray not to enter into temptation is primarily about their

preservation *from succumbing* in the coming temptation, but that in connection with Jesus' own prayer that the 'cup should pass' there is an echo of the petition to be spared temptation; in other words, Jesus, who knows the human weakness of his disciples, also intends his admonition to make sure that their prayer stands in the way of the temptation to flee, to deny him. By contrast, conversely, in the Our Father the petition to be spared temptation lies in the foreground, and only in connection with the submission required in any prayer, which it can produce, does it issue in the subordinate clause 'deliver us from evil', which with its general formulation implies a petition for support in temptation.

190. Augustine vacillates over the question whether there are six or seven petitions. Carmignac, *Recherches sur le 'Notre Père'* (n.60), 313, points out that he does not always express the same opinion. Martin Bucer (*In sacra evangelia enarrationes perpetuae*, 1536) and Calvin (*Institutes*) assume six petitions.

191. Grelot, too, regards the petition in this way as a correction of the petition to be spared temptation. But in keeping with his general preference for the Lukan form, in which this clause is missing, he regards it as a secondary expansion through the Matthaean form.

192. It is correct that in Judaism the Semitic equivalent (*rasha*) occurs very rarely. At any rate M.Black, 'The Doxology to the Pater Noster with a Note on Matthew 6.13b', in *A Tribute to Geza Vermes*, 1990, additional note, 333ff., demonstrates its occurrence on the one hand in the Qumran texts 4QAmram[b] and 4Q280, 286, and on the other hand in Targum Isaiah 11.4, and thinks that this designation was probably more frequent than its attestation suggests.

193. It has been pointed out that in the New Testament ῥύεσθαι ἀπό elsewhere always refers to human beings and never to the devil. But that is an argument from silence. If with Lochman, *Unser Vater* (n.21), 128, who refers to many passages in the psalms, we translate 'deliver us' instead of 'redeem us', this fits particularly well with the personification of evil in the devil.

194. But not Luz, *Matthäusevangelium* (n.60), who assumes the neuter.

195. *Hatima* (see Jeremias, 'Abba' [n.74], and *New Testament Theology* [n.53], 203).

196. Elbogen, *Der jüdische Gottesdienst* (n.87), 249.

197. A.Schlatter, *Der Evangelist Matthäus*, 1929, 217.

198. Jeremias, *New Testament Theology* (n.53), 203.

199. See K.Seybold, 'Zur Vorgeschichte der liturgischen Formel "Amen"', *TZ* 1992/1, 109ff.

200. Also in Didache, I Clement, Martyrdom of Polycarp.

201. Black, 'The Doxology to the Pater Noster' (n.192), 327ff.

202. J.J.Wettstein, *Novum Testamentum Graecum*, 1781.

203. F.H.Chase, *The Lord's Prayer in the Early Church*, 1891.

204. Granted, in contrast to the 'Amen', the doxology is not a confirmation by the assembled believers of the words spoken by one of their number, but is added by the speaker. Nevertheless, in the light of the liturgical character of the doxology it would make sense if today, as I have proposed on 155, n.58 above, for quite a different reason (a practical one) only the six or seven petitions were spoken by the pastor and the doxology were the response of the community.

205. This connection is also shown by the word ὅτι, for.

206. Lochman, *Unser Vater* (n.21), 145ff.

207. It should also preserve us from an exaggerated Protestant anxiety about a *theologia gloriae*, as though the emphasis on the divine glory, the resurrection and exaltation of Christ, detracted from the cross, which is certainly to be given special emphasis.

208. E.g. the earlier one by F.Ménégoz, *Le problème de la prière. Principe d'une révision de la méthode théologique*, Strasbourg and Paris 1925, ²1932.

209. From an earlier period, E.von der Goltz, *Das Gebet in der ältesten Christenheit*, 1901; now A.Hamman, *La Prière I: Le Nouveau Testament*, Tournai 1959.

210. G.Harder, *Paulus und das Gebet*, 1936.

211. Roland Gebauer, *Das Gebet bei Paulus. Forschungsgeschichtliche und exegetische Studien*, 1989.

212. Some of his own exegetical investigations are also worth noting. Unfortunately, however, in his discussion of Rom.8.12–27, a passage which in my view and that of others is quite fundamental to the understanding of prayer in Paul, and to which I accord a key position, he puts forward an interpretation which does not seem to me (and others) to do justive to the originality and depth of the apostle's view (see below, 72ff.)

213. δεήσεις, προσευχαί, ἐντεύξεις, εὐχαριστίαι.

214. Karl Barth rightly sees here in the predominance of the prayer of thanksgiving in Paul the advantage that intercession is not too exclusively envisaged. But the present-day situation requires that intercession should be defended.

215. This is especially emphasized by Senft, *Le courage de prier* (n.16), 59f.

216. See H.Lietzmann, *Messe und Herrenmahl* (1926), ⁴1962, and O.Cullmann, *Early Christian Worship* (1944), London 1953.

217. This does not contradict the saying of Jesus 'where two or three are gathered together in my name . . .' (Matt.18.20), since here what matters is not the (small) number but the gathering.

218. Among others see J.M.Robinson, 'Die Hodajot Formel in Gebet und Hymnen des Frühchristentums', *FS E.Haenchen*, 1964.

219. P.Schubert, *Form and Function of the Pauline Thanksgivings*, BZNW 1939. But O.Roller, *Das Formular der paulinischen Briefe*, 1933; J.M.Lieu, ' "Grace to You and Peace." The Apostolic Greeting', *BJRL* 68, 1965, 161ff., have demonstrated that the combination χάρις καὶ εἰρήνη comes neither from Jewish nor from Hellenistic formulae.

220. Gebauer, *Das Gebet bei Paulus* (n.211), shows this in his exegesis of the long prayer report in Phil.1.3–11, which at the same time gives a preview of the content of the letter. M.Arnold, 'Luther, imitateur de Paul: ses letters aux communautés évangeliques', *RHPR* 72, 1992, 103–6, shows well that Luther takes over Paul's introductory thanksgiving formula, and in particular its Pauline stamp.

221. By contrast, W.Bieder, 'Gebetswirklichkeit und Gebetsmöglichkeit bei Paulus. Das Beten des Geistes und das Beten im Geist', *TZ*, 1948, 27, which comes very close to my view, puts too much emphasis on it.

222. αὐτὸ τὸ πνεῦμα.

223. τὸ πνεῦμα ἡμῶν. The 'bearing witness together' is expressed in v.16 in the verb συμμαρτυρεῖν.

224. Thus rightly E.Käsemann, *Commentary on Romans*, [2]1982, 226; also A.Schlatter, *Gottes Gerechtigkeit. Ein Kommentar zum Römerbrief*, [5]1976, 266; E.Schweizer, *TDNT* VI, 433; also O.Kuss, *Der Römerbrief*, 1963, ad loc. By contrast, R.Bultmann, *Theology of the New Testament* I, New York and London 1952, 208, and F.Leenhardt, *L'Epître de S.Paul aux Romains*, [2]1967, 123 n.2, assume that a distinction is made here between God's Spirit and the natural human spirit. Leenhardt comments that otherwise one would arrive at the 'subtle' assertion that the Spirit is speaking to itself. But this in fact is Paul's view (and that of Tillich, see below, 169 n.230), though a distinction should be made between spirit 'in us' and spirit 'outside us' (αὐτὸ τὸ πνεῦμα), just as a distinction should be made between 'Christ' sitting at the right hand of God and 'Christ in us', although it is the same Christ; I have spoken above (17f.) in another context of 'God in us' and 'God outside us' (ubiquity).

225. Armin Dietzel, 'Beten im Geist', *TZ*, 1957, 12ff., cites as a parallel from the Qumran *hodayot* texts which like Paul know a praying of the spirit in human beings and of human beings in the spirit.

226. It is forgotten that the assertion that this is an acclamation rests on an assumption which is only one (possible) hypothesis: '*abba*', like '*maranatha*' (and also Kyrios), was an ecstatic cry in the liturgy. Gebauer, in whose argument it plays such a major role, takes over this explanation, which has become customary today; it is also taken almost for granted e.g. by Käsemann, *Commentary on Romans* (n.224), 226.

227. Thus rightly U.Wilckens, *Der Brief an die Römer*, EKK, 1978ff., II, 137.

228. See Grundmann, χράζω, *TDNT* III, 898f.

229. The hypothesis has been argued for by many scholars, e.g.T. Zahn, *Der Brief des Paulus an die Römer*, 1910, 396; H.Lietzmann, *An die Römer*, ⁴1933, 83; C.H.Dodd, *The Epistle of Paul to the Romans*, 1973, ad loc., but disputed by Käsemann, *Commentary on Romans* (n.224), 225. Also by Gebauer, *Das Gebet bei Paulus* (n.211), 155. However, his argument that in Matthew and Luke there is only the Greek translation of Abba does not seem to me to be convincing. For in a translation of the *whole* Our Father into Greek the word to be translated could not really also be translated. Also the fact that only the word 'Father' is cited here would not tell against an allusion to the Our Father; for in arguing in Rom.8.15 that we are children Paul could limit himself to the opening word of the Our Father. Gebauer's arugment that the Our Father was not regarded as being inspired by the Holy Spirit seems to me equally untenable.

230. Paul Tillich expressed the understanding of Rom.8.12ff. advocated here in a particularly apt way. In *Systematic Theology* III, Chicago 1963, reissued London 1978, 192, he emphasizes that 'the subject-object scheme of "talking to somebody" is transcended; He who speaks through us is he who is spoken to.' Ibid., 'The paradox (that God can only become object if he is at the same time subject) is resolved if we become clear that the divine Spirit which seizes those who pray is God himself, and that one can say that God speaks through us to himself.' For the reciprocal effect (we pray for the Holy Spirit, and at the same time the Spirit prays) see also K.Berger, 'Gebet', *TRE*, 50.

231. 'Console-toi, tu ne me chercherais pas, si tu ne m'avais pas trouvé', Pascal, *Pensées*, ed. Leon Brunschvig, 552. The editor refers in a note to St Bernard, *De Deo diligendo* VII, PL 182, col.987; only he can seek you who has already found you.

232. For the eschatological character of the prayer see H.Greeven, *Gebet und Eschatologie im Neuen Testament*, 1931.

233. χληρονόμοι.

234. ἀρραβών; as a synonym 'firstfruit', ἀπαρχή, Rom.8.23.

235. ἀρραβὼν τῆς χληρονομίας ἡμῶν.

236. O.Michel, *Der Brief an die Römer*, ¹⁴1978, rightly assumes the connection (which is disputed by Gebauer, *Das Gebet bei Paulus* [n.211], see his whole chapter on Rom.8.26, 166f.).

237. This is emphatically disputed by Gebauer in his whole chapter on Rom.8.26. In his view neither vv.14f. nor v.26 refer to praying in general. Rather, the two verses, which are not to be connected, are special cases: in v.15 about the acclamation 'Abba', which is to be distinguished from prayer,

and in v.26 about prayer and the future hope. Thus neither verse is about the general inability of human beings to pray as they should. By contrast W.Niederwimmer, 'Das Gebet des Geistes Röm 8,26', *TZ* 1964, 252, following Bieder, 'Gebetswirklichkeit und Gebetsmöglichkeit bei Paulus' (n.221), 27, rightly takes up this basic inability. This interpretation is indispensable for the view which I propose. It is also suggested by I Cor.12.3, cited above, 'No one can say "Jesus is Lord" except by the Holy Spirit.'

238. Käsemann, *Commentary on Romans* (n.224), ad loc.; Gebauer, *Das Gebet bei Paulus* (n.211); and also Senft, *Le courage de prier* (n.16), 70, stress that only τί, the object, and not the nature of prayer is envisaged. It does not say how we pray, but what we are to pray. This is correct, and also applies to my view. For even the subject of the prayer is inspired by the Spirit if it happens 'as it should' (καθ'ὃ δεῖ, v.26, or κατὰ θεόν, 27). But prayer as it should be is included in what we pray. Both go back to the Spirit when this prays in us. That is also the case in the saying of Jesus in Matt.10.20, quoted above (75): 'how and what you will pray'.

239. συναντιλαμβάνεται, 'he comes to help' and ὑπερεντυγχάνει, 'he intercedes for us'. Intercession and representation, which are implied in these latter verbs, fit the talk of the Spirit in our praying (Käsemann, *Commentary on Romans* [n.224], 241, puts it well: the 'intercession' in the Spirit takes place 'in heaven'; the glossolalia is the Spirit, as the 'earthly presence of the exalted one').

240. To demonstrate the supposed impossibility of taking vv.26 and 15 together, Gebauer argues as follows: if the Spirit speaks in prayer, no imperfection is possible (n.340). But the speaking of the Spirit in human prayer is necessarily bound by human inadequacy.

241. By contrast Rudolf Bohren, *Predigtlehre*, [5]1986, 331ff., devotes a detailed and instructive section to speaking in tongues.

242. In Acts 10.46; 19.6, the fact that believers begin to speak in tongues at baptism is regarded as an indication that the Holy Spirit has fallen on them.

243. προσεύχεται.

244. Käsemann, *Commentary on Romans* (n.224), 240, similarly explains the sighing as glossolalia, like others before him, e.g. T.Zahn, *Der Brief des Paulus an die Römer*, 1930, ad loc.; Harder, *Paulus und das Gebet* (n.240), 169, also mentions it as a possibility. By contrast, Gebauer, *Das Gebet bei Paulus* (n.211), 60f. and 168, and Leenhardt, *L'Épître de S.Paul aux Romains* (n.224), 131 n.4, reject this assumption (Leenhardt with remarkable rapidity in a note); so too do Schlatter, *Gottes Gerechtigkeit* (n.224); Michel, *Der Brief an die Römer* (n.236), 178; and Senft, *Le courage de prier* (n.16), 70, without going into it in more detail (here Gebauer is the exception).

245. ἀλάλητος.

246. As Gebauer, *Das Gebet bei Paulus* (n.211), 168f., indicates in connection with his rejection of a reference to speaking with tongues.

247. ἄρρητα ῥήματα. Käsemann, *Commentary on Romans* (n.224), 240, also accepts this connection.

248. Tillich, *Systematic Theology* III (n.230), 116f., puts it well: 'He (Paul) knows that every successful prayer. i.e., every prayer which reunites with God, has ecstatic character. Such a prayer is impossible for the human spirit, because man does not know how to pray; but it is possible for the divine Spirit to pray through man.'

249. Karl Barth, *CD* IV.2, 141f. gives a very good definition of speaking with tongues as a 'limit case of Christian discourse as such, as wanting to express the inexpressible, in which the tongue to some degree anticipates and expresses the vividness and conceptuality necessary for normal discourse, which can only be perceived as a sigh or exclamation'.

259. ἀποκαραδοκία, 'with raised head'.

251. συστενάζειν.

252. συνωδίνειν.

253. The solidarity is often emphasized in Judaism, cf. IV Esdras 7.11.

254. A.Jülicher, *Der Brief an die Römer*, Schriften des NT, 1907; Zahn, *Der Brief des Paulus an die Römer* (n.229), ad loc.; Forster, *TDNT* 3, 1030, decides for Adam.

255. Beginnings of this are to be found in Orthodox theology.

256. πάντοτε, ἀδιαλείπτως.

257. ἐν πάσῃ σοφίᾳ καὶ συνέσει πνευματικῷ.

258. E.Trocmé, 'L'apôtre Paul et Rome: réfléxions sur une fascination', *RHPR* 72, 1992, 41–51 (esp.43ff., 50), refers to the great importance which Paul attached to this journey.

259. κωλυθέντες ὑπὸ τοῦ ἁγίου πνεύματος.

260. παρρησία, a term the application of which to prayer is important (see Schlier, παρρησία, *TDNT*, 871ff.).

261. Rapture to the third heaven, where he heard 'words which cannot be uttered' (ἄρρητα). Paul's ecstatic experiences also include – albeit in weaker form – his capacity to speak in tongues (mentioned above, 77ff.).

262. ἀσθένεια.

263. Since Tertullian, interpreters have usually – and rightly – thought in terms of an illness. The hypothesis of P.Menoud, 'L'écharde et l'ange satanique', *FS F.de Zwaan*, 1953, that the reference is to the impossibility of converting the Jews seems to me hardly compatible with the image of the thorn. However, M.Carrez, *La deuxième épître de St Paul aux Corinthiens*, 1986, 230f. takes it up. Gal.4.13 very probably also alludes to an illness, there in connection with his missionary work in Galatia.

264. Carrez, *La deuxième épître de St Paul aux Corinthiens* (n. 263), 230, reports that so far more than 150 illnesses have been conjectured.

265. See Grundmann. δύναμις, in *TDNT* II, 284ff.

266. ἀρκεῖ.

267. Gebauer discusses the question of the hearing of prayer in Paul in connection with his interpretation of II Cor.6.43ff., but without any mention of II Cor.12.5ff.

268. Cf. Tillich, *Systematic Theology*, III (n.230), 191: 'a prayer in which this happens (the presence of the divine Spirit) is heard, even if subsequent events contradict the manifest content of the prayer'.

269. ἐπικαλεῖν.

270. E.Fuchs, *Die Freiheit des Glaubens, Röm. 5–8 ausgelegt*, 1949, brings out the special relationship of the event of II Cor. 12.8ff. to Jesus in a different way: Paul's weakness repeats the weakness of Jesus. In his section on 'Praying Through Christ', Gebauer, *Das Gebet bei Paulus* (n.211), 120, explains the fact that prayer to Christ occurs only once, in II Cor. 12.8, by saying that at this point Paul was still under the impact of the Damascus experience, in which he had heard the voice of Christ.

271. But see Gebauer, *Das Gebet bei Paulus* (n.211), 141. In an excursus, 139ff., on the basis of an investigation of the passages in which the formula appears (Rom.1.8; II Cor.1.20; also Col.3.17 and outside the prayer texts, Rom.7.25), he comes to the conclusion that the formula is to be related to the saving action in Christ 'as the ground of possibility of Pauline thanksgiving and praise' (141). This conclusion does not really do justice to the present sense, which he allows throughout the 'through Christ phrases' (139).

272. Given by Gebauer, *Das Gebet bei Paulus* (n.211), 140 (without excluding a simultaneous reference to Christ's saving work as well), but with the comment that the authenticity of Colossians is disputed.

273. Paul concedes to the Corinthians continence in marital sexual intercourse if both are agreed – but for a limited period – so that they can devote themselves fully to prayer (during such a period, I Cor.7.5).

274. πάντοτε.

275. I Thess.2.2; II Cor.3.12; 7.4; Phil 1.20; Eph.3.12; 6.19; Philemon 8; I Tim.3.13.

276. Even redactors need to be taken seriously by theologians. See O.Cullmann, 'The Theological Contents of the Prologue to John', in *FS J.L.Martyn*, ed. Fortna and B.Garvta, 1990, 295ff.

277. See A.Dahl, *Anamnesis. Mémoire et commémoration dans le christianisme primitif*, Studia theologica, 1947, 94ff.; id., *Early Christian Worship* (n.216), 48f.

278. The temple, which was probably built in the fourth century, had been destroyed in 128 by John Hyrcanus. The mountain remained (and still

remains) the holy cult place of the Samaritan community. Recently the religious community has become the object of thorough investigations. See the bibliography by L.A.Meyer and D.Broadribb, *Bibliography of the Samaritans*, 1962, and P.Sacchi, *Studi Samaritani*, RSLRS, 1969. In addition to the early work by M.Gaston, *The Samaritans. Doctrines and Literature*, 1925, see J.McDonald, *The Theology of the Samaritans*, London 1964; F.Dexinger and D.Plummer, *Die Samaritaner*, 1991. For their relationship to early Christianity see C.H.H.Scobie, 'The Origins and Development of Samaritan Christianity', *NTS* 1972/73; O.Cullmann, *The Johannine Circle* (n.3), and id., 'Von Jesus zum Stephanuskreis und zum Johannesevangelium', *FS W.G.Kümmel*, 1975, 44f., now reprinted in Dexinger and Plummer, 393ff.

279. Following his ordering of the material.

280. Cf. L.Gaston, *No Stone on Another. Studies on the Significance of the Fall of Jerusalem in the Synoptic Gospels*, 1970.

281. B.Gärtner, *The Temple and the Community in Qumran and the New Testament*, 1965; G.Klinzing, *Die Umwandlung des Kultus in der Qumrangemeinde und im Neuen Testament*, 1971. Also R.Schnackenburg, *The Gospel according to St John*, I, 1968, 350f. The three authors could not have been aware of the 'Temple Scroll' (11Q Temple) edited in 1977/1978 by Y.Yadin.

282. Y.Yadin, *Megillat ha-miqdal*, 1977/78.

283. See A.Caquot, 'Qumrân et Temple', *RHPR* 1992, 4ff.

284. For the connections between Jesus, Stephen, Qumran, Samaria and the Gospel of John, in addition to my *The Johannine Circle* (n.3), cf. my 'Von Jesus zum Stephanuskreis und zum Johannesevangelium', in *FS W.G.Kümmel*, 1975, now reprinted in Dexinger and Plummer, *Die Samaritaner* (n.277), 1991.

285. For the significance of the Johannine 'remembering', see above, 172 n. 276.

286. This applies even if the words καὶ νῦν ἐστιν should be a gloss, as is often assumed.

287. R.Bultmann, *The Gospel of John* (1941), Oxford 1971, 191, understands the word ζητεῖν, seek, probably rightly, not as 'be concerned for' but as 'demand' (as in Mark 8.12). At all events, since God has created human beings as free beings in his communication of himself out of love, so that they may freely enter into his love, 'seeking' in the sense of the divine intention in creation cannot be included.

288. 'Such' worshippers: similarly Paul, Rom.8.26 ('as we ought').

289. ἐν Ἱεροσολύμοις, ἐν τῷ ὄρει.

290. According to Bultmann's commentary, worshipping in the Spirit in John 4.23 is no more a repudiation of all cultic prayer than are Isa.1.11 and Amos 5.21f.

291. It can certainly also be assumed that the evangelist used the saying in 1.51 (see above, 94) about the angels who ascend and descend upon the Son of Man instead of in the cult place of Bethel in connection with the answer to the Samaritan woman.

292. τὸ πνεῦμα τῆς ἀληθείας.

293. Here we must leave out of account the adverbial use of the expression ἐν ἀληθείᾳ, in the sense of 'really', which we perhaps have in II John 1 and III John 1 (thus Bultmann, *Johannine Epistles*, Hermeneia, Philadelphia 1973, ad loc., and R.Schnackenburg, 'Zum Begriff der Wahrheit in den beiden kleinen Johannesbriefen', *Biblische Zeitschrift*, 1967, 259ff.). This is opposed by Bonnard, *Les Epîtres Johanniques*, Neuchâtel 1983, 120, 130, who both times gives the words ἐν ἀληθείᾳ a meaning full of Johannine theological content and sees them as a polemical point against the heretics who are being combatted.

294. I.de la Potterie, *La vérité dans St Jean*, Analecta biblica (2 vols), 1977, is a very thorough work; it has been preceded above all by R.Bultmann, ἀλήθεια, *TDNT* I, 245ff. and *The Gospel of John* [n.287], passim), who puts particular stress on the influences from special streams of Judaism. It is important that these appear in Palestine and not first in the Diaspora. They cannot simply be subsumed under the term 'Gnosticism', which is too narrow (see my *The Johannine Circle* [n.3]).

295. M.Dibelius, *RHPR* 1933, 42, opposes this interpretation.

296. According to Bultmann, *The Gospel of John* (n.287), 656 n.2, the indifference of the representatives of the state, who are not interested in the ἀλήθεια.

297. ἐγένετο.

298. The heretics combatted in the Johannine epistles have not remained in the truth. According to Bultmann, *Johannine Epistles* (n.293), ad loc., those in II John 1 who are said to have recognized the truth are all Christians, whereas P.Bonnard, *Les Epîtres Johanniques* (n.293), 120, sees them as the special Johannine group and assumes that the view of the truth which they represent is a focus against the heretics.

299. ἐντολὴν καινήν.

300. παράκλητος.

301. Bietenhard, ὄνομα, *TDNT* V, 242ff.

302. Lochman, *Unser Vater* (n.83), 30ff. See also what is said above, 00f., on the first petition of the Our Father.

303. John 14.9: 'He who has seen me has seen the Father.'

304. See O.Cullmann, 'Alle, die den Namen unseres Herrn Jesus Christus anrufen', in K.Froehlich (ed.), *Oscar Cullmann, Vorträge und Aufsätze*, 1966, 605ff.

305. Schnackenburg, *The Gospel according to John*, III, London 1982,

73, cites this particular text on John 14.3, prayer in the name of Jesus.

306. Here the preposition before the mention of the name can change: usually εἰς (Matt.28.19; Acts 8.16; 19.5; I Cor.1.13); but also ἐν (Acts 10.48) and ἐπι (Acts 2.38– variant BD ἐν).

307. Here without a preposition, only in the dative: τῷ σῷ ὀνόματι.

308. Perhaps this could explain the difficult verse 16.26: 'In that day you will ask in my name; and I do not say to you that I shall pray the Father for you; for the Father himself loves you, because you have loved me and believed that I am come from God.' Perhaps this can mean that Christ as the exalted one is so closely connected with the Father that every prayer spoken in the name of Christ automatically includes the intercession of Christ, and thus implicitly brings the disciples into direct contact with the Father, because with their prayer in the name of Jesus they make known their love of Jesus and their belief that he proceeds from God, and in this way manifest the love of God which he shows to them.

309. παράκλητος.

310. See O.Cullmann, 'Der johanneische Gebrauch doppeldeutiger Ausdrücke als Schlüssel zum Verständnis des vierten Evangeliums', in Fröhlich (ed.), *Vorträge und Aufsätze* (n.304), 176ff.

311. Without identifying them, as Paul does in II Cor.3.17.

312. Schnackenburg, *Gospel According to John* III (n.305), 134, also assumes this reference.

313. If the Spirit which according to 14.17 is 'in us', is at work in our prayer, this could recall Paul in Gal.4.6; Rom.8.15. However, we must not overlook a difference: in the Gospel of John the Spirit does not show itself in the utterance of the prayer, as it does in Paul.

314. Thus also C.H.Dodd, *The Interpretation of the Fourth Gospel*, 1956, 349.

315. παρρησία.

316. Quite apart from the reference to prayer, the expression 'believe in the name of Christ' occurs often in the Gospel of John: 1.12; 2.23; 3.18.

317. But what is difficult to explain here is the qualification (pray for) 'what is not a mortal sin' (v.16: ἁμαρτία μὴ πρὸς θάνατον) and especially the conclusion of verse 16, which has to be explained: 'There is sin which is mortal; I do not say that one (the brother) is to pray about that.' Bultmann, *Johannine Epistles* (n.293), ad loc., regards this qualification as a redactional addition (contrary to Bonnard, *Epîtres Johanniques* (n.293), 14, who attributes this 'terrible restriction' to the author and applies it to the heretics who are so vigorously attacked throughout the letter, especially those who have forsaken the community of the brethen). Judaism already assumed a distinction between sin and mortal sin. In the Christian sphere one might

think about the 'second' (final) death. As the divine verdict has already been spoken here, in this case human prayer has lost its significance. But the qualification remains difficult within the Johannine writings and the New Testament generally.

318. See Cullmann, 'Der johanneische Gebrauch doppeldeutiger Ausdrücke' (n.310).

319. ποιήσω.

320. ὑμῖν γενήσεται.

321. Schnackenburg, *The Gospel according to John* III (n.305), 433 n.2, points out that two church fathers already emphasized the 'high priestly' character of the prayer. For one of them, Cyril of Alexandria, see also R.Brown, *The Gospel according to S.John (XIII–XXI)*, 1970, 747.

322. Hallowing of the name, John 17.6,26; Matt.6.9; deliverance from evil, John 17.15; Matt.6.13.

323. Thus Bultmann, *Gospel of John* (n.287), 350f. For the positioning at the end, see Brown, *Gospel according to S. John* (n.321), 741; Schnackenburg, *Gospel according to John* III (n.305), 167.

324. Contrary to a present-day tendency, historical conditioning should not be regarded as a negative aspect in the application of the Bible to our problems, but it should also disclose the continuity in the historical development.

325. This is the meaning of καρπός, especially in the Pauline epistles, see *TDNT* III, 618.

326. Cullmann, *Christ and Time* (1944), esp. 115ff.

327. ἐκ τοῦ κόσμου.

328. By contrast, J.Willebrands, the former President of the Secretariat for Unity, rightly put the petition in its context in his address in Cambridge (Ecumenical Conference, 18 January 1970).

329. The thorough book by Hamman, *La prière du Nouveau Testament* (n.209), which has been cited often, is far more than a lexicographical survey; the author also aims at a theological understanding. However, his procedure is different from that in my book; he often puts forward different explanations, and the two investigations can supplement each other. Hamman devotes more space to semantics and the theological context of the passages on prayer, but sometimes he goes rather a long way from what in my view is the special theme of the work.

330. 6.1ff. speak only of the prayer which is uttered with the laying on of hands after the election.

331. There is a theological analysis of this prayer in Hamman, *La prière du Nouveau Testament* (n.209), 174.

332. It is probably because of the vision of Christ and the content of these prayers, which take up the words spoken by the crucified Jesus (only

according to Luke 23.46, 34), that in contrast to the other prayers in Acts, all of which are addressed to God, Stephen calls on the 'Lord Jesus' (Κύριε, Ἰησοῦ).

333. It is the Spirit which instructs him there to go with the two people (v.19).

334. ἡ εὐχὴ τῆς πίστεως.

335. δεήσεις καὶ ἰκτηρίας.

336. λατρεύειν.

337. προσέρχεσθαι.

338. παρρησία.

339. ὁμολογία is often mentioned in Hebrews: 3.1; 4.14; 10.23.

340. See Cullmann, *Early Christian Worship* (n.216).

341. Apart from E.Lohmeyer, *Die Offenbarung des Johannes*, 1926, in particular P.Prigent, *L'apocalypse de Saint Jean*, ²1988, has emphasized the liturgical character of the Revelation of John.

342. παντοκράτωρ.

343. For the formula see T.Klauser, *Realenzyklopädie für Christentum und Antike* I, 228.

344. Note that here too a communication of the prayers – though not by Christ – is assumed.

346. The designation 'new' appears in the Psalms (see Ps.33.3), also Rev.14.3.

346. Introduced by εὐχαριστοῦμεν σοι.

347. See O.Cullmann, *Early Christian Worship* (n.216).

348. ἔρχου κύριε is a Greek translation of *maranatha*.

349. Henry Mottu, 'Apocalypse 2–3 comme modèle homilétique', *Bulletin du centre protestant d'Etudes* (Geneva), March 1991, 5, refers to this. What he says about preaching also applies to prayer.

III. Synthesis. What Answer does the New Testament give to Today's Questions?

1. There is a similar objection to confession, which is a form of praise: I Cor.12.2f. Here Paul rejects the objection that the Spirit could drive someone possessed to say, 'Cursed be Jesus'.

2. Granted, it is acknowledged by others that this false prayer is condemned by the New Testament itself, but they wrongly infer from this condemnation the right to reject other elements of prayer, all of which belong to the New Testament. See above, 12f.

3. προσκαρτερεῖν.

4. πάντοτε.

5. ἀδιαλείπτως.

6. εὐχαριστεῖν.

7. Thus also S.Haussammann, 'Atheistisch zu Gott beten. Eine Auseinandersetzung mit D.Sölle', *Evangelische Theologie*, 1971, 425, and H.Schaller, *Das Bittgebet. Eine theologische Skizze*, Einsiedeln 1979, 97.

8. 'From Jerusalem to Jericho', as D.Sölle repeatedly says.

9. D.Bonhoeffer, *Letters and Papers from Prison*, London and New York 1971, 282.

10. λατρεύειν.

11. This also applies to intercesionns for fellow men and women who are in need. Sölle generalizes this, without being specific in any way, as 'the most mendacious information if Christians respond to the question what they did for the Jews when they were being persecuted by saying, "We prayed for them"' (*Atheistisch an Gott glauben*, Olten and Freiburg 1968, 111). Of course it is hypocritical and mendacious if these Christians could have done something by exposing themselves to danger and did nothing. But the generalization should not give the impression that prayer should be condemned even if there was no real possibility of supporting the Jews actively.

12. In his recent book, Theodor Gut, *Der Schrei der Gottverlassenheit*, Zurich 1994, sees Jesus' cry on the cross as an expression of Godforsakenness and protest against God. However, it should also be noted that the question 'Why?' with the psalm is addressed to God as a prayer.

13. See 135 below.

14. As we neither see nor hear God with our usual human organs, it is not in fact a matter of course, as D.Sölle, *Thinking about God*, London and Philadelphia 1990, 171ff., rightly remarks; but it is not the case, as she suggests, only today, nor is it just a result of modern science and modern experience. (See also H.Gollwitzer, *Von der Stellvertretung Gottes. Zum Gespräch mit Dorothee Sölle*, 1967, 19, 142.) Nor does the theism which she contests see God as a 'matter of course'. As a witness to the repudiation of God envisaged in 'theistic' tems she cites Paul (*Die Wahrheit ist Konkret*, Olten and Freiburg 1967, 106), who, as she thinks, according to Rom.8.26 can no longer make contact with this God when he writes: 'We do not know how to pray as we ought.' But in the context, through this negative statement the apostle simply arrives at the positive fact of the necessary support of the Holy Spirit (see 76f.).

15. The elimination of passages which have not been 'selected' can be justified only if these are really views which apply only to a particular historical framework which, as people used to say, is 'historically conditioned' and can therefore be abandoned, but not if it relates to those which clearly, as with the biblical view of God, belong to the centre.

16. This is the passage in which D.Sölle sees the New Testament

foundation for contesting the view of God which she calls theistic. In his important book, *Von der Stellvertretung Gottes* (n.13), Gollwitzer investigates her christological comments in this connection in terms of the concept of representation and comes to the conclusion: 'It is striking how sharply Sölle attacks the central view of Christianity, and equally striking that she evidently is not aware that she is contradcting the centre of the New Testament and has this against her' (112). She interprets the cross and resurrection of Christ on the basis of the sociological principle of interpretation with which she wants to develop the historical-critical use of the Bible (*Thinking about God* [n.13]:, 22ff.). Here, too, I cannot help applying to these remarks, in which she attempts to be true to the New Testament, the verdict of Gollwitzer mentioned above, although she quotes with approval Gollwitzer's reply to a questionnaire 'Who is Jesus of Nazareth for me?' in order to do justice to the 'orthodox tradition' in which she sees Gollwitzer 'deeply rooted' (141).

17. For the relationship between the omnipotence and the love of God, see below, 137ff.

18. Sölle, *Thinking about God* (n.13), takes over this correct formulation by M.Buber: relationship and transcendence are not opposites.

19. ἦν.

20. ἐγένετο. For the relationship with the perfect γέγονεν in v.4 see the instructive work by E.L.Miller, *Salvation History in the Prologue of John*, Leiden 1989.

21. Sölle, *Atheistich an Gott glauben* (n.11), 112.

22. To supplement her earlier publications D.Sölle now (see *Thinking about God*) attempts to take account of the transcendence of God. But with her fight against the caricature of the 'theistic' view of God and 'reified' transcendence, important though it is, (*Thinking about God* [n.13], 184) and her formula 'transcendence is radical immanence' (ibid., 186), she seems to me in the end to be maintaining the same line and not doing justice to the biblical origin of immanence from transcendence. The 'theistic' God whom she so passionately contests is the God of the New Testament. I have quoted Sölle often, because her publications are so widely circulated – albeit only in German-speaking countries and North America – and fit in with present-day tendencies. Within the framework of the present work we have to ask only whether she reproduces the view of the New Testament. My criticism relates only to this question.

23. The Catholic theologian K.Koch, *Gelämte Ökumene*, 1991, 147ff. a book which is well worth reading, discusses this side of the problem.

24. See below, 137ff.

25. The justified rejection of prayer to a God imagined in anthropomorphic terms should not lead to cheap polemic against 'childish faith' in God's omnipotence.

26. See the apt remarks of Gollwitzer, *Von der Stellvertretung Gottes* (n.13), 142, on the emphatic rejection of the words of this hymn by D.Sölle. First he quotes the beginning of her speech at the Cologne Kirchentag in 1965: 'I too do not know how after Auschwitz one is to praise the God who rules all things so gloriously', and 'there is no way back to the father of children who gives way and course to clouds, air and winds'. Gollwitzer comments: 'Have these words become untrue through false usage? How is there no way back to them? If they are untrue today then they were also untrue earlier, even during the atrocities of the Thirty Years War, which contradict what these hymns say no less than the atrocity of Auschwitz . . . Was the excess of believing in the promise "I will be there" in the midst of atrocities less then than it is today? . . . As if such hymns of former centuries, as if the talk of divine guidance, rule and fatherhood, owe their rise to naive optimism! They are prayed *in extremis*, in the hardest tribulations; they know the situation of Job; they speak in the face of the godforsakenness of Golgotha.'

27. Martin Buber, *I and Thou*, whom Sölle quotes in *Thinking about God* (n.13), 183, puts it in a pointed way. We need God, God needs us. One could agree with this formulation if one presupposed with Emil Brunner (see *Dogmatics* III, 373; cf. also I, 272ff.) that 'of his own free will God makes himself dependent on what his child says to him' (see what is said above on God's communication of himself). So in the case of prayer I say the opposite: God does not need our prayer, but wants it.

28. Similarly Karl Barth, *CD* II.1, 510, writes that 'God positively wills that man should call upon Him in this way, in order that He may be his God and Helper.'

29. Only *mutatis mutandis* again the relationship between parents and children may serve as an incomplete example; the parents are to prevent the children having inhibitions about asking for such things as they assume their parents can give them, but without being certain that they will do so.

30. Karl Barth emphasizes impressively that petition is the centre of prayer. 'That (the one who prays) comes to God with his petition makes him a suppliant' (CD III.3, 280). This does not contradict his high evaluation of thanksgiving and praise. See 167 n.214 above.

31. What has not been resolved is the question whether our intercession may also be extended to the dead, as if we had to pray for them (not to them). The Reformers answered this question in the negative, and we must consider their arguments seriously. It is correct that nowhere in the New Testament is there evidence of prayer for the dead – the enigmatic passage about 'baptism for the dead' (I Cor.15.29), of which there is perhaps no satisfactory explanation, cannot really be regarded as evidence. On the other hand there is no New Testament text which directly rejects intercession for the dead.

The argument that the dead are in God's hands and therefore do not need our intercession is not completely convincing, in that the living for whom we pray are also in God's hands. But what is correct about this argument is that according to the evidence of the whole of the New Testament the dead are nearer to God (see my *Immortality of the Soul or Resurrection of the Dead?*, London 1958) and that this creates a fundamentally new relationship between the living, the dead and God. The question needs to be discussed from this perspective,

32. See above, 1of.

33. O.Cullmann, *Salvation in History*, London and Philadelphia 1967, 122ff.

34. Chosen by Paul Claudel as a motto for his play *Le soulier de satin*: 'Dieu écrit droit, mais en lignes courbes.'

35. Thanks to the Basel Germanist K.Pestalozzi I was able to see a manuscript from the posthumous unpublished works of J.C.Lavater in which under the title 'Prayers that have been heard', the author reports prayers the hearing of which he could not explain in natural terms.

36. ἀσθένεια means at the same time both 'weakness' and 'sickness'.

37. See what is said above, 60f., in the explanation of the sixth petition about the two kinds of temptation.

38. Theologians have created the term *felix culpa* to explain the context of this event.

39. ἀρχαί, κυριότητες, θρόνοι, δυνάμεις. We still do not have a detailed investigation of the role played by these invisible powers in the New Testament environment, especially in late Judaism. Such a work would perhaps allow us to make a distinction between their functions. For in all probability we should reckon that the authors of the New Testment writings had such knowledge.

40. See O.Cullmann, *The State in the New Testament*, London 1957, Excursus I, on the most recent discussion of the *exousiai* in Rom.13.1ff., 95ff.

41. 'We are not contending against flesh and blood, but against principalities, against the powers, against the world rulers of this present darkness, against the spiritual hosts of wickedness in the heavenly places.'

42. See O.Cullmann, *The Earliest Christian Creeds*.

43. Pluralistic singular.

44. In II Thess. 2.8 the same verb καταργεῖν denotes the future final annihilation of the devil.

45. For which further examples could be found.

46. For the question of duration see my discussion with Fritz Buri in K.Froehlich (ed.), *O.Cullmann, Vorträge und Aufsätze*, 1962, 414ff.

Index of Names

Index of Biblical References

OLD TESTAMENT

NEW TESTAMENT

EXTRA-CANONICAL WRITINGS: OLD TESTAMENT

EXTRA-CANONICAL WRITINGS: NEW TESTAMENT